THE
Multimedia Authoring
Workshop
with Director 5

THE
Multimedia Authoring
Workshop
with Director® 5

William D. Harrel

SYBEX®

San Francisco • Paris • Düsseldorf • Soest

Associate Publisher: Carrie Lavine
Acquisitions Manager: Kristine Plachy
Developmental Editors: Dan Brodnitz and Suzanne Rotondo
Editor: Suzanne Rotondo
Technical Editors: Amy Shelton and Jeffrey Southard
Book Designers: Jack Myers and Tracy Dean at Design Site
Graphic Illustrator: Catalin Dulfu
Desktop Publisher: Tania Kac at Design Site
Production Coordinator: Anton Reut
Indexer: Nancy Guenther
Cover Designer: Adrian Morgan at Red Letter Design, Design Site

Screen reproductions produced with Collage Plus.

Collage Plus is a trademark of Inner Media Inc.

SYBEX is a registered trademark of SYBEX Inc.
TRADEMARKS: SYBEX has attempted throughout this book to distinguish proprietary trade-marks from descriptive terms by following the capitalization style used by the manufacturer.

Netscape Communications, the Netscape Communications logo, Netscape, and Netscape Navigator are trademarks of Netscape Communications Corporation.

Library of Congress Card Number: 96-68700
ISBN: 0-7821-1799-6

Manufactured in the United States of America

10 9 8 7 6 5 4 3 2 1

Acknowledgments

I owe a lot of people for their invaluable help in making this book a reality.

First, thanks goes to my beautiful wife (and assistant) for her tenacity in untangling the sometimes confusing and time-consuming web of securing all the licenses and contracts required to place the product demos and clip media samples on the CD-ROM. Without her help, the book would have taken much longer to finish.

Deeply felt thanks also goes to Suzanne Rotondo, who developed and edited this book. Her dedication and unfaltering eye for quality and detail helped me tame what sometimes seemed like an impossible subject to cover in so short a space. Without her, *Multimedia Authoring Workshop* would not have been nearly as focused. Thanks, too, to Dan Brodnitz at Sybex for his clear-headed guidance through this project. Also, thanks to Anton Reut for coordinating the production process, and Tania at Design Site, for her patient and creative layout of the book.

The technical reviewers, Amy Shelton and Jeffrey Southard, knew this subject so well that, at times, I felt the reader would have been better served if they had written this book. Many thanks to both of them. It's not often that I can submit my work through the technical editor grind with the confidence that my mistakes and oversights will be so be readily worked out.

Finally, thanks to the good people at Macromedia, Adobe, Sonic Foundry, Corel, Image Club Graphics, and Jasmine Multimedia for their help in putting together such an interesting suite of applications and samples. Thanks, too, for their support through my times of confusion.

Contents at a Glance

Table of Contents

Part Two: Hardware and Software

Chapter 3: Monitors and Graphics Cards 35

Chapter 4: Sound and Video 45

Chapter 5: Storage Devices:
CD-ROMs and Removable Media 57

Part Three: Bringing It All Together

Chapter 13: Working with Graphics and Text 227

Chapter 14: Making Your Title Interactive 257

Introduction

For years multimedia has been the battle cry of many a computer pundit, but its entry into the mainstream has been slow in coming. Only recently have reasonably priced computers become powerful enough to process this system-taxing form. In this era of super-fast Pentiums, 6- and 8-speed CD-ROM drives, and SurroundSound systems, the splendors of multimedia have become available to a wide range of computer users.

At the moment, we see multimedia everywhere—games, edutainment titles, presentations, on the Internet, even on our TV screens. It is the wave of the future, and the future is upon us.

What Is Multimedia Authoring?

Multimedia authoring is the combining of several different types of media—graphics, text, sound, animation, digital video—into multimedia titles. Multimedia titles can be many things, and here are some places you're sure to find them:

- On the shelves at your local book and video store, mostly in the form of multimedia games.
- In marketing, where companies are producing extravagant CD-ROM brochures or electronic presentations to show off their wares and services.
- In reference books, such as encyclopedias, magazines, atlases, and medical books, which have come alive with animated and digital video demonstrations.
- Throughout education, where the learning process is being enhanced with edutainment titles that make teaching easier.
- In corporations that train employees with computerized courseware.

Is This Book for You?

If you want to learn how multimedia components—such as graphics, text, video and sound—come together as impressive works of art, this book is for you. If you think you want to enter the brave new world of multimedia authoring, but aren't sure about what type of hardware you need, or you are a little bit intimidated by the plethora of available software, carry this book over to the cash register. All of the information necessary for you to get started resides on these pages.

As a seasoned multimedia author, I have tried to create a book that demystifies the terms, concepts, and sometimes complicated system configuration issues involved in the process of creating and distributing multimedia titles. It answers questions such as: What are the equipment and software essentials required to write multimedia titles? How do sound, digital video, and animated graphics get into computers? What's involved in creating and distributing CD-ROM titles? I also introduce you to the wealth of multimedia software available, and provide comparisons between the most popular and most powerful multimedia solutions.

Throughout this book you'll find countless tips and tricks to get you up and running. On the CD-ROM, you'll find all of the applications you'll need to take your first crack at authoring a full-fledged title.

What's on the Multimedia Authoring Workshop CD?

The CD-ROM that comes with this book is full of demonstration copies of some of the leading multimedia and graphics applications, including Macromedia Director 5, a popular multimedia authoring program, and Adobe Premiere, an industry-leading digital video editing application. Also included are several graphics, sound, video, and text files you'll use when creating your first multimedia title.

To help you create future titles, we've also thrown in several photographs, clip art, and digital videos from vendors such as Corel, Image Club, and Jasmine Multimedia.

NOTE Instructions for installing the demo applications and using the clip media files are included in each chapter and listed on the page opposite the CD. You can also check out the readme.txt file in the root directory of the CD-ROM itself.

How This Book Is Organized

Multimedia Authoring Workshop is organized into three parts: Part One, *Getting to Know Multimedia*, introduces you to the world of multimedia authoring, and describes the computer and components you'll need to get started.

Part Two, *Hardware and Software*, covers peripherals and the software available in multimedia. Chapter 3 looks into the best monitors and graphics cards. Chapter 4 covers using sound and digital video, both from hardware and software perspectives. Chapter 5 discusses CD-ROM technology, as well as other types of storage devices. Chapter 6 explores two types of multimedia authoring programs: Multimedia Presentation software and Multimedia Authoring software. Chapter 7 introduces you to the editing software available for clip media, graphics, and video.

Part Three, *Bringing It All Together*, is the Workshop portion of the book, where you'll create an actual multimedia title. Chapter 8 provides the information you'll need for the Workshop, such as how to use the CD-ROM and supporting files. Chapter 9 introduces you to Macromedia Director and lays the groundwork for our title. Chapter 10 introduces you to Sonic Foundry Sound Forge XP and shows you how to use, edit, and enhance sound files. In Chapter 11, you'll use Director to animate objects. Chapter 12 introduces you to Adobe Premiere and the exciting world of digital video editing, so you can use video in your title. In Chapter 13, you'll create text and graphics, using the industry-leading Adobe Photoshop, for your ongoing Director title. Chapter 14 introduces you to Director's Lingo scripting language and shows you how to make your titles interactive. In Chapter 15, you'll learn how to turn your work in Director into stand-alone, self-running titles that will play on any Windows machine. Here we also cover turning Director titles into Shockwave movies that can play on the World Wide Web.

There's also a Glossary at the back of the book. This will serve as a reference where you can find definitions for the multimedia terms and buzzwords used throughout the book.

Conventions Used in This Book

This book uses several conventions to help you find important information readily: Tips, Notes, Warnings, and Sidebars.

TIP

Tips point out useful shortcuts and alternatives to the methods introduced in the text of the book.

 Notes include reminders, asides, and helpful information designed to make the Workshop easier to follow and trouble-free. You'll also find important information on application idiosyncrasies and tricks of the trade.

 Take heed. Warnings help you arm yourself against time-consuming mishaps and potential trouble.

To introduce related concepts, this book uses Sidebars. They are also used to provide additional information on a given topic.

This Is a Sidebar

Sidebars introduce useful information that you will benefit from knowing, but can do without when you're in a hurry. You'll find product comparisons and "Behind the Scenes Authoring" in Sidebars scattered throughout the text. This information will be useful when evaluating products and when preparing your own files to include in multimedia titles.

1

PART

Getting to Know Multimedia

CHAPTER 1

What Is Multimedia Authoring?

Featuring

- Multimedia business presentations
- Educational and training multimedia
- Multimedia advertising
- Authoring multimedia entertainment
- Multimedia and the Internet

What is multimedia authoring? Now there's a good question. Before going into that, we must first define *multimedia.* On a computer, *multimedia* means the bringing together of many, or multi(ple)*,* types of media—in this case digital sound, animation, and video on a computer. (Technically, on a computer, text and one other medium is multimedia, but that's a bit too simplistic.) *Multimedia authoring* is the process of combining several multimedia elements into a coherent form, such as, an interactive multimedia children's book, an interactive encyclopedia, a game, and so on. In other words, it is the act or process of creating *multimedia titles*.

That's the short answer to the question, but there is, of course, more to it than this brief explanation. Multimedia is a lot of things and has many applications. To better understand multimedia authoring we'll look at how it's used in business, education, and entertainment.

How Long Has Multimedia Been Around?

When I ask myself this question I imagine a Neanderthal chiseling a caption beneath an etching of a dinosaur. He grunts, smiles a broken-tooth grin, and says, "Hmp. Multimedia!" (Remember that the technical definition for multimedia is the combining of two or more types of media.)

The real question is, of course, when did people begin combining sound, animation, and video in their computer documents? Answer: About the same time the Macintosh began supporting sound with the release of the Mac II in 1987.

Shortly after, two presentation programs, Forethought PowerPoint and Aldus Persuasion, began supporting embedded sound files in electronic presentations. Forethought PowerPoint went on to become Microsoft PowerPoint, a leader in the presentation market and Persuasion is now owned by Adobe, the desktop publishing and graphics giant. Shortly after the first presentation software started integrating sound, we began seeing animation programs, such as AutoDesk Animation and Gold Disk Animation Interactive.

Full-motion video didn't appear on the desktop until a few years later, when Apple introduced QuickTime (again on the Mac). It wasn't until the debut of Windows 3.1, and the release of Microsoft Video for Windows, that movies got a strong foothold on the IBM-compatible PC.

Unfortunately, multimedia applications do not lend themselves to these neat little categories. In almost all aspects of multimedia authoring, each category overlaps with others. Business presentations, for instance, are designed primarily to persuade, but often they do so through educating. Education and entertainment often happen simultaneously, especially in multimedia titles. I've broken multimedia authoring applications into these compartments to make them easier to discuss. But remember while reading this, that just as you can learn from cartoons, you can be entertained by a multimedia application designed to sell you on some product or idea.

Multimedia Business Presentations

Whether you're selling yourself, your company, a product, or pitching your superiors on a program or idea, image counts. Look at the city of Atlanta, which not too long ago won the 1996 Olympics bid with a resplendent multimedia presentation. The presenters razzle-dazzled the Olympic site selection committee with intense computer-generated sound, animated graphics, and digital video clips.

Most business people learn early in their careers that a well-prepared *business presentation*, supported by slides or by overheads, helps deliver an effective message. The right presentation adds pizzazz to your message while helping you deliver your message clearly, concisely, and cohesively. Today, however, more and more business and sales presentations are done electronically from a computer, instead of with slides or overheads, or drawing on oversized paper that the presenter flips while making his or her presentation. Ugh!

Typically, a presentation consists of a presenter—or narrator—operating some kind of device, such as a slide projector or computer. As he or she speaks, supporting data and graphics are displayed on a screen. The screen presentation serves two purposes: one, to increase interest for the audience by adding visual stimuli; two, to guide the presenter as he or she delivers the presentation.

Since the release of Windows 3.1, an ever-growing slew of *presentation software* has clamored for a place on your hard disk. Because of its support for millions of colors, its ability to display screen fonts respectably, and *Object Linking and Embedding (OLE)*,

Windows is perfect for these graphics-intensive applications. The Macintosh, of course, has always been a graphics application stalwart with a few strong contending presentation programs. We take a closer look at these presentation programs in Chapter 7. Figure 1.1 shows an example of the title slide for a business presentation in Lotus Freelance Graphics. The primary benefit of this type of presentation is that the programs that create them are very easy to learn and use—and relatively inexpensive. This is especially true when compared to full-blown multimedia authoring programs.

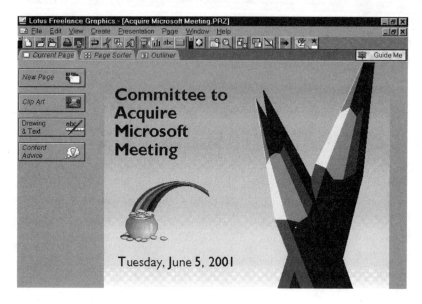

FIGURE 1.1:
An example of a business presentation created in Lotus Freelance Graphics.

The Slide—Building Block of Your Presentation

While companies and organizations create presentations in different ways, most business presentations rely on the slide metaphor. Each presentation—even a multimedia presentation—consists of a series of slides, with each slide displayed on your PC's screen. One of the key advantages of presentation graphics programs is the wide variety of output they let you generate. Nowadays, most presenters still choose to create the ever-familiar 35mm slide shows, something done easily with any presentation program. Another way to give a presentation, and one that's growing in popularity, is with the use of a projection panel. These are electronic display devices that connect to the video port on your laptop or notebook and sit on top of an overhead projector, displaying everything that appears on your PC's screen. Presenting on a TV screen is also an option, and we are seeing it more and more. Of course, you can also just give the show right on your notebook's screen, an attractive option for people who have notebooks with color, active-matrix screens.

NOTE The reason, I think, that most business people like to use presentation packages, rather than authoring software, to create their electronic presentations is that these programs mimic so closely the typical slide-show approach. In other words, it's not such a big leap from one type of medium to another. The truth is that you can create much more sophisticated presentations with a multimedia authoring program, such as Macromedia Director or Asymetrix ToolBook. But using these programs often requires you to think more like a movie director or film editor, rather than as a typical business presenter. This is not to say that some companies do not put on more sophisticated presentations created with authoring programs—it happens all the time—but they usually pay a professional multimedia author to put the thing together for them. After going through the tutorial in Part Three, you should be in good standing to go beyond these more simplistic slide shows, and move on to author your own dazzling multimedia presentations.

Most presentation programs also support multimedia in some form or another. Microsoft PowerPoint and Harvard Graphics, for example, allow you to create on-screen presentations complete with sound, animation, and video, as shown in Figure 1.2. Typically, the multimedia files, or *events*, in these presentations are embedded on a slide and are initiated in some manner by the presenter—either by switching slides or by selecting a *hot link* or text on a slide. These hot links usually activate small *applets*, such as Windows Sound Recorder or MultiMedia Player, which in turn play the file.

Viewer-Interactive Presentations

Another name for this form of presentation might be user-activated presentations. The difference between these and the straight slide show is primarily the absence of a presenter. Instead, the person for whom the presentation is intended loads it onto their computer

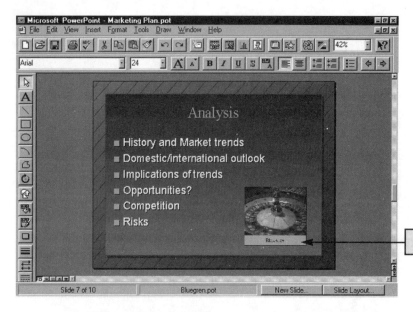

FIGURE 1.2:
Microsoft PowerPoint (top) with an embedded video clip and SPC Harvard Graphics (bottom) with an embedded sound clip. To activate the event, all you do is double-click on the hot link.

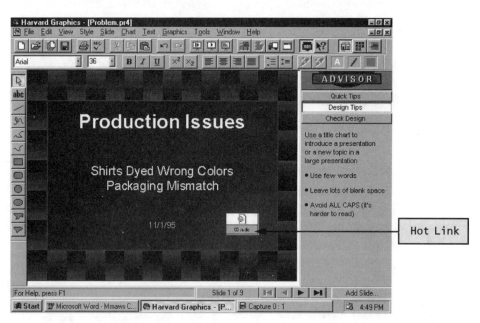

and navigates through it on their own by clicking the mouse, or with the PageUp and PageDown buttons. Figure 1.3 shows a typical screen from a *viewer-interactive presentation*.

This type of presentation is possible due to the runtime applets that ship with many of today's presentation packages. Basically, these applets bundle up a presentation into small executable files. All that's required of the person viewing the presentation is that they double-click on the icon and navigate the presentation by following the on screen directions. Viewer-interactive presentations are a great way to distribute promotional material. We'll look at this type of presentation more closely in Chapter 7.

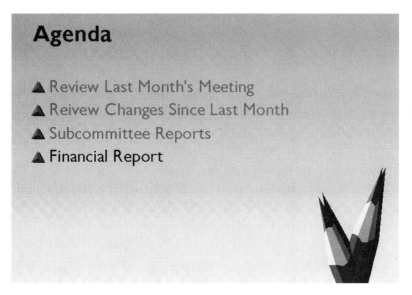

FIGURE 1.3:
A typical screen from a viewer-interactive presentation. The viewer controls the flow of the presentation by clicking on the agenda buttons with a mouse.

Self-Running Multimedia Presentations

Yet another type of presentation you can create is automated, self-running presentations. All your intended viewer does is double-click on the presentation icon and the show begins. While this is not the same caliber as a movie or a sophisticated show created with a multimedia authoring package, you can still create some pretty dynamic effects, such as transitions from slide to slide that fade from one into another, wipe from side to side, glitter, and so on. You can also create *build slides*—slides that introduce topics point by point, where each point, or bullet, flies in from left or right, along with a lot of other dramatic effects. This type of presentation can also *loop,* or run over and over, making them ideal for a store front, display window, or trade show. Again, we'll see more of this type of presentation in Chapter 7.

Corporate Multimedia Presentations

OK, I can hear your brain churning. *What's the difference between a business presentation and a corporate presentation? Business is business, right?* Semantically, there is no difference, I guess, but I needed some way to make this distinction. Let's define it this way: A business presentation is a short talk in front of some potential clients, at a business meeting for a group of colleagues. An example of a corporate presentation would be Bill Gates giving an hour-long keynote address at COMDEX (an annual computer trade show) or PC-Expo before a room full of computer professionals, industry analysts, and computer journalists.

When thinking about it that way, the difference is obvious: the software's different; the equipment's different; everything—right down to the multimedia author creating the show. Typically, business presentations are created *by* the presenter. Corporate presentations are created *for* the presenter. All he or she does is stand there and recite memorized lines while the computer operator behind the curtain runs the show.

As you can imagine, a lot more goes into this type of presentation. In many cases (as in the Bill Gates example), all aspects of the presentation are created especially for *that* presentation with *multimedia authoring software*. Artists draw and paint the images and backgrounds; camera and video professionals film and edit video…you get the idea. This is a multimedia author's dream world, where the money's good and the stakes are high.

Multimedia Authoring and Education

Of all the applications for multimedia, education appears to be the most promising. Computers and multimedia have virtually taken the hum-drum out of classroom learning, through a new type of learning software called *edutainment*. In addition, another multimedia phenomenon, *courseware,* allows people to learn on a computer without the necessity of an instructor. The software teaches, checks answers, and monitors progress, allowing the student to learn at his or her own pace and convenience. Let's look at these two types of multimedia applications separately.

Edutainment

The concept behind edutainment is that students learn more if the mode of instruction is entertaining and engaging. In other words, instead of a stodgy old teacher (from a young student's perspective, that is) lecturing before a classroom, what you get instead is a far less painful means of conveying information. Small children, for example, are more likely to pay attention to a cute clown or adorable puppy than a teacher at the chalkboard. As we've seen through the use of television, filmstrips, and VCRs, older children and even adults gain immensely from entertaining forms of instruction. Information just seems to sink in better if it's visually and audibly stimulating, which keeps us interested and gives us something to remember.

This idea, that students—especially young students—learn more from entertaining forms of instruction, is certainly not new. We've seen it kindergarten classes for quite some time. Television capitalized on the edutainment gravy train early in that medium's development, with entertaining instructional programming like *Captain Kangaroo, Mr. Wizard,* and later to an even greater degree on Public Broadcasting, with *Sesame Street.* In fact, the *Sesame Street* experiment proved so successful, it all but revolutionized how we teach small children.

The sights and sounds of multimedia make instruction on a computer lively and interesting. The interactivity provides the instant gratification children (and many adults) need to help them learn and perhaps best of all, multimedia lets the student learn at his or her own pace, in the privacy of one's own home or office. Nowadays, there are literally hundreds of multimedia edutainment titles, mostly in the form of interactive references, such as encyclopedias. Some of the biggest are *Microsoft Encarta* and *Compton's Interactive Encyclopedia*, shown in Figure 1.4.

These titles contain a multitude of information, including animated demonstrations, filmstrips of animals, and historic events. It's one thing when studying President Kennedy, for example, to read about the "Ask not what you can do for your country..." speech, but it's another thing altogether to actually see him delivering it. Likewise, when looking through an Atlas, it's much more helpful to actually hear the computer pronounce a country's name than to merely read it.

The computer's ability to create hot links allowing you to jump from related topic to related topic and back again cannot be matched by a hard copy book. The best a book can do is cross reference, forcing you to flip pages and use bookmarks (or fingers) to save your place.

Edutainment titles come in many forms, including famous novels, plays, and other literary works. Several classic movies, including the Beatles' first flick, *A Hard Day's Night*, shown in Figure 1.5, have been digitized and burned (with a laser) onto CD-ROM discs. The beauty of watching a movie this way is that you can jump from scene to scene with a mouse click, get information on characters and actors, and find trivia about the making of the movie, which turns watching your favorite classic into a more interactive experience.

Another important multimedia authoring venue is multimedia titles designed to teach specific skills. These too come in many forms, from beginner's art programs to children's dictionaries and other references. A couple of popular ones are Big Top Production's

FIGURE 1.4:
Examples of edutainment titles: *Compton's Interactive Encyclopedia* (top) and *Microsoft Encarta* (bottom)

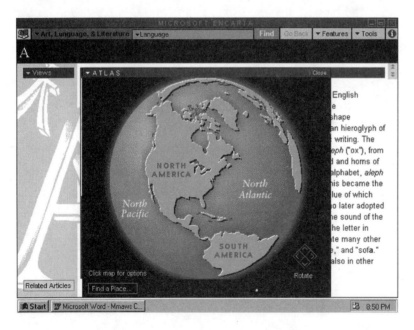

Cartoon Toolbox and Micrografx *Crayola Art Studio,* as pictured in Figure 1.6. Creating these types of titles is a good place to start for the beginning multimedia author. They rarely require sophisticated graphics and media clips.

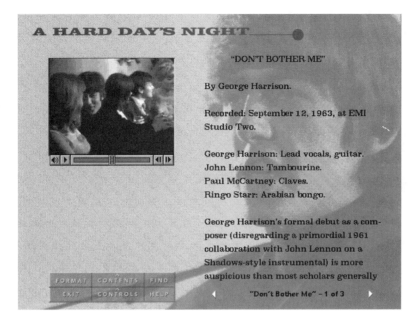

FIGURE 1.5
The Beatles' *A Hard Day's Night* as an interactive edutainment title.

Courseware

While computers may not ever replace the instructor and the classroom, multimedia courseware certainly provides a viable alternative. Courseware is software that teaches or trains, and its first applications were in corporate training. Chain restaurants, for example, use courseware to instruct new employees in company rules, the menu, and work procedures. Large corporations often use courseware to train people for new positions.

Today's courseware combines several aspects of the classroom into a visual, easy-to-use software application. The courseware title often provides the reading material, multimedia descriptions and demonstrations, workbooks, and *kudos* all in one package. Courseware can also be programmed to control the rate of advancement. You can, for instance, restrict moving on to advanced topics until the student masters the current lessons, and you can tailor the course to provide additional material to reinforce a student's weak areas.

While we haven't really seen an insurgence of commercially distributed courseware, the day is likely to come. Again, it's most widely used among mid-sized and large companies to train employees. Often companies make the courses available over a network, allowing employees to train in their spare time.

FIGURE 1.6:
Micrografx *Crayola Art Studio* is a popular edutainment title for children.

The versatility of this approach to teaching is limitless, and the benefit of courseware is that it doesn't get sick, doesn't require expensive healthcare benefits and vacations, doesn't have bad days, and you don't have to keep it on the payroll or a retainer. In other words, it'll be available when you need it.

Multimedia Authoring and Advertising

Virtually all aspects of our lives are affected by computers in one way or another. One area where computers are thoroughly pervasive is in advertising, from print media to TV commercials. Display ads, for example, are created in desktop publishing and graphics applications. Video tape is edited in digital video editing applications, and commercial graphics and animation are created with multimedia authoring and animation software.

Two of the most popular forms of advertising created with multimedia authoring are point-of-sale *kiosks,* and sales and marketing demos. This section looks at these two forms of multimedia advertising.

Point-of-Sale Kiosks

These are becoming increasingly popular in shopping malls and discount warehouse stores. There are basically three types of point-of-sale kiosks: self-running kiosks, kiosks with buttons beside the monitor, and touch-screen kiosks. Some kiosks display product information or provide directions, while others allow you to order products or services directly. (I saw one on TV the other day that processes divorces.)

Consider wedding list kiosks that allow you to reserve and purchase wedding gifts. The computer displays each item and tells you whether or not somebody has already purchased it for the lucky couple. There are, of course, many other types which, for the most part are quite simple, displaying graphics and text designed for user-interactivity.

I've also seen some rather elaborate kiosks—for instance, in museums and visitor pavilions—complete with sound, animation, and video, that are effective and entertaining. Surely, you have too.

Sales and Marketing Demos

We see these all over the place. Perhaps the most common are demos that run on display models in computer and electronics stores. Software companies also distribute demos of their products in multimedia form. Figure 1.7 shows an example of a ToolBook marketing demo.

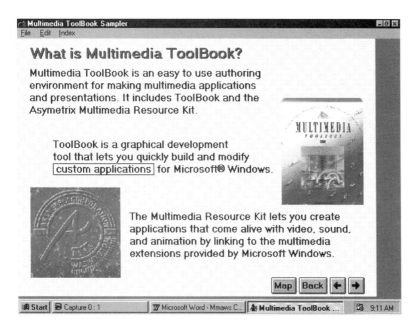

FIGURE 1.7:
An example of a marketing demo

The computer is ideal for this type of multimedia authoring, and serves as an effective tool to sell products. Along the same lines are the product demos that accompany software applications. These usually come in the form of multimedia help or animated demonstrations that show you how to perform certain tasks with the software. Adobe, the desktop publishing and graphics software giant, includes hot demos with PageMaker, Photoshop, Illustrator, and other programs, as shown in Figure 1.8.

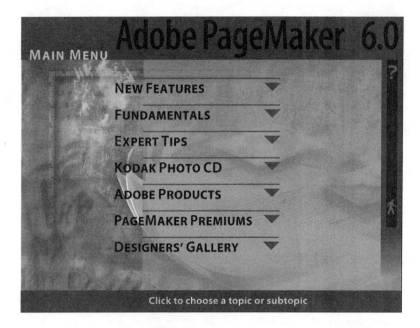

FIGURE 1.8:
Adobe's multimedia help demonstrations

Computers and software are, of course, not the only products advertised through multimedia marketing demos. You can create multimedia titles describing and displaying just about anything you can think of, from fishing lures to motorcycles. With so many people owning computers today, you can easily mass produce a CD-ROM for distribution among potential customers.

Multimedia Authoring and Entertainment

Multimedia authoring is responsible for several types of entertainment, including many of the cartoons you see on TV and even some of your favorite full-featured films, such as *Beauty and the Beast* or *Batman*. But the type of entertainment most appropriate to multimedia authoring is multimedia games, one of the fastest growing forms of software and entertainment today. There is a tremendous opportunity for authors in this area.

Multimedia games range from the simple and silly to intricate and sophisticated, and are a lot of fun to create. There are all kinds of games—war games, futuristic star flight games, logic games, and many more.

Some of the more popular multimedia games, such as *Myst* or *Where in the World is Carmen Sandiego,* are puzzles or mysteries, where you figure out options and make decisions that move characters through mazes or around the globe. In *Carmen Sandiego*, for instance, the user flies around world finding clues to solve mysteries. In *Myst,* you slay foes and solve puzzles, moving up in levels of difficulty and sophistication.

While these types of games are technically easy to create, they provide a challenge in terms of script writing. It takes a lot of creativity to plan out the intricate plots and subplots. Other types of games, such as action games, provide additional challenges to the author. In a starship battle game, for instance, you must perform some intricate animating, as well as event programming.

Beyond games, some titles are designed for artistic or literary expression, such as "Freakshow" or "Bad Day on the Midway", while others are just pure fun, like "Monty Python's Complete Waste of Time."

Multimedia Authoring and the Internet

One of the newest and more exciting applications for multimedia authoring is the *World Wide Web*, a popular graphical environment on the Internet. The most attractive aspect of the Internet is its nearly unlimited potential for distribution options. As I write this, because of data transfer limitations over phone lines, creating multimedia events for the World Wide Web is challenging, at best. However, emerging technology, such as fast ISDN phone lines, television cable modems, and other technology will soon improve the multimedia author's lot on the Internet. The problem we face right now is that most people don't yet have access to high bandwidths.

Because of the enormous amount of data required to display full-color images, video, animation, and sound, the phone line can't play live clips (even with the fastest modem—28.8bps). Instead, your computer downloads the files from the server computer, and then the clip is played from your hard disk.

This limitation, however, has not stopped many innovative Web page designers from creating some sophisticated pages with integrated sound and video, as shown in Figure 1.9. You should keep in mind, too, that technology on the Internet is advancing faster than my fingers can type this. The future of multimedia on the Internet is exciting. The information highway *will* include live (fast) full-motion video and sound, and then the possibilities for multimedia authoring will become virtually limitless. Already we've seen the introduction of multimedia technologies, such as Macromedia Shockwave, for playing movies and multimedia titles on the Web. You'll see how to setup your multimedia masterpieces for view on the Web in Chapter 17.

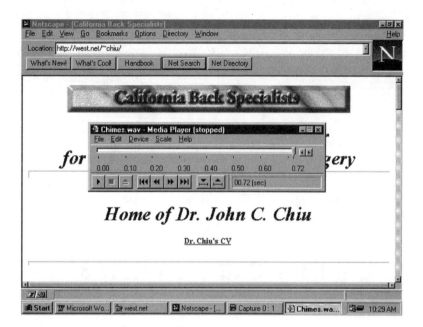

FIGURE 1.9:
Netscape Navigator playing a sound file on the World Wide Web.

As with the beginning of every emerging technology, multimedia on the Internet can be frustrating and challenging. But I stuck around for the desktop publishing revolution, and what a ride that was. Today some of the best graphics the world has ever seen are being produced on desktop computers, and there's no reason to believe we won't see similar advancements on the Internet. If you're new to the world of multimedia authoring and are interested in publishing for the World Wide Web, hold onto your hat—we're on the brink of some exciting times.

CHAPTER 2

The Anatomy of a Multimedia Machine

t's said in the real estate business that the value and salability of property are defined by three equally important factors:

1. Location
2. Location
3. Location

In other words, above all else, it's where a piece of property sits that determines whether the seller can get a good price and sell in a reasonable period. We computer journalists advise people to buy hardware and software based on three all-important considerations:

1. Application
2. Application
3. Application

This is especially true of multimedia and graphics. For these resource-intensive applications, and depending on the kind of multimedia authoring you intend to do, not just any computer and software will work. There is, after all, basic multimedia authoring, such as creating simple presentations, which requires a less sophisticated set up. And then there is multimedia authoring, those sound, animation, and video extravaganzas that I told you about in the previous chapter—remember the Atlanta Olympics proposal? In order to do something along those lines, you need to have a set up that meets multimedia authoring requirements.

In this chapter we look at the equipment you'll need to create your own multimedia titles, and touch briefly on putting together the ultimate dream machine to give you a sense of the potential of multimedia authoring (and so we can all drool a little).

If you're planning on designing multimedia presentations to take to potential clients, you'll want to consider using a notebook computer. They are the easiest way to get your work in front of would-be customers. We'll look at some of the notebook computers available and other portable display devices that you'll need to give successful presentations, and I'll also provide you with a brief overview of the types of presentations for which these devices are best-suited.

As you can see, we've got a lot of ground to cover—let's get started.

The Multimedia Authoring Machine

Just as you cannot make rabbit stew without first catching a rabbit, you can't author a computerized multimedia show without a computer. So if you don't already have one, go out and catch a computer. But before you do, read this section; it can save you some money and grief. (Isn't it funny how those two so often show up together?)

The Basic Multimedia PC

What makes a Windows computer a multimedia machine? A few years ago an organization known as the Multimedia PC Marketing Council (MPC) got together and came up with some guidelines for defining a multimedia PC. Machines that meet the guidelines are said to be MPC-compliant. Table 2.1 lists the minimum requirements for a Level 2 MPC multimedia PC.

Table 2.1: MPC Level 2 compliance requirements	
Component	**Configuration**
CPU	486SX25mhz
RAM	4MB
Sound (discussed in Chapter 6)	8 or 16-bit sample size; 11, 22, and 44 Khz sample rate; input mixing and MIDI In, Out, and Through.
Video (discussed in Chapter 3)	640x480 with 16-bit color or 24-bit.
Keyboard/mouse	101-key and two-button mouse
Writable storage (discussed in Chapter 5)	Floppy drive, and 160M hard drive
CD-ROM (discussed in Chapter 5)	Transfer rate of 300K/sec; seek time of 400 ms or better. CPU usage no more than 60 percent at 300K/sec; CD-Audio, CD XA multi-session, and Subchannel Q standards; (a basic dual-spin device)
I/O ports	Serial, parallel, MIDI, joystick

NOTE Actually, the council came up with two sets of guidelines: MPC Level 1 and MPC Level 2. Technology advances so fast that as soon as the council ironed out MPC Level 1, along came faster CD-ROM drives, more powerful sound cards, and so on. So we have Level 1 and Level 2. You probably couldn't find a Level 1–compliant machine in any retail store today, though. And multimedia has come so far since Level 2 was defined that it, too, is not altogether pertinent. We can, however, use it as a minimum requirement measurement.

If you know anything about computers, you can see that MPC Level 2 is a minimum configuration. Actually, if you went into a department store or another computer retailer looking for a machine with this configuration, you probably couldn't find one. Only second-hand stores and the classifieds would have these systems. Many of them are already dangling from the ends of ropes, anchoring small fishing boats.

The Typical Multimedia Machine

In actuality, people buying computers today are getting Pentiums with at least 4x CD-ROM drives. But there are still a lot of 486 machines out there, which are a lot slower. It's important to remember that many people never change the default resolution and color depth on their computers, and most manufacturers ship PCs set at 640x480 resolution with 256 colors. When authoring multimedia titles, you should always keep the minimum standards in mind—unless you know for certain they'll be displayed on machines comparable to yours, with high resolution and color depth settings.

Nowadays, almost all new computers have a minimum of 486/DX2/66mhz CPU, at least 8MB RAM, SuperVGA displays (or better), at least a 500MB hard drive, a quad-speed CD-ROM drive, and a super-duper stereo sound card with great quality speakers. My Altec Lansing Multimedia speakers are nearly powerful enough to blow me away from the computer. And they sound almost as good as the Kenwood stereo in my living room.

Well, I said *almost*.

So if you're in the market for a new multimedia computer, almost any new computer on the shelf will do, but the one described in the above paragraph will suit you nicely and, as I write this, you can find one for well under $2,000. (I always hate to quote prices for computer equipment—they change faster than I can type.)

There's a general rule of thumb that you can always purchase a basic state of the art computer, complete with monitor and keyboard for $2,500. With rapidly advancing technology and early obsolescence, what that buys you keeps getting better and better. If you're in the position to go all out, read the next section on *The Ultimate Multimedia Dream Machine*.

Regardless of which system you choose, the one thing you'll want to be mindful of is the modem. If you plan to do multimedia authoring for the Internet, your new system should have the fastest modem available. Right now that's a 28.8bps modem, and even at that speed transferring media clips can be painfully slow.

The Ultimate Multimedia Dream Machine

If you've got a bottomless pit for a wallet, this is the section for you. Figure 2.1 shows you a powerful multimedia computer system. Here's a list of what you should buy if you're serious about multimedia authoring and money is not an object. (Know anybody like that? I don't.) A professional multimedia developer will more than make back their investment in increased productivity, not to mention better quality of life associated with less frustration stemming from slow, obsolete hardware and software.

- 166mHz Pentium (or faster)
- 32MB RAM
- 64-bit PCI video graphics accelerator with at least 2MB VRAM (see Chapter 3)
- 1GB (or more) hard drive (see Chapter 5)
- 17" (or larger) monitor (see Chapter 3)
- 24-bit bed scanner
- Windows 95
- 32-note sound card and at least 10 watt speakers (see Chapter 4)
- 6x CD-ROM Drive (see Chapter 5)
- Video capture board (see Chapter 4)
- Stereo 4-head VCR
- Iomega JazDrive removable drive or some other type of removable media, such as magneto optical, Syquest, Bernoulli, or CD-ROM writer (see Chapter 5)
- 28.8bps modem for working on the Internet (see Chapter 15)

If some of these components seem unfamiliar, don't worry, we'll be covering each of them in detail in upcoming chapters, as indicated.

FIGURE 2.1:
This is an example of an ultimate multimedia machine: a 166mHz Pentium with ampllified speakers, 15-inch Trinitron Monitor, and microphone.

Before leaving this section on the dream machine, let me say that this configuration isn't required for effective, painless multimedia authoring—these are the ideal specs. Any machine somewhere between the basic system and the one described here will serve most people fine. Multimedia authoring is really an application specific endeavor so the system you end up with should ultimately be suited to the type of multimedia authoring you intend to do.

Making Your Old Clunker Multimedia-Ready

Chances are that if you bought this book, you already have a computer. And, if you bought your computer within the past two years, it's probably already multimedia-ready since almost all PC manufacturers ship their PCs with CD-ROM, sound cards, and speakers. If you bought your PC earlier than a couple of years ago, or if, for some other reason, your computer is not multimedia-ready, read the section on upgrading. If you're happy with your PC in general, but are considering making some specific improvements, read *Breathing New Life into Your PC* a bit further down.

You bought your computer a couple of years ago, and it came multimedia-ready, or maybe you've since added multimedia components. You just read the preceding paragraph and you figure you're out of the woods, right? If you're committed to this multimedia authoring thing, you'll want to look twice at your equipment. Just a couple of years ago computer manufacturers were shipping their supposed multimedia-ready computers with 8-bit sound cards, double-speed CD-ROM drives, and some really cheap, tinny-sounding speakers. Take it from me, you probably won't be happy with these components in the long run. The CD-ROM drives are too slow (video and animation are slow and jerky) and the sound quality stinks. Think twice, even three times, about upgrading your multimedia components—there's some good, relatively inexpensive stuff out there.

Multimedia Upgrade Kits

If you're making a non-multimedia-ready PC multimedia-ready, the only way to upgrade that makes sense is to buy a multimedia upgrade kit. They come with everything you need: CD-ROM drive, sound card, speakers, microphone, and a slew of utilities and multimedia titles to get you started. If your PC is already multimedia-ready, but you are not satisfied with the performance of one component or another, read the next section.

NOTE   If you (like me) are asking yourself when it will stop, the answer is— never. And while it's true that few of us can afford to keep up, this ever-evolving computer industry is exciting. We are doing things today few of us dreamed of five years ago—this is especially true in multimedia.

When upgrading your system, keep these two things in mind:

1. You probably won't be happy with a CD-ROM drive slower than 3x (and you probably won't be able to find a brand new one slower than 4x).
2. Pay close attention to the speakers in the box, some companies still slip in cheap, tinny ones. Look at Chapter 4 on speakers if you're not sure.

Breathing New Life into Your PC

If you've been using your PC for awhile, there's a good chance that you've already added components here and there. In my Pentium, for instance, I've got a brand new 3-D sound card, a 4x CD-ROM drive (which so far is plenty fast enough), and my speakers are 10-watt Altec Lansings with a woofer. However, the computer I started out with had an entirely different set of equipment. In effect, I rolled my own multimedia PC, and am quite happy with the results.

You, too, can create your own custom multimedia PC. Before doing so, though, you should do a little research on the different components, their features, and what they're capable of. Not all multimedia components are created equal. Upcoming chapters will give you an in-depth look at each of the components mentioned in earlier sections. Skip ahead to the ones you're considering adding or upgrading; for example, see Chapter 4 on sound cards. If you're building a multimedia PC from scratch, it's worth spending some time looking through each one, they'll help you sort out what's what in hardware.

TIP

Getting more information about video: Video capturing and editing is a specialized application in itself, and a bit beyond the scope of this book, except where it pertains to multimedia authoring. From a multimedia authoring standpoint, all we're really concerned with is importing the clips into our multimedia titles. For a more detailed description of video importing, see Chapters 4 and 12.

Taking Your Multimedia Authoring Titles on the Road

As I've already said, much of the multimedia activity going on today is in the area of business presentations. As you can imagine, it can be a real drag toting your desktop computer from prospect to prospect (especially a full-size tower and 20-inch monitor). The way most road warriors handle this is with a notebook computer capable of playing sound and connecting to a larger monitor, a TV screen, or a projection unit. Notebooks are easier to carry and don't require a lot of fuss to setup.

Windows Road Warriors

Most Windows notebooks don't come multimedia-ready, though an ever-increasing number are starting to. You can find IBM ThinkPads, some of Panasonic and Toshiba's top-of-line machines, and others with built-in sound and speakers. Some of the later models also come with built-in CD-ROM drives. The machines I've seen with this configuration are good, strong road warriors because they are fast and easy to use. The important thing to remember, though, is that you should try to get the components you need already built-in. It can be costly and frustrating to upgrade a notebook, and some can't be upgraded to sound capabilities at all.

Keep the following list in mind when looking for a multimedia Windows notebook:

- At least 256 colors on-screen and through the external monitor port (this is important, they're often different); HiColor is better. The external port should also support a higher resolution than the built-in screen. (See Chapter 3 for more details on display systems.)

- Removable hard drive or at least 500MB
- Sound built-in
- 8MB RAM
- CD-ROM (if your application calls for one)
- PCMCIA (PC cards) level 3 (for removable drives)

Be aware that the speakers in most notebooks are squeakers—you'll get better sound from external speakers. If your machine does have internal stereo speakers, you should also make sure it has an external jack.

Other Portable Equipment

Depending on your application, in addition to a good notebook computer, you may also need a few other pieces of hardware, such as a *digital-to-analog converter* for displaying your presentation on a TV screen or copying it to video tape, or an *LCD screen* for overhead projecting.

Digital-to-Analog Converter

A digital-to-analog converter is a device you connect to the video adapter port on your notebook (or desktop) that converts the data to a format usable by a TV or VCR. There are many good ones available, and they run from about $200 to upwards of $1,000—as with most things, you get what you pay for. Some are small boxes that fit neatly into your laptop case, while others are relatively large desktop models capable of running more than one TV at a time.

You should keep in mind, though, that this is not a perfect solution. TV monitors are low-resolution devices designed for viewing from a distance. Computer monitors are high-resolution devices designed for detailed, up-close work. In order to make this conversion, the converter must filter out some of the data, or resolution, intended for the computer screen. This works reasonably well for multimedia and graphics, but not so well for displaying text. And one last thing—you can forget transferring sound through one of these devices. You'll get audio out directly from the sound out port on your sound card. Some users might prefer a video capture board, they're discussed in Chapter 4.

LCD Screen

Like a digital-to-analog converter, an LCD screen connects to the video port. It then lays on an overhead projector, which in turn projects the computer data onto a screen—similar to using transparencies. This is, of course, a large-audience solution that works better for shows that don't contain a lot of sound and animation. The display quality is not nearly as good as a computer monitor. You can find them from just under $500 to upwards of $1,500.

What About Windows 95?

One of the selling points Microsoft has used to persuade people to switch to Windows 95 is "enhanced multimedia capabilities." Just what does that mean? Well, it comes down to three things: speed; better multimedia applets included with Windows 95; and Plug-n-Play peripherals.

Let's look at each of these separately.

Speed Thrills

Multimedia applications—playing sound, animation, and video—can really tax a computer's resources. Windows 95 and applications designed to run under it are 32-bit applications, as opposed to the previous version of Windows and its 16-bit processing speed. On the surface, this looks as though programs should run at twice the speed in Windows 95, right? Not exactly.

The graphics subsystem (video card) and hard disk speed still greatly affect how fast the system runs, and all the fancy software in the world can't change that. Where you really notice a difference is in memory-intensive processing, or when the computer doesn't have to access the hard disk to process data. Windows 95 is much better at handling RAM than earlier versions. The more RAM in your machine, the faster Windows 95 can run.

The bottom line? Windows 95 *is* faster, especially when running applications written specifically for that platform (although 16-bit applications run a little faster too). As you've undoubtedly gathered, speed is important in multimedia authoring. If you're upgrading, the path can be a bit arduous—be sure to read *Upgrading to Windows 95* later in this chapter.

Better Multimedia Applets

With the release Windows 3.1, we saw a number of applets, such as Sound Recorder, CD-Player, and a few others, that enabled Windows to record and play sound. A short time later, Microsoft introduced Microsoft Video for Windows, which allowed us to capture and play video. Next, other vendors, such as Intel and Autodesk, began releasing products that created and played multimedia files. Within a short time, you had to scrounge up drivers from all over just to get your sound, animation, and video files to work properly.

One way in which Windows 95 makes for a better multimedia platform is that most of the known multimedia drivers for multimedia files are already part of the Windows 95 package. (Although now that multimedia is taking hold on the Internet, we're coming up with a bunch of new file formats from UNIX and other platforms you'll need to find and install soon.) But the real story is the new 32-bit applets Microsoft has included for recording and playing multimedia files. Figure 2.2 shows Windows 95 Media Player with a Video for Windows files loaded. The 32-bit applets are faster, more reliable, and they allow third-party vendors to create bigger and better multimedia utilities.

FIGURE 2.2:
Windows 95's Media Player provides a smoother, faster, and more reliable way to play multimedia files.

Plug-n-Play

If you've ever installed a sound card or some other peripheral, such as an internal modem, in your computer, you'll appreciate this feature. In the pre-Windows 95 days, you had to figure out which IRQs and I/O addresses were available in the computer and then set the jumper switches of the new hardware to make it work in the system. No simple task.

Plug-n-Play (PnP) eliminates this process. All you do with a PnP device is plug it in and then tell Windows to find and configure it, as shown in Figure 2.3. In some cases you don't even have to perform the second step, Windows 95 sees the new hardware while booting and asks you if you want it configured.

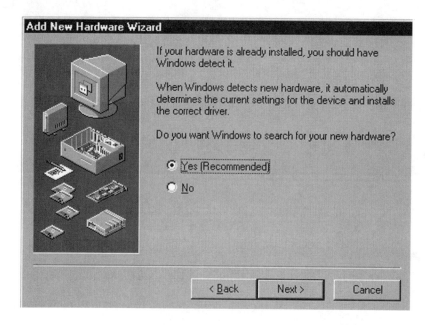

FIGURE 2.3:
The Add New Hardware Wizard in Windows 95 allows you to tell Windows to search for new hardware in your system, and then Windows will configure itself to use the new peripheral.

Sounds good in theory, right—but how well does it work? Well, since I've been using Windows 95, I've installed three PnP devices: a modem, a SCSI card, and the sound card I spoke of earlier—all three went in without a hitch. Windows saw them upon booting, asked me if I wanted them configured, and the next thing I knew I was computing again. This is a far cry from the hours (sometimes days) and numerous calls to technical support for installations I've experienced in the past.

WARNING Not just any device will support Plug-n-Play. In order for Windows 95 to find and configure hardware as I've described here, the product must display the PnP logo on the box.

Upgrading to Windows 95

From the description above, you'd think that Windows 95 is perfect. Well, the old adage remains true—nothing's perfect. And the most imperfect aspect of Windows 95 is its rocky upgrade path from Windows 3.x. The more hardware and peripherals you have installed and connected to your computer, the greater your chances for an unsuccessful upgrade to Windows 95.

For example, I've installed Windows 95 on five machines so far, and only one of them—my notebook—went without a hitch. In one machine, Windows 95 didn't support the sound card properly; in another it couldn't use the CD-ROM drive; and in another the modem didn't work. You get the idea.

Usually, this is not a problem—all you do is call the manufacturer of the device and they'll send a driver, or you can locate their BBS (Bulletin Board System) or CompuServe and download it in a few minutes—but not always. AT&T took about two weeks to get me the modem drivers, while the manufacturer of my sound card has not sent anything, and told me they will not develop Windows 95 drivers for their product (hence the new sound card).

Let's not forget the 16-bit software applications that either won't run or don't run properly under Windows 95. Most run OK, but a few don't (like Photoshop 3, for example). Your only alternative in these cases is to upgrade the application, providing an upgrade is available. Be sure to check with the manufacturers of your favorite and essential applications to see if they run under Windows 95.

The point is, be prepared for some frustration when upgrading to Windows 95. If you buy a new computer, though, you can probably rest assured that any incompatibilities have already been worked out. Undoubtedly, by the time you read this, Microsoft will have ironed out many of the buggy drivers, while software and hardware vendors will have taken steps to make their products compatible. You should not let a few early compatibility snarls stop you from taking advantage of Windows 95's increased power and flexibility.

> **WARNING** When installing Windows 95, the installation wizard asks you if you want to create an uninstall backup from your current installation, which will return your system to its original state before you installed Windows 95. Do yourself a favor—say "yes." It takes only a few minutes and a measly 6MB of disk space.

PART

2

Hardware and Software

CHAPTER 3

Monitors and Graphics Cards

Featuring

- Computer display systems 101
- What to look for in a graphics card
- Maintaining compatibility among components

Wh_en designing titles for playback on computers, there are many compatibility issues to consider. One of the more important configuration concerns is computer display systems. This chapter looks at the different types of systems and points out what to look for when considering monitors and graphics cards for multimedia work. We will also cover possible design snafus that can arise from the various display options available in the computer world.

Monitors and Graphics Adapters

To display information, be it text or graphics, all computers require two components: a display adapter and, of course, a monitor. Display systems run in various *modes*. Keep in mind during this discussion that to get the most from a display system, your monitor and graphics adapter must support the same modes. It does you little good, for example, to spend the extra money on a Super VGA display adapter if your monitor supports only *VGA*.

Getting a Better View

What is there to say about computer monitors? You hook them up and they display what's happening on the computer, right? Actually, there's more than meets the eye when it comes to monitors. Nowadays, computer monitors come in various shapes and sizes, with numerous bells and whistles. When it comes to multimedia authoring, however, only a few features really matter. In the following list of descriptions, key monitor features appear in order of significance for mulitmedia authoring:

- **Resolutions Supported**—Most of your multimedia titles will be created at 640x480, because that's the *resolution* of most computer displays in most offices. However, the higher resolution settings allow you more screen real estate to work in. In Figure 3.1, for example, I'm working in Macromedia Director at two different resolutions, 640x480 and 1280x1024. Notice that at the higher setting there's more room for my palettes and I can see more of my stage—the area where the actual title is being created. (Since the resolution of your monitor depends greatly on your graphics card, resolution sizes are discussed in detail in the next section.) Believe me, if you spend a lot of time in applications that use multiple palettes, like Macromedia Director, you'll need the extra space.
- **Screen size**—Currently, most computers ship with 15" monitors. If you bought your computer a few years ago, it may have a 14" monitor. The problem with small

monitors is that when you crank the resolution up, text, dialog boxes, and everything else gets smaller. In the bottom example in Figure 3.1, on a 15" monitor you'd have to squint to see many of the elements on the screen. For working at high resolutions—1024x780 or better—you really do need at least a 17" monitor, with 19" or 20" being ideal. However, there's a gigantic price jump (as much as $1,000) between 17" and 19" monitors.

- **Dot pitch**—This refers to the size of pixels that comprise the image on the screen. The smaller the *dot pitch*, the finer the display. Most of the monitors shipping today are .28, which provides a clear, crisp picture. Some are .26, which is even better. Beware of monitors over .28, though, the display is rough and ragged.

TIP

If you've spent any time with your nose buried in computer ads lately, you may have noticed some of the new "multimedia" monitors available. These monitors come with speakers and microphones built in. Be careful when considering this solution, often these speakers and microphones are of low quality. Check out Chapter 4 and make sure the microphone and speakers are good enough for multimedia authoring.

Pick a Card

Often called a graphics card, the display adapter is usually an incredibly simple-looking circuit board that slips into a bus slot (bus types are discussed in the next section) on the motherboard of your computer (some computers have display adapters built onto the motherboard). The graphics card processes information from the computer and sends it to the monitor.

When looking for a graphics card, you should consider these features:

- Whether your computer supports ISA bus, VESA local bus, or PCI local bus
- Resolution
- Number of colors (or bits-per-pixel); this is sometimes called *color depth*
- The screen refresh rate
- Software utilities

Let's look at each of them.

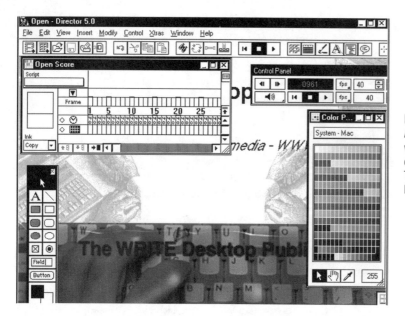

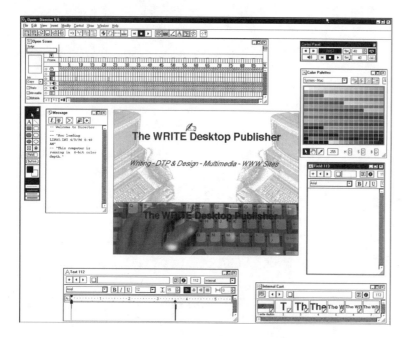

FIGURE 3.1:
An example of the expanded work area available at higher display resolutions.
Top: 640x480;
bottom: 1280x1024.

Bus Type

In order to constantly paint and refresh the thousands of pixels that make up a computer screen, your CPU (Central Processing Unit) must process and send millions of data bits to the monitor via the display adapter. Your display adapter connects to the mother-board by plugging into what's called a *bus slot*. The kind of bus slot your computer has determines how quickly these data bits flow from motherboard to monitor. Depending on how recently you bought your computer and how much money you spent, your computer has an ISA bus, a VESA local bus, or a PCI local bus. One of the reasons that Windows runs so gruelingly slow on yesterday's computers is due to the old AT/ISA bus standard, which transfers data from the CPU to the graphics card on a 16-bit path, as opposed to the 32-and 64-bit paths of today's computers.

> **NOTE** If your computer is so old that it has only an ISA bus video connection, you can still run multimedia, but you'll be much happier if you rush out to the nearest CompUSA and get a newer machine. If that's not feasible, read on, the rest of this discussion (after the material on bus types) also pertains to you.

To replace ISA (up until late 1993 to early 1994), computer manufacturers used VESA (Video Electronics Standards Association) local bus (VL-Bus) in all 486 and Pentium computers. The speed boost was tremendous, up to 132 megabytes per second (MBps), as compared to ISA's 1.5 to 3 MBps. In other words, VESA is more than forty times faster.

In late 1993, Intel released a new standard: PCI (Peripheral Component Interconnect). There is a major performance difference between PCI and VESA standards. PCI peripherals on a PCI bus can operate asynchronously. In other words, the CPU can send out instructions and access memory without waiting for the peripheral to respond. They don't keep the CPU (or you) waiting for the screen to redraw, as VL-Bus peripherals can. Now most computers (including Macs) use the PCI standard.

Resolution

Resolution refers to the number of dots, or pixels, on the monitor. The higher the resolution, the more information you can fit on the screen, and the better the image. In Windows, that means that you can view more open windows at the same time, and for multimedia you get better-looking graphics.

Standard VGA has a resolution of 640 pixels across and 480 pixels down (640x480). Super VGA mode is 800x600. VGA and Super VGA are the most common resolutions, but 1024x768 and even 1280x1024 (sometimes called Ultra or Extended VGA) are becoming increasingly popular. Some cards support resolutions up to 1600x1200. Remember, though, that your monitor must support the resolution of the card to benefit from the additional dots. If your monitor supports only 800X600, don't waste money on a card that pushes the resolution barrier up to 1280x1024.

When you choose a resolution, you'll also need to consider the screen size of the monitor. If you cram too many pixels onto a 14" monitor, text becomes too small to read easily. A good rule of thumb is to use a system that approximates the size of the final printed text. Table 3.1 should help you match resolution and monitor sizes.

Table 3.1: Matching monitor sizes to screen sizes	
Resolution	**Screen Size**
VGA (640x480)	14"
Super VGA (800x600)	15" or 16"
Extended VGA (1024x768)	17" or higher
1280x1024	19" to 21"

If you edit graphics in CorelDRAW, Adobe Photoshop, or some other application (and use a small monitor), you should choose a card that lets you switch resolutions, so that you don't have to strain your eyes when editing text. Presentations and multimedia applications also benefit from high resolutions. As I said, graphics look much better on a fine display monitor than they do on a coarse one.

Millions of Colors

Perhaps even more confusing than resolution is *display color*. Graphics cards are rated by the number of distinct colors they can display on a screen at one time. The range is from 16 to 16.7 million colors, with 256 being the most common. The number of colors a card is capable of displaying on the monitor depends on its bits-per-pixel rate, also known as its color depth. Today's graphics cards come in four color standards, as depicted in Table 3.2.

Table 3.2: Color depth ratings for graphics cards		
Bits Per Pixel	**Color Mode Name**	**Number of Colors**
4 bits	Minimum Color	16
8 bits	Pseudo Color	256
16 bits	Hi-Color	32,768 or 65,536
24 bits	True-Color	16.7 million

TIP

This color depth and resolution thing just gets more and more confusing, doesn't it? How do you know which standard to design your titles to? Well, the answer is, do what the professionals do—design to the lowest common denominator. (I'm jumping ahead a little bit, but it's important for you to keep this in mind when you are thinking about authoring titles.) Most computers come from the factory configured at the fastest display setting (640x480 with 256 colors.) You'd be surprised how many people never change them (or even know they that they can). So, design titles aimed for the general public at the lowest settings. The only time you should design at higher resolutions and colors is when you have some control over the system on which the title is to be displayed.

Just because a graphics card is capable of only 16 or 256 colors, it doesn't mean unsupported colors do not display. In Windows, for example, when an image calls for more colors than the graphics card is capable of, the approximation of these additional colors are displayed through a process called *dithering,* in which two or more solid colors are mixed together to form another. Figure 3.2 shows the difference dithering can make. If your graphics card doesn't support many colors, you've probably noticed that some hues are coarse or speckled—this is the result of dithering. In many applications, dithering is not a problem, but in graphics and photo processing, where color purity is critical, it's not acceptable.

TIP

Many of the stock photography and clip art images you'll use in your titles are True-Color images. Instead of depending on your audience's display systems to dither the images included in your masterpieces, it's a good idea to resample the images in your photo editing software to 256 colors before placing them in your layouts.

For most applications, including many multimedia applications, 256 colors are fine. However, most graphics look better at Hi-Color, though many multimedia applications and titles don't support more than 256 colors. Most people, except for users of high-end photograph editing software, such as Photoshop or Corel Photo-Paint, don't need 24-bit color.

FIGURE 3.2:
Notice the difference in image quality before (top) and after dithering (bottom).

If you're shopping for a new card, keep in mind that there's more to the way a card performs than the number of colors it can display. I've found that many cards with the same bits-per-pixel rate were not comparable in terms of clarity and purity of color. If at all possible, see the card in action before you buy it. Even then, looking at how the store's monitor performs hooked up to this card is only half the battle. The ideal situation is to see how the card performs with *your* monitor.

> **WARNING** Just because a display adapter claims 32,768 or 16.7 million colors doesn't mean it supports them at all resolutions. When you increase the number of colors, the display adapter needs more memory to store the additional information. When looking at a card's color and resolution specifications, make sure it's capable of the number of colors you need at the desired resolution. Sometimes you can add RAM to a graphics card to increase resolution and color capabilities—in both PCs and Macs.

Refresh Rate

If you spend a lot of time at your computer, be on the lookout for a card with a high refresh rate, your eyes will be forever grateful. (The *refresh rate* is the speed at which the screen gets repainted.) If the refresh rate is too low, your monitor flickers, which is annoying and hard on the eyes. It can cause headaches and long-term visual problems.

Refresh rates are measured in hertz (Hz). A rate of 72Hz means the screen is refreshed 72 times per second. Anything less than 72Hz can cause noticeable flicker. Just because a card claims to run "up to 72Hz" doesn't mean it supports that rate in all modes. Match the refresh rate to the number of colors and resolution at which you plan to use the card.

Software Features

It used to be that when you bought a graphics card, all you got was high-resolution and lots of colors—not any longer. Some of today's display adapters provide several useful features, including *panning, on-the-fly-resolution switching,* and *Green PC* energy saving.

- Panning, or virtual desktop, allows you to work in a larger area than displayed on your monitor. For example, in 640x480 mode, your desktop can actually be 1280 pixels wide by 1024 pixels high. You can then use your mouse or hot keys to scroll around in the virtual desktop area. There are several advantages to this feature, including the capability to have more open windows on your desktop. You can use virtual desktops to easily move text and graphics between programs.

- On-the-fly resolution switching has been available with several Macintosh graphics adapters for quite some time, and is a standard feature in Windows 95. Since many people typically work in word processors at lower resolutions and graphics applications at high resolutions, it is important to be able to change resolution and number of colors displayed without shutting down the computer or rebooting Windows. On-the-fly resolution switching allows you to switch back and forth without closing all your programs.
- Green PC is an energy saving feature built into most new monitors. In order to use the Green PC energy saving feature, you'll need a monitor capable of taking advantage of this technology. This is a simple concept that we should have thought of a long time ago. Basically, the graphics card puts the monitor and itself to sleep after specified periods of inactivity. While asleep, the display system uses about 90 percent less power. To wake the display system up, all you do is move the mouse or press a key. Not only does this save energy, but also prolongs the life of your monitor.

CHAPTER 4

Sound and Video

Featuring

- Sound card technology
- Tips on speakers
- Overview of microphones
- Understanding video capture technology
- Capturing your own video

So you're serious about multimedia authoring—you're ready, but your computer's not quite there yet. Either it's not multimedia-ready because it's lacking a component or two, or you're just not happy with the quality of the sound and video you're getting so far. If any of that sounds familiar, then this is the chapter for you. Over the next few pages we'll look at the most basic multimedia equipment: sound cards, speakers, microphones, and video capture cards. You can't create multimedia titles without them.

You can use this chapter as a reference for getting the sound and video portion of your system up and running. Other components, such as CD-ROM drives, multimedia authoring software, and supporting utilities, are discussed in detail in upcoming chapters.

Sound Card Technology

Most sound boards can produce 16-bit, 44.1kHz audio—the same level of digital audio you get from a compact disc player. The 16-bit rating depicts how much data the board can store in each sound sampling; 8-bit sound is okay for voice, but you need 16-bit for the higher-fidelity audio required for music. The 44.1kHz rating refers to the number of times (44,100) per second the sound board can process incoming or outgoing sound.

The technology used to reproduce musical instruments on a computer sound card is called *MIDI*—which stands for Musical Instrument Digital Interface. MIDI was established in 1982 by electronics manufacturers to provide simple, low-cost solutions for connecting synthesizers to computers. Essentially the connection allows devices to send and receive MIDI messages that signal which notes to play, how loud to play them, and for how long.

Today's sound cards support two types of MIDI sound: *wavetable* and *FM synthesizer*. Wavetable uses prerecorded samples of actual instruments to recreate sound. FM synthesizer imitates instrument sounds, producing an artificial sound that works fine for many games, but doesn't sound very good as music. Most multimedia authors want the richer sounds associated with wavetable MIDI.

TIP

Getting wavetable sounds from your existing sound card: Many cards, including some SoundBlasters, do not support wavetable on a board, but instead support optional daughter cards that plug into the sound card to give it wavetable compatibility. If you already have a sound card and want wavetable access, you might want to find out whether your card can be upgraded to provide this feature.

Another feature to consider is *3-D sound*. There are two types—surround sound (SRS) and Q-Sound. Basically, these two effects try to simulate the theater-like sounds you get at the movies, or from surround sound home entertainment centers. Based on two slightly different technologies, they perform very similar functions, and cost about the same. 3-D sound separates audio signals to create a more life-like effect. Once you've heard sound cards with 3-D sound, you'll be spoiled and won't want settle for anything less—particularly if you plan to create multimedia titles that contain lots of music.

Finally, you want to look for a sound card with 32-note polyphony capability, which provides even more of a concert-hall effect by allowing the card to store up to 32 different sounds simultaneously—this is especially important when playing back music. In addition, you can upgrade the memory with some wavetable cards, which allows you to save additional MIDI sounds, called *SoundFonts,* on your card. The Sound Blaster AWE32, for example, can be upgraded to 28MB, so you can save many additional sounds. Figure 4.1 shows an example of software that is used for creating and saving SoundFonts.

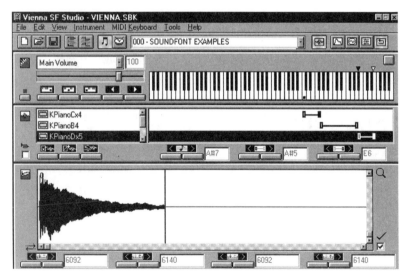

FIGURE 4.1:
An example of a software application that is used for creating and saving SoundFonts to a sound card.

Much of multimedia authoring doesn't actually require technology as sophisticated as I've discussed so far, which is really designed for composing music. However, even if you aren't planning to focus on music composition, you'll be happier with a sound card that supports wavetable—you'll have more options and the music will sound noticeably better.

SoundBlaster Compatibility

In addition to MIDI, you'll want a card that is SoundBlaster compatible. While the Adlib card was the first PC sound card, Creative Lab's SoundBlaster set the standard and became the most popular. In fact, for a long while, one of the requirements for purchasing a sound card compatible with multimedia applications was to make sure it played SoundBlaster files.

> **TIP**
>
> When a sound card claims that it is "backward compatible" it usually means that the card is SoundBlaster compatible. Even though many of today's computer sounds are not necessarily SoundBlaster sounds, some still are—so if you want to be able to play all sounds, make sure your card is SoundBlaster compatible.

Since Creative Labs keeps up with evolving sound technology, SoundBlaster will continue to be a player in the world of sound cards. The Sound Blaster AW32 PnP, for instance—one of the first Windows 95 cards—supports all of the latest technology and is considered to be a quality product.

Speaker Technology

Most computer speakers are petite enough to sit cozily next to your computer or hang off your monitor with the aid of brackets. However, don't expect hi fidelity from a 3" cone. You'll find any multimedia experience greatly enhanced by amplified speakers, surround sound, and a *subwoofer*. With the proliferation of the home computer market, we're just entering the age where the computer playback environment is trying to replicate the home theater setup. All good speakers will also contain magnetic shielding that keeps them from distorting the image on your monitor.

When shopping for speakers, sound quality should be your primary concern. Most speakers can't handle throbbing bass. You'll often need to include a larger external speaker called a subwoofer, which greatly enhances the depth of the speaker tone. Try listening to your prospective speakers with and without a subwoofer before settling on a set. Many speakers attempt to make up for poor bass response through tone controls (the little knobs and wheels that boost or cut the low and high frequencies). You should look for speakers with dual controls: one for treble and one for bass. It's convenient, too, if the controls are on the front of the speakers rather than on the subwoofer, which many people then place on the floor beneath their desk. You don't want to have to keep bending over to adjust the volume and tone.

On a similar note, it's a good idea to have headphone jacks on the front of the speakers. Why is location so important? You'll probably be plugging in and unplugging your headphones a lot to cut off the external sounds through your speakers, so it's better if the jack is easier to reach.

Microphones

Unfortunately, the microphones that come with most multimedia upgrade kits and multimedia PCs leave a lot to be desired. In order to record sounds into most of them you must get very close—so close that your breath also gets recorded. The good news is that the human voice doesn't require an expensive microphone capable of a wide sound range. If you want to do any serious voice recording, you should consider springing for a new one, which will set you back between $25–$100, depending on the quality. But as is the case with most things, you get what you pay for. A quality mic can make a voiceover sound richer, and though professional mics cost as much as $1,000 or more, you can find a suitable one for much less.

Video Capture Boards— the Talkies on Your Computer

As far as I'm concerned, one of the more exciting aspects of multimedia is the ability to capture and display full-motion video. For many applications, especially presentations and edutainment, video provides a great vehicle for enriching your titles with compelling and entertaining content. The next few sections take a look at the fundamentals of video capture technology, the types of video capture boards currently available, and the benefits realized with their use.

Overview of Video Capture Technology

Video capture cards convert the analog signal from a video or audio source into digital files for use in producing computer-based video clips. In the most basic sense, the video capture samples an incoming analog video signal at a specified frequency and converts that signal to a digital file (also known as *digitizing*), which you can then run on your computer, as shown in Figure 4.2. Like graphic cards, video capture cards rely on a balanced integration of hardware and software to efficiently manage your system's CPU and other resources. However, unlike graphic cards, the use of video capture technology places a tremendous strain on your system because of the requirements of processing converted video files. A comprehensive discussion of desktop video production (DVP) is beyond the scope of this book. However, there are two DVP concepts that are important for the beginning multimedia author to understand: *capture variables*, and *compression/decompression algorithms* commonly referred to as *CODECs*. Both of these concepts play an important role in determining the file size of video clips.

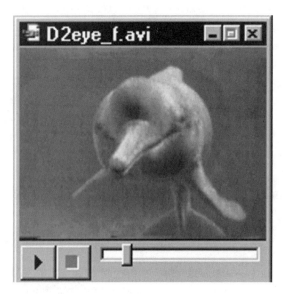

FIGURE 4.2:
Here you see a frame from a movie running on a computer monitor.

Capture Variables

Capture variables are those elements that impact the quality of a captured video sample, and include items such as *frame rate*, frame size, color depth, and image quality. These factors play an integral role in the appearance of your final product.

Frame Rate: Video delivery relies on the perception of motion. When a series of still images displays in rapid succession, an illusion of continuous motion is perceived by the human eye. In the television and film industries, the presentation of a rapid succession of still images is measured in frames per second, or fps. Standard television broadcasts are delivered at between 25 and 30 fps, while the standard delivery for film is about 24 fps. Consequently, each still image in a series of images comprising a video segment is termed a frame. Frame rate is the number of frames per second required to create the illusion of motion to the human eye. For digital video, it is recommended that a capture card be capable of supporting a minimum of 15 frames per second.

TIP Capturing video at less than 15 frames per second produces a noticeable jerkiness in the playback quality of the captured segment.

Frame Size: As covered in our discussion of graphic cards, standard VGA presents a screen frame display of 640x480 pixels. While it is possible to capture video at this resolution, it is unlikely that the hardware used to replay a video segment will be able to accommodate a video clip of this size, resulting in slow, jerky playback, and data loss. Common practice is to make sure that your capture card can maintain frame sizes for digital video in the range of 160x120 pixels to 320x240 pixels so that yor clip can be viewed as intended. Most mainstream cards support these resolutions. The most common practice is to capture at the largest frame size and use your video editing software to resize the frames downward. You won't have much success trying to go from smaller frames to larger frames, computers aren't very good at guessing where to add data.

Color Depth: Most video capture cards are capable of acquiring video segments in 8-bit, 16-bit, and/or 24-bit color. The rule of thumb here is to capture high and reduce. In other words, capturing a video segment in 24-bit color provides the best color sample possible, but in order to keep your files a manageable size, you will need to reduce them to 8-bit in the editing process. This is essentially the same concept as capturing bigger frame sizes and editing down.

Image Quality: Another factor that affects file size is image quality. As with color depth, it takes a lot of data to reproduce crisp, clear pictures, frame after frame. Creating clips at manageable file size and acceptable playback rates can be a precarious balancing act. As shown in Figure 4.3, video editing software allows you to reduce file size by compromising picture quality. The trick is to reduce size (and by definition, quality) by removing the redundant or unnecessary information. If you choose the right elements, the clip won't suffer much at all—in fact, the human eye will not even see a difference.

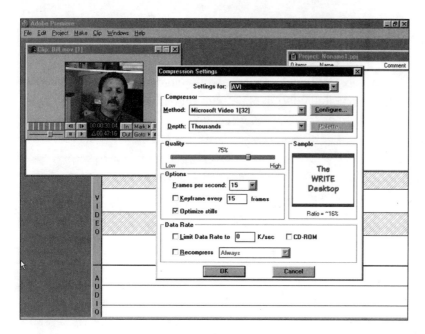

FIGURE 4.3:
Video editing software allows you to reduce the size of your file.

Compression and Decompression

In addition to controlling file size by adjusting frame size and rate, color depth, and image quality, you can also make movie clip files smaller by using compression and decompression routines built into your video editing software. A number of formats are available, but the ones most commonly used in multimedia video editing are Microsoft Video (AVI) and Apple QuickTime. It's beyond the scope of this book to define and discuss them in detail, however, it's a good idea to use AVI files for titles designed to playback on Windows machines, and QuickTime for Macs. Also, since Quicktime can play on both platforms (with some preperation in your video editing software), you should use it when designing titles for playback on both platforms. Compression and decompression (*CODEC*) can be understood in terms of the method and mechanism relationship. Compression is a method used to facilitate the use of captured digital video segments for desktop video production; decompression refers to the method used to play back the clips on the desktop. These concepts are covered in more detail below.

Lossless and Lossy Compression Methods: Working with captured digital video requires the use of compression techniques during the editing process to enhance the quality of the playback image. Today there are two compression methods in common use, they are the Lossless Method and the Lossy Method.

Capture cards using the lossless method of compression keep all the data from the captured video file in tact. This means that the image quality of the digital file is high, but the file size is large. This method is called *lossless* because when the file is decompressed, all of the data contained in the file is there.

Typically, lossless data compression can make a file as much as half its original size. However, since 60 seconds of video can take up several megabytes of disk space, 50 percent size reduction does not entirely solve the video file size dilemma. Lossless is preferable when creating video for large storage mediums, such as CD-ROM. But even then, you won't be able to create long clips—if you do, you won't have room for the rest of your title. For this reason, in most multimedia applications, lossy is a preferable method.

Cards using the lossy compression method use compression algorithms to eliminate specific data from the captured video file. This means that the image quality of the resulting digital file may be degraded, however, file size is greatly reduced. This is not as bad as it sounds. As I alluded to earlier, many clips contain far more data than is needed to play well on a computer display system. For example, 24-bit images contain a lot of unnecessary repeated data, and display a lot of subtle color differences people cannot perceive. It does little to the image quality to drop this data from the file, but it helps tremendously in terms of file size manageability.

Unlike lossless, lossy data compression is capable of compression rates as high as 100:1. In other words, you could compress a 5MB file down to 50K—this is a radical squeeze. The extent to which a file can stand to be compressed depends solely on the clip and the level of degradation you can live with. New video editors must experiment with compression to find the right balance between quality, practicality, and file size.

CODEC: CODEC is an abbreviation for compression/decompression, and refers to the algorithm used to reduce the size of video, sound, and graphic files. CODEC drivers may be firmware existing on a video capture card, or they may be software supplied—as in the case of Video for Windows which ships with RLE and Video 1 CODECs. When deciding on a video capture card, it is advisable to make CODEC compatibility between different hardware types a basis for your selection.

Capturing Your Own Video

Before you begin assembling digital files for your desktop video epic, it's prudent to realize that there is a certain amount of preparation to be done. First, let's look at the set up you'll need to capture video, and then we'll walk through the steps for capturing your own video.

1. Inspect your system.

A multimedia computer system configured for desktop video production should meet the following requirements (don't worry if you don't recognize some of these components, they'll be covered in upcoming chapters):

System Component	Minimum Requirement	Recommended Requirement
CPU	386/33	486/DX/33 or better
RAM	8 MG	16 MG or better
Monitor and Graphic Card	8 bit (256 colors at 640x480 pixels)	24-bit (16.7 million colors) at 800x600 pixels or better
Hard Disk Drive	540 MG (more is better)	1 GG or better
CD-ROM Drive		Windows compatible quad-speed or better
Video Capture Card	Supports Microsoft Video for Windows drivers	Support for Microsoft Video for Windows, *Apple QuickTime for Windows*, and MPEG full-screen video
Sound Card	8-bit SoundBlaster compatible	16-bit SoundBlaster compatible
MS-DOS	5.0	Windows 95
Windows	3.1	Windows 95

2. Defragment your hard drive.

As you copy, delete, and move files around on your hard disk, files and your disk itself get fragmented. In other words, files are scattered around on the disk, and you have noncontiguous gaps that must be filled in with new data. This process of the computer figuring out where to put data next can slow down the capture process, causing loss of data. Performing a defragmentation will create contiguous disk space facilitating the capture and playback process. Windows 95 comes with a defragmentation utility, called an optimizer.

3. Capture at a higher frame rate than the target playback rate.

When designing a title for playback on an unknown source, such as somebody else's computer, you'll have to ensure that the clip will play optimally. Typically, CD-ROM and other titles designed for playback on a computer work well at 15 fps. However, you'll have better luck if you capture at a higher rate and use your video editing software to sample the frame rate downward. Remember that you can remove data, but it's difficult to replace it. I usually capture at about 20 or 24 fps, and then I have plenty of disk space at my disposal.

4. Estimate the size of your capture file.

This will enhance capture performance. Capturing a file larger than you intend to display can introduce image garbage when you reduce the image for playback. You can control file size by adjusting color depth, image quality, and compression method before you capture. Also, be sure that you have enough disk space available to hold the file.

Realtime Verses Frame-per-Frame Capturing

The procedure described here is a typical realtime capturing process. In other words, the computer captures all of the data in a stream, leaving out only what you setup in your compression and frame rate settings. An alternative method is frame-per-frame, which allows you to designate which frames to capture. You can, for example, capture every other frame, ever third frame, and so on. With this method, you get more precision in starting and stopping the capture, allowing you to easily skip portions of the tape.

To perform this type of capture, you'll need a special controller video capture card, and a device, such as a controllable video deck, that will respond to signals from the controller card. The advantage of this method is that it gives you much more control over what you capture and its quality. However, the board and control device can add considerable costs to your mulitmedia workshop—as much as a few thousand dollars.

5. Set your video source.

This is the easy part. Most capture cards come bundled with software that lets you set your video source (signal from a VCR, videodisc player, camcorder, etc.) to the first frame of your capture sequence. The way you connect to the video capture board will depend on the board itself, as well as the playback device.

6. Begin the capture process.

This varies slightly from software to software. In Adobe Premiere, for example, you initiate the capture by choosing the Capture Movie command, setting your compression, frame size, frame rate, and then clicking Start and turning on the playback device (VCR, camcorder, etc.). The video will display (at a very slow rate) in the capture window as it is saved, going to either memory or disk, depending on the program preferences you set. When you get all the footage you want, simply click the mouse and turn off the playback device. You are now ready to edit the video and set the final compression, frame, and other settings before saving the clip in its final file format—QuickTime, AVI, etc.

After capturing the video, it will probably need editing. While most capture boards come with some sort of video editing software, often it is inadequate for achieving professional results. Be sure to checkout Chapter 7 for an overview of video editing software.

CHAPTER 5

Storage Devices: CD-ROMs and Removable Media

Featuring

- Choosing a mass storage solution
- What to look for in a CD-ROM drive
- Why use a CD-Recorder?
- Comparing Syquest drives
- Transportable hard disks

Typically, when people think of mass storage, data backup comes to mind. But desktop publishers, multimedia authors, and other folks who deal with large multimedia and graphics files appreciate the need for alternative methods to store and transport computer files. At 1.44MB a pop, those little 3.5 plastic disks you stick into the front of your computer quickly become woefully inadequate. (I know what you're thinking—you'll just use PKZIP or Stuff-It to make the files fit. Well, that will only work for very small multimedia titles—remember the discussion of compression in Chapter 4?) Few computer files are larger than multimedia video-, sound-, and animation-filled multimedia creations. Multimedia titles often range in the 500MB to 600MB and beyond—that's why most come on CD-ROM discs.

In fact, it wasn't until the introduction of the 650MB CD-ROM disc that distributing multimedia titles really became a viable prospect. Before then, getting multimedia files from one computer to another was too expensive and time-consuming. CD-ROM discs solved the commercial multimedia titles distribution problem, but for the multimedia author, marketing and distribution of his or her wares addresses only a small part of the storage issue. The CD-ROM disc is often the last stage, or the end of the line, in multimedia authoring. It's where you house the finished product, but you still need a way to transfer, share, and back up your files during the production process, as well as a way to get your multimedia titles to the *service bureau* to get a master CD created.

Since CD-ROM discs are write once/read often media, you cannot conveniently store dynamic or editable versions of your titles on them. As a result, most multimedia authors prefer to work with rewritable devices, such as Syquest or Bernoulli drives, transportable hard disks, or some other type of removable storage device.

Data storage, transportation, and distribution are crucial issues in multimedia authoring applications; therefore, this entire chapter is devoted to storage devices. You've got a lot of solutions at your disposal.

Choosing a Mass Storage Solution

The title of this section might suggest that you don't need a CD-ROM drive for multimedia authoring. Well, you do—you need a CD-ROM drive to garner multimedia programs, media clips, and to play other multimedia authors' wares. However, you will most likely need an additional form of storage for saving and transporting your multimedia files. No matter how big your hard disk, when working with multimedia files, eventually you'll need some other medium to remove the multimedia title and supporting files to make room for your next project.

What is a Service Bureau?

Service bureaus (sometimes called *imaging centers* or *desktop publishing service bureaus*) are companies that provide support for computer users. Their most common uses are printing high-end color proofs from thermal wax or dye sublimation printers, printing high resolution output on imagesetters, scanning, and slide making. They offer a number of multimedia services, from printing specialized color output to CD-ROM mastering, and are cost effective for developers if they only need these services occasionally, and therefore, can't justify buying that particular output device. If you don't plan to create many master CDs, for example, you wouldn't want to spend the $1,000 to $3,000 purchase a CD-Recorder when you can have one created through a service bureau for a fraction of the cost. Most of them also provide CD-ROM recording.

While these devices come in numerous shapes and sizes, for multimedia authoring purposes there are basically three types of storage devices: CD-ROM, removable media (which includes tape back up drives), and transportable (or external) hard disks. The type you should choose depends on several factors, and in some cases, you may need more than one storage device. For example, I use removable media to transport files to the service bureau and a tape backup drive to store files over the long hall. The reason is that the Iomega Bernoulli drive that I use for transporting files uses disks that can hold only 150MB of data—and they cost close to $100 each. I simply can't afford to fill them up with data and then store them away somewhere. Especially when you consider that my tape backup drive uses tapes that hold up to 2GB, and the tapes cost only about $10. Doesn't take a mathematician to figure out which method is cheaper, does it?

So let's look at these different types of storage devices.

CD-ROM Drives

In my years of reviewing software and hardware for computer magazines, it hasn't been often that I could say that most of the products in a category are comparable. But for the most part, that's true of CD-ROM drives. Unless you compare different speed drives to one another (say dual-spins to quad-spins), performance-wise CD-ROM drives are pretty much the same. Where they differ primarily is in the CD titles bundled with them, the way the CD-ROM disc loads into the front of the device, whether they are internal or external, and—a relatively new feature—whether they are multi-disc changers. With Windows machines, it is also worth paying attention to whether the device is SCSI (see note on p. 63 for more information on SCSI) or IDE. The following is an overview of what I consider to be the most important CD-ROM features for you to consider as you prepare for your multimedia authoring trip.

FIGURE 5.1:
Examples of external and internal CD-ROM drives. External drives (top) come in cases suitable for sitting on the desktop. Internal drives (bottom) mount inside your computer.

Speed Demons

Quad-speed drives provide all the pep you need for playing back multimedia files, they play sound and video files quite efficiently. While multimedia files don't run any multimedia clips any faster on 6x and 8x drives, they do load more quickly, so you don't have to wait as long to see a video or hear a sound after making a selection (this is also known as the drive's data *transfer rate*). For instance, programs like Encarta contain humongous databases. So with a faster drive you can load the data search engines and find the data you're looking for sooner.

Where you really see the difference is when you're opening large image files in Photoshop, or when you're transferring a lot data from a CD-ROM to your hard disk or a removable disk. Nowadays, it's nearly impossible to buy a new 2x or 3x CD-ROM drive. As I write this, 4x drives are the norm, and 6x and 8x drives have just begun to appear. As you can see from Table 5.1, the drive's speed determines its data transfer rate.

Table 5.1: CD-ROM drive transfer rates	
Speed	**Transfer Rate**
4x	600 KB per second
6x	900 KB per second
8x	1200 KB per second

Multi-disk Drives

Perhaps you've seen those 5-, 10-, 25- and 100-disc changers that come with some stereo systems. Wouldn't it be nice if you get one that works with your computer so you wouldn't have to keep swapping those disks in and out each time you wanted to access a file not currently on disc? Well recently, several CD-ROM drive vendors, including NEC and Turtle Beach, have released 3- and 7-disc changers.

As a writer, the first benefit that comes to mind from these drives is the ability to keep several reference volumes mounted at the same time, that way you don't have to switch disks in an out each time you need different types of information. For multimedia authoring, the benefit is that you can access several different types of clip media without fussing with the disks, and you can run some large programs without having to install them on your hard drive. A complete installation of the CorelDRAW package, for example, can take upwards of 100MB.

A problem with trying to run a program from a single-disc drive is that if you need to import something—an image or multimedia file, for example—from a CD other than the one containing the program files, you must remove the disc from which the program is running. This is never a good idea; it can be disastrous if the computer tries to read from the missing program disc, causing your computer to crash.

These drives can cost a little more than single-disc drives, so you might want to weigh the benefits against the expense.

To Caddy or Not to Caddy

No, I'm not getting ready to tee off. A *caddy* is a small case, or carriage, in which some types of drives require you to put the CD-ROM disc before you slide it into the drive. Drives that do not require caddies simply accept the bare disk. Whether you need a caddy or not is strictly a matter of taste, like deciding whether to carry your own golf clubs. Some people consider caddies (for disk drives) a nuisance. However, I prefer them—here's why:

- You're more likely to damage the disc putting it into the drive without the caddy.
- It's much easier to put the disk into the drive incorrectly without the caddy.
- You can purchase extra caddies and keep your disks in them so you don't have to take them out of the cases before use.

The last point is a real time-saver. For example, the other day while working on a project, I used several stock photography collections. Instead of fumbling with the cases, taking the CD-ROM discs in and out of the drive when I needed a new photograph, I simply kept them in separate caddies, switching them in and out of the drive as needed. (Since stock photography discs cost about $200 each, I wasn't about to leave them lying on the desktop.)

CD-Recorders (CD-R)

CD-R technology is used to record CD-ROM discs. Unfortunately, you can't use the CD-ROM drive that came with your computer to record CDs, it's a read-only device. In other words, you can only copy data to CD once, but you can read it over and over. So once you "burn" the CD (files are placed on the disc with a laser beam), you can't change it. If you don't get it right the first time, or if you want to upgrade your files, you'll have to burn another disc. This is not only time-consuming, but also expensive. If you're getting your CDs done at a service bureau, it can cost up to $200 per disc.

There are two ways to access CD-R storage (well, three, if you have a friend or relative with a CD-R drive): buying your own CD-R device or using a service bureau. If I were writing this book a couple of years ago, the first option would not be available to most aspiring multimedia authors—CD-R devices used to cost as much as $40,000. Now, if you shop around, you can find them for under $1,000.

The question, of course, is whether your application justifies this kind of expense (although at $1,000 to $3,000 per drive, it probably seems like an easy choice). However, if you plan to burn several multimedia titles within a year or two, spring for the CD-R drive. If you spend about $150 per CD (if you fill them up) at the service bureau, it won't take but a few discs to add up to the cost of a recorder. The $1,000–$3,000 price does not, however, include multimedia authoring software or blank discs, but most CD-R drives come with some sort of software for organizing and transferring files to the CD. In terms of buying additonal disks, the best part of this solution is that the blank discs cost only a few bucks each ($7–$10)—a tremendous advantage over other types of mass storage disks. You could easily spend a few hundred dollars for comparable storage on other types of media, such as SyQuest drives.

If price isn't enough to persuade you, there are a host of other reasons to consider recording your CD-ROMs on your own CD-R: inexpensive and plentiful storage space means there is no need to risk image degradation by using compression schemes—such as JPEG, ZIP, Stuff-It, and so on—to archive art and media libraries; you can test your multimedia titles while in progress; and by burning a CD-ROM, you can check factors like interface ease of use, interactivity, how the content plays—whatever questions you may have—before committing to a master title. You could not, of course, afford such experimentation by taking your work to the service bureau.

Sounds great so far, right? Well just for balance, here are some other things to consider before deciding on this technology:

- First, do you really need your own recorder? As I said earlier, the service bureaus in most metropolitan areas will make a CD-ROM for about $150. If you need CD-ROMs primarily for storing scanned photos, a local lab can make a packed Photo CD (100 images) for less than $100. The issue here is, how many CDs will you make? If you foresee the number going over 10, you should probably consider investing in your own device.

- Next, consider your computer. Because a computer must maintain a steady throughput to the CD-Recorder to ensure you don't get data errors on your CD, you'll need a fast one with at least 8MB of RAM. Remember that an 80486DX-based PC is a minimum Windows machine.

- Publishing software should play a large role in your purchasing decision as well. This software controls the recorder, properly organizes and names files, and pre-masters the CD-ROM on your hard drive. You can save yourself a lot of headaches by making sure your drive hardware comes with a compatible software package.

So, does it seem far-fetched, all this talk about writing your own CDs? Welcome to the future. It's very likely that by the end of 1996, most graphics designers and multimedia authors will have CD-Recoders sitting on their desks (or installed in their computers). As I write this, you can find 2x CD-Recorders for about $1,200. In addition to recording (or writing) CDs at double-speed, they can also serve as 2x CD-ROM readers.

4x recorder/readers are also available, costing in the neighborhood of $3,000. However, if you already have a 4x or faster CD-ROM drive, you shouldn't shell out the money for the 4x recorder. Whether your drive records at 1x, 2x, 4x, or whatever, that has no bearing on how well the CDs playback on faster drives. And let's face it, in most cases, recording CD-ROMs is not something you'll do often enough that it matters how fast they pop out of the recorder. You've probably figured out that desktop CD-Rs are not meant for mass producing CD-ROM discs—you burn the disc only after your multimedia titles are finished and take them to a service to have them reproduced. (Although you *can* use the CD-R to backup data, as well as create multimedia titles.)

It's In the Software

Despite what I said a few paragraphs back about speed and CD-ROMS, speed is a secondary issue when looking for a CD-Recorder; your most important consideration should be the software that ships with the drive used for burning CD-ROM discs. (Few applications require you to burn CD-ROMs often enough to gain much from the extra speed.) Basically there are two standards: Corel's CD Creator on the PC (also available for the Mac), and Astarté's Toast on the Mac. Both programs, shown in Figure 5.2, have received rave reviews and are considered the industry-standard for ease-of-use and reliability. However, this does not mean that other programs do not work well, too. What's important is the data formats supported by the drive and the software.

For maximum flexibility, you should look for drives and software that support the CD-ROM data formats in Table 5.2. Note however, that Macintosh software (because Macs can read PC formatted disks) is typically capable of more formats than Windows software. So, if you have your choice between hooking your CD-R to a Mac or Windows PC, choose the former—you'll be able to burn both types of discs.

Table 5.2: CD-ROM data formats	
Format	**Platform Supported**
ISO9660	Standard PC format supported by both Mac and Windows, supports standard DOS character naming format of 8.3 characters.
HFS	Macintosh format, support associations, links, and other Mac features—can't be read by Windows machines.
Mac/ISO Hybrid	Can be read by both Macs and Windows machines, common data is read by both machines.
Audio CDs	Used to copy and make audio CDs like those used by stereo CD changers.
Mixed Mode CD-ROMs	Used to make combination Audio and Data CDs.
Generic format	Copies information exactly as saved on the CD, typically used to make copies of existing CDs.

Removable Media

This category of storage devices—*removable media*—has become so diverse that it would be impossible to discuss all of them in this chapter. Rather than trying to provide comprehensive coverage of all the various removable media types, this section looks at a couple of the most popular technologies among multimedia authors—their advantages and disadvantages.

Though diverse, there are two basic types of drives: disk (random access) and tape (sequential). The main difference between them is that your computer programs can usually read disk drives directly, so you can easily copy files to and from them; in fact, you can even run programs directly from the disk. Tape drives, on the other hand, usually require some type of specialized software to copy the files to and from the tape. Your computer programs can't read and write to the tape directly, nor can you execute programs from them. Tape drives work best for backing up files (though some multimedia authors use them for transporting data to the service bureau). The bottom line is: Disk drives are much more flexible.

It's easy to understand the difference between these two devices if you think about the difference between the cassette player on your stereo and the unit's CD or record player. The cassette player is linear. In order to access songs toward the back of the tape, you must first fast forward through the songs preceding them. On a CD or record, which are flat and accessed by a floating arm, you can easily pick and choose by placing the arm on the desired song, regardless of where the song lies on the medium.

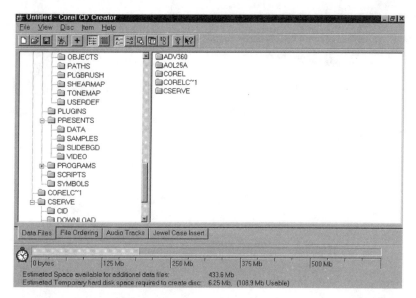

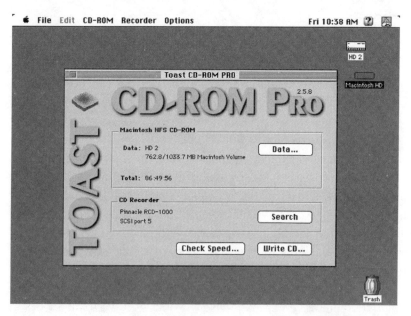

FIGURE 5.2:
The two CD-R software standards: Corel's CD Creator on the PC (top), and Astarté's Toast on the Mac (bottom).

This is also true of backup tape drives and disk-type removable media. While the tapes used in tape drives can hold upwards of two gigabytes of data, they are linear. The removable disk drives are much more flexible and faster, but they're also more expensive. Still, I can't really recommend a tape drive unless you have the money for two drives—the removable disk drives are a must for multimedia authoring. As a result, the next few sections focus exclusively on disk drives.

Removable Disk Drives

As I've already said, there are many different types of removable drives. Remember from the discussion earlier that there are two basic types: disk (random access) and tape (sequential). Tape drives are more often used for data backup, rather than moving and temporarily storing data. This section concentrates on the most popular random devices, which are the following:

- Syquest drives
- Syquest EZ drives
- Iomega Bernoulli drives
- Iomega Zip drives
- Iomega Jaz drives

NOTE Removable drives are almost always SCSI: "SCSI" stands for Small Computer System Interface. SCSI (pronounced "scuzzy") devices are accessed through Windows machines via a bus card, commonly called a SCSI card. Because of the SCSI interface's ability to chain up to seven devices on the same card, removable media are almost always SCSI. Some manufacturers, when configuring packages for Windows machines, include SCSI cards in their kits. Since Macs are already SCSI-equipped, Macintosh-configured kits do not contain SCSI cards. You should note when buying a drive whether the SCSI interface is included. If it's not, buying one will add $70–$300 to the cost of your drive.

WARNING Before purchasing a removable drive, confer with the vendors who will be processing your data at your service bureau. Don't buy a drive they don't support, you'll be up a creek and searching for a new service bureau. Also make sure that their drive supports the size disks your drive uses. If you have clients that use removables, you should also check with them.

SyQuest Drives: Syquest removable cartridge drives are based on technology invented by Syquest, Inc. But several vendors (including Syquest) actually make the drive, including MicroNet and APS. Basically, the drives themselves are the same. Price and bells and whistles, such as software utilities, determine the value of each vendor's drive.

This technology is based on a sturdy, plastic-encased removable hard disk. The disks come in storage sizes of 44, 88, 200, and 270MB.

Syquest drives are the most widely used drives in the graphics design and desktop publishing fields, and are also widely used in multimedia authoring. I've never found a desktop publishing service bureau or imaging house that didn't support them—especially on the Mac platform. So, if compatibility with a wide range of services is important to you, you can't go wrong with this drive.

However, I've been using these drives for years and have found them to be somewhat quirky. The disks don't always mount properly, and I've had a number of them fail, losing valuable data—despite the five year warranty. (And I know other designers who have experienced similar problems.) While they're great for transporting files, I don't recommend them for storing data over time, unless you're prepared to keep two copies of everything, which is a good idea for important material anyway.

At press time, the 270MB version of these drives sold for about $500 or less. There are also some dual-drive units that will run 44, 88, and/or 200 disks from the same drive mechanism, which are available for slightly more money. If you purchase an internally mounted model, you may save yourself about $100. The disks themselves run between $40 and $100 dollars, depending on capacity and the amount you buy.

SyQuest EZ135 Drives: The SyQuest EZ drive uses a smaller version of the Winchester hard disk and comes in 135MB configurations. They are much faster than the original SyQuest technology (and slightly faster than the popular Iomega Zip drive discussed later in this section), and this time SyQuest held onto the technology. You can't buy an EZ135 drive from any other manufacturer.

Though SyQuest has sold a bunch of these devices, at this point, you won't find them in as many service bureaus as the SyQuest drives. They seem to appeal mostly to small home offices, and are used predominately for storage and backup, for which they are well-suited.

Iomega Bernoulli 230 Removable Disk Drive: The Bernoulli 230 is a 5¼" removable 230MB cartridge drive, and is available in a number of different subsystem configurations: internal, external, and dual drive. The Bernoulli 230 is also capable of reading and writing to the earlier 150, 105, 90, 65, 45, and 35MB versions of Bernoulli disks.

Like the original SyQuest drive, this is another popular drive among service bureaus and imaging houses. The disks are more dependable than the original SyQuest disks but not as widely supported. At press time the drives sold for around $500 and about $80 for the disks themselves. Iomega frequently runs "Service Bureau Specials" where if you buy several disks (usually 3 or 5), they will give you the drive free.

My service bureau and I have been using Bernoulli drives for a couple of years and are pleased with their durability and performance. However, at $80 a pop for disks, they're much more suited to transport and temporary storage, rather than long-term.

Iomega Zip Drive: The Zip drive, shown in Figure 5.3, uses 100MB and 25MB 3.5" disks that are slightly thicker than traditional floppies. The best part of this drive is that it costs less than $200 dollars and the 100MB disks are about $20.

Two Zip models are available—Zip SCSI and Zip Parallel. Zip SCSI is compatible with both Macs and Windows PCs. Iomega offers a SCSI interface card for PCs, and Zip Parallel uses any common PC parallel port. The Zip drive itself is about the size of an external notebook computer hard disk and weighs less than a pound. They are extremely easy to transport between computers, making it unnecessary to worry about compatibility.

These drives are very popular among home-based businesses and are widely used by service bureaus, but you should call ahead to make sure.

FIGURE 5.3:
The Iomega Zip drive
and disks

The Iomega Jaz Drive: Unlike the Zip drive, which uses a flexible magnetic medium encased in a floppy-sized enclosure, the *Jaz drive*, shown in Figure 5.4, uses standard 3.5" Winchester hard-disk technology enclosed in a cartridge, similar to products from SyQuest. The external Jaz drive costs about $600, and an internal version costs about $500, with its 1GB cartridges selling for about $125 apiece, or $100 if you buy several.

These drives are a great value, and the 1GB storage cartridges are almost economical enough for long-term storage, as well as transporting files. This is a new drive; as I write this I really can't say what their success will be in the drive market, though it looks promising. One problem I have run across, however, is that it's tough find a vendor who can keep them in stock. Also, several other drive manufacturers have begun selling them.

As I write this, Syquest is gearing up to release its SyJet drive, which is similar to the Iomega Jaz, except that it supports 1.3GB and 540MB disks. But for now, Iomega has the jump on this exciting new technology. For multimedia authoring, one of these large-capacity removables is the best bet. With additional disks running about $100 dollars, we're looking at an unprecedented 10¢ per megabyte. It's hard to beat that!

FIGURE 5.4:
The Iomega Jaz drive

Transportable Hard Disks

This solution has long been popular on the Macintosh. That platform's built-in SCSI drive mechanism makes it easy to add and remove peripheral devices, which is another reason why the Mac has found a strong footing in graphics, multimedia authoring, and film editing. With this solution, you simply unplug the disk from the computer and take it wherever you need to go. As long as the computer you're transporting to is SCSI compatible, you can plug the disk into it and away you go. Transportable hard disks can run as large as 9 or 10GB, and nowadays, at just over $300 a gigabyte, they're also becoming more affordable.

This is also the fastest solution available. In most cases, transportable hard disks are as fast as (or almost) the hard disk in your computer. You can easily and quickly copy files and run programs. In fact, you can keep your multimedia titles and the program you created them in (Director, Authorware, etc.) right on the disk and take the whole thing to the service bureau or another computer. It doesn't get much easier than this.

There are some drawbacks, though. Transportable hard disks are often big and bulky, making them difficult to store and transport, especially if you have to ship them to various service bureaus. Additionally, since the drive mechanism is connected to the disk, they are a bit fragile. Also, when you leave them at your service bureau, you're without the drive until the data or output is processed, which can be a bit disconcerting to leave in somebody else's hands if you've got lots of valuable data stored on it.

CHAPTER 6

Business Presentation vs. Multimedia Authoring Software

Featuring

- An overview of presentation software
- Director, Authorware, and ToolBook
- Linking multimedia titles to the Internet
- Internet programming languages

Essentially, this book is about using multimedia software, though up to this point much of it has focused on getting your system ready to meet the challenges of multimedia authoring. By now you have probably gathered that the software is, of course, a vital component in the multimedia authoring process. In essence, multimedia software is the stage upon which you create your multimedia titles. However, it comes in many shapes and sizes, from toy-like programs that allow you string a few multimedia clips together, to full-blown production packages, such as Macromedia Director 5.0, with which you can create highly professional multimedia titles. There are several programs that fall somewhere in between, like Microsoft PowerPoint, a popular business presentation program, and Asymetrix Compel, a powerful multimedia presentation program—each of which lend themselves well to some pretty impressive *screen shows* (presentations on your computer screen).

This chapter compares three general types of software packages: business presentation software; multimedia presentation software; and multimedia authoring software. We'll look at a couple of specific programs in each category, highlight their main features, and finally, identify the types of presentations or titles for which they are best suited. Since this book focuses primarily on authoring multimedia titles, Part Three of the book will be entirely devoted to a hands-on tutorial doing just that, using some of the authoring software we'll be discussing here.

Business Presentation Software

When it comes right down to it, almost all computer software is business-related in one way or another. Software is most often used for creating business documents, accessing business information, training, and so on. When it comes to multimedia software, it's almost always used for creating some type of business application, too—except for games and reference titles, such as interactive encyclopedias.

Presentations created with business presentation software typically appear in meetings with someone clicking through a series of screens in succession. These screens can contain text and graphics, and their strength lies in the ability to format and display help charts, graphs, and other presentation graphics (e.g., bulleted lists).

Another place where this type of show appears is during sales presentations. Rather than using a huge, feature-rich multimedia authoring programs to create them, most people find it easier to use a presentation program, such as Microsoft PowerPoint or Lotus Freelance Graphics 96. There are several programs available for Windows, and all of them are generally comparable in their performance. Although they have limited capabilities compared to multimedia presentation and authoring software, this type of program might make sense if the message you want to convey needs to be slightly jazzed up, but doesn't require any kind of sophisticated implementation of sound and graphics. To create the kind of slide show described here, there are three main techniques used: creating slides and transitions, Object Linking and Embedding (OLE), and employing multimedia events. Let's look at each of them in a bit more detail.

Sliding into Success

NOTE As we saw in Chapter 1, business presentation programs rely on a slide metaphor for creating presentations. Each presentation—even a presentation containing multimedia elements created with these programs—consists of a series of slides, with each slide displayed on a PC screen, one after the other. One of the key advantages of presentation graphics programs is the wide variety of output they let you generate. Nowadays, most presenters still choose to create the ever-familiar 35mm slide show, something done easily with any presentation program. However, for creating electronic presentations, you rely on the program's "screen show" feature, which allows you to create presentations designed for computer screens. Screen show is simply the name many presentations programs use for electronic presentations or slide shows—in Freelance Graphics, for example, you use Start Screen Show to begin the presentation.

Most presentation programs also support multimedia in some form or another. Microsoft PowerPoint and Harvard Graphics, for example, allow you to create on-screen presentations complete with sound and animation. Typically, the multimedia files, or *events*, in these presentations are embedded on a slide and triggered in some manner by the presenter—either by switching slides, or from a "hot button" or text on the slide. These hot buttons (or hot links) usually activate small applets, such as Windows Sound Recorder or MultiMedia Player, which in turn play the (sound) file. Figure 6.1 shows an example of a slide displayed with PowerPoint's screen show feature.

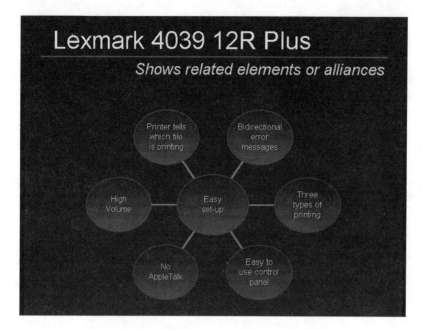

Presentation programs provide a variety of options for creating interesting screen shows, among them are slide transition special effects, OLE links to other applications, and the ability to embed multimedia events, such as sound, animation, and video. Additionally, as is the case with Freelance Graphics 96, some provide the user with a feature that delivers your presentations via a network. Freelance Graphics calls this feature TeamShow; other programs use different names. With it, you can deliver your presentations to other computers on the network.

Transition Effects

While this seems like a fancy term, it simply refers to the way sound and/or graphics are used to animate the changeover between slides. Some of the simplest include wiping away the current object and replacing it with another, while the more complex effects include venetian blind or barn door closing effects. One of the more useful transition effects is called *build*, and it is used most often with bulleted lists. Instead of showing all of the items from a bulleted list on a single slide, you can add impact by utilizing the dim feature, which exposes only one point at a time. Most software tools have a library of built-in transitions, while others give you the ability to create your own. Macromedia Director 5.0, for example, has an extensible architecture called "Xtras" for adding special code and effects. There is even a third party product for Director 5.0 called Killer Transitions, that functions as a plug in and supplies the user with some hip new transition effects like shark bites and clock turn wipes.

While transitions *are* rudimentary forms of animation (in that pixels move on the screen), they do not produce movement in the same way that animation programs do (as discussed in the next chapter). Nonetheless, transitions are one of the more useful business presentation tools when creating electronic screen shows. (You'll get a chance to create animated characters in Chapter 11.)

Object Linking and Embedding (OLE)

Most presentation programs let you integrate your presentations with other Windows applications in one of two ways: by launching the *source application* that created the file you want to include by clicking on a hot button (linking); or by placing the file you want into the *destination application*, or your current file (embedding). The first method actually lets you go to the other application to display and edit an object in its native environment. The latter lets you edit the element directly in the presentation file (the destination application). Both methods have distinct advantages: linking keeps the size of your file down by allowing you to jump to the source application, rather than placing the file directly into your presentation file. Additionally, when you edit the source file, you automatically edit it in your presentation file. With embedding, on the other hand, you essentially copy the desired file into your presentation file, so you are able to leave the original file intact in its source application, while keeping your presentations current and available for hypothetical audience queries (e.g., plugging new numbers into a spreadsheet).

The ability to launch applications allows you to display a spreadsheet to elaborate on data, or perhaps respond to audience questions by jumping to a word processor document containing pertinent text without having to have all of the information contained in one file. You can also link to other presentations, or hop around in the same presentation, which are handy ways to tailor presentations to each audience or respond to audience questions.

OLE2 is the latest version of OLE, which provides a smoother relationship between OLE-aware applications, such as the ability to edit an embedded file in place, in the destination application. Let's look at embedding an OLE object and then look at how to use OLE2 to edit the object.

The Power of Object Linking and Embedding

If you're familiar with Windows, you probably know that you can move text and graphics from one Windows application to another on the Clipboard with the Cut and Paste functions. OLE and OLE2 provide the presenter with much more muscle. Not only can you copy and paste graphics, text, and other objects between applications, but you can also create hot links between the source application, or OLE *server*, and the destination application, or OLE *client*.

The advantage of object linking is that you update your presentations—such as an Excel chart—automatically, no matter how many applications or documents they are linked to. For example, if you link a CorelDRAW drawing to a Harvard Graphics presentation, the linked drawing in the Harvard Graphics presentation will automatically be updated each time you change it in CorelDRAW—without you having to remember to import the object again.

Object embedding lets you temporarily launch a second application from within a Windows program and use it to create a new object. Typically, you do this with the client application's Object command. When you finish creating the object, it is pasted into the destination (or client) application. You can then edit the object anytime by simply double-clicking on it in the destination application. The server application then opens to let you edit the embedded object. (Note that you embed the object as either a document or an icon that opens the server application.)

Multimedia Events

What's a multimedia business presentation without multimedia? While business presentation software doesn't provide as much control over multimedia clips as does full-blown multimedia authoring programs, it does allow you to considerably beef up your electronic screens shows. In most instances, multimedia events (which, in this case, means playing a clip) can occur in one of two ways: you can create hot buttons on the slide that a presenter (or viewer of an interactive presentation) clicks on to play the sound, graphic, or movie file; or you can set up the events to execute in a linear sequence. Depending on the software, direct support for various multimedia clips are built in, meaning that the clip plays inside the presentation. Other file formats can be accessed through OLE. One of the benefits of presentation software is that these types of simple events are easy to include in your presentations.

Choosing the Right Multimedia Program

You need to create presentations and you're not sure what to buy? Let's see if I can make it any easier. As is usually the case when comparing software packages, there are trade-offs depending on what you consider to be a priority. In this case, the differences lie most often in the cost of the software itself and ease of use. The following description of the pros and cons of each type of software may help you determine where to allocate your financial and learning resources.

Business Presentation Software

This type of application works best for creating the electronic screen shows that you will be delivering at board meetings, sales meetings, and committee meetings. It also works reasonably well creating self-running linear presentations if they don't contain a lot of interactivity.

Advantages:

- Easy to learn and use.
- It's relatively inexpensive.
- Allows you to chart and graph data.
- Comes with many predesigned templates.
- Works in conjunction with other business software packages, such as word processors and spreadsheets.
- Often comes integrated into business office suites, such as Microsoft Office and Lotus SmartSuite.
- Fast development cycle—easy to organize your data to produce a quality product.

Disadvantages:

- Gives user limited control over multimedia clip behavior.
- Provides very limited ability to create interactive titles and movies containing custom dialog boxes and other user input options, such as questionnaires, quizzes, and the like.
- Inability to access databases and perform calculations to return responses to user input.

Multimedia Presentation Software

This genre gives you more flexibility over animation and multimedia events than standard business presentation software. It combines a limited timeline with slide-type controls, yet still maintains relative ease of use and added multimedia power.

Choosing the Right Multimedia Program (continued)

Advantages:
- Easy to learn and use.
- Costs a bit more than business presentation software, but still relatively inexpensive.
- Allows you to chart and graph data, as well as animate these types of graphics.
- Comes with many predesigned templates.
- Provides wider multimedia control than standard business presentation programs.

Disadvantages:
- Provides very limited ability to create media clips.
- Provides limited ability to create interactive titles and movies containing custom dialog boxes and other user input options.
- Inability to access databases and perform calculations to return to user input.

Multimedia Authoring Software

These programs are powerful and often complicated, sometimes requiring some programming skills. At the same time, they allow you the most flexibility in creating multimedia titles, especially interactive titles, such as games, books, and training titles.

Advantages:
- Provides widest control over multimedia clips—control or jump to individual frames of video, fade in or out sounds, and a score of other multimedia actions.
- Allows you to create titles with a full range of interactivity, including responding to user input, custom dialog boxes, and performing complex calculations.
- Allows you to access databases and other applications to perform functions outside of the title, such as returning quiz scores, or answering user queries.
- Provides ability to program virtually any Windows function as part of the application title.

Choosing the Right Multimedia Program (continued)

Disadvantages:
- More expensive than the previous two types of software listed.
- Takes up large amounts of room on your hard drive.
- Steep learning curves.
- Often requires some programming savvy to create sophisticated titles.
- Longer development cycles—the more complex your program, the more debugging time you need.

Multimedia Presentation Software

During the past few years we've seen a new gang of presentation packages that fall somewhere in between business presentation programs and multimedia authoring software. For lack of a better term, we'll call them *multimedia presentation software.* By intermingling slide-based and *timeline*-based metaphors, this type of software is more conducive to creating robust presentations. What separates them from standard business packages is that they provide more multimedia options, such as the ability to animate objects within the presentation, and create movie-like events and transitions, such animating various objects on the slide itself.

Two of the more popular programs are Macromedia Action and Asymetrix Compel. The primary difference between this type of software and standard business presentation packages is that, while both allow you to create 35mm slide and transparency presentations, multimedia presentation software is geared primarily toward creating computer-based delivery. In this regard, you can add simple animation, such as movement or shrink and grow, to almost every object in your presentation.

Macromedia Action

In Action, you can apply transition effects to titles, bullets, and graphics, and also animate charts. If you want to draw attention to a bar or show a trend, you can make the bar grow, flash, or apply any of several similar effects. Another important feature is its utilization of the timeline concept. This means that sound, for instance, can be played over the course of several slides or scenes, rather than only when a slide appears or a mouse click initiates it. The bottom line is, you get much more control over media events with this type of software than you do with standard business programs. As you can see in Figure 6.2,

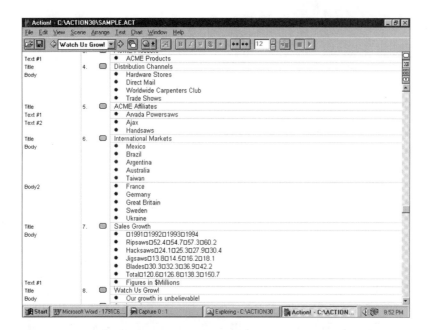

FIGURE 6.2:
An example of Macromedia Action's timeline (top) and scene-based (bottom) approach to creating presentations.

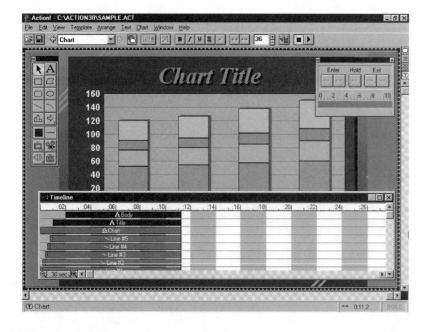

Action lets you build your presentation based on both slides and time sequences. The slide, or in this case, scene, is the basic background, and the timeline controls the behavior of individual objects over a specified period of time.

Asymetrix Compel

Like, Action, Compel provides wider controls over the animation of objects inside the presentation, as well as a sequential approach to initiating multimedia events, as opposed to the slide-activated events used in standard business presentation programs. You can also emphasize points with by growing and shrinking objects. Additionally, the program provides more extensive controls over multimedia clip events, such as when to play them and for how long.

Depending on the type multimedia titles and business presentations you want to create, this type of software may be all you need. It's more powerful than traditional business software, and easier to use than full-featured multimedia authoring programs—not to mention cheaper.

Multimedia Authoring Software

If you want to create a wide range of multimedia titles, or highly interactive ones, you'll need a full-featured multimedia authoring program. While there are several available, three have really set the industry standard—Macromedia Director, Macromedia Authorware, and Asymetrix ToolBook. There is often a steep learning curve when mastering these products, but you'll more than make up for the time investment with the added sophistication of the titles you produce.

In the next few sections I'll introduce you to each of these programs and discuss how they work, and then we'll briefly examine some of the lesser-known multimedia solutions.

NOTE In the workshop section of this book (Part Three), we use both Director and Authorware (as well as a host of other multimedia-related wares). These programs approach authoring in different ways, and it's worthwhile to get a feel for the strengths and limitations of each.

Macromedia Director

If you're interested in high-end multimedia authoring, Director 5.0 is probably the most complete solution. It allows you to create highly interactive multimedia presentations, along with animation, movies, and games. Additionally, Director 5.0 contains a built-in paint applet for creating bitmap graphics directly in your titles, and built-in frame-based animation tools. (Animation is discussed briefly in the next chapter, and you'll get a chance to animate a graphic with Director in Chapter 11.)

NOTE A major consideration for anyone who wants to work with Director 5.0 is that to achieve anything other than simple self-running shows, you must learn how to use Lingo, Director's built-in programming language. It is not considered to be a simple language, but you can learn it on a need-to-know basis, and accumulate knowledge slowly as it applies to your specific title requirements.

How Director Works

Director is based on the metaphor that you are a director creating a movie. You work with a cast that contains all of the elements you plan to include in your performance, and then arrange them upon a stage. When creating titles in Director, you work with four major components: the internal cast, the score, the stage, and the script. As shown in Figure 6.3, the stage is where you build and rehearse your titles (or movies, as Director calls them), and the internal cast and score are floating windows you can resize and move around the screen. The following is a list of Director's key components:

- **Internal cast**—Also known as the cast palette, the internal cast holds all elements of your presentation including graphics, animation, video, sound, text, *scripts*, and color palettes.
- **Score**—The score is the grid for laying out cast elements over time, consisting of 48 channels for graphics elements and special channels for controlling tempo, color palette, transitions, two sound channels, and scripts.
- **Stage**—This is the area on screen where the presentation takes place.
- **Script**—Consists of a small program written in Director's Lingo language that allows you to include interactivity in your titles.

These next few sections provide an overview of the process for creating a Director movie. In the Workshop section, Part 3, you'll actually use Director to create a short movie.

After setting up the stage by defining size and color depth, the construction process begins by creating casts. Casts are composed of text or simple graphics you create inside Director in the paint window, or graphics, sound clips, and movies you import from other programs.

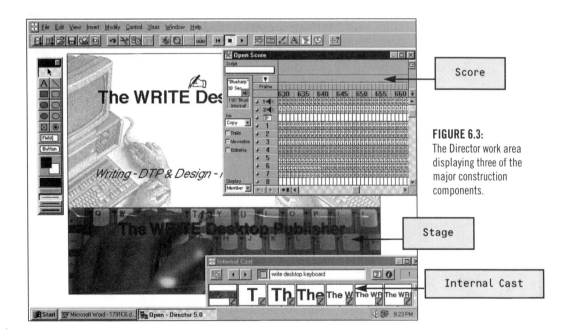

FIGURE 6.3:
The Director work area displaying three of the major construction components.

After you've created a cast, you move objects from the cast palette to either the stage or to the score, where the actual movie creation occurs. You control the way an object behaves—how long a graphic is displayed, how long a sound or movie file plays, and numerous other variables—from the score. As you become more familiar with the program, you'll discover that you can also work with numerous commands on the menu bars to achieve your authoring goals.

Director and Interactivity

Most of Director's powerful interactivity features are based on Lingo commands, the program's scripting language. Depending on your level of experience (and the time you have to devote to learning Lingo) you can make Director movies do just about anything. For more complex operations like tallying user responses to questions, hooking into databases, and returning answers to queries, you will need to use Xtras (formerly called Xobjects for the Mac and DLLs for the PC, written in C code). Fortunately, there are a number of off-the-shelf Xtras already created that you can purchase, or that ship with Director. These Xtras perform many commonly needed tasks, and simply need to be called up by your Lingo script.

Some Key Points to Keep in Mind with Director

Once you master Director, you can create just about any type of multimedia title you want: courseware interactive training titles, games, edutainment, kiosks, and presentations, to name a few. One of the primary benefits of Director 5.0 is that its movies are self-contained. However, there are some key points to keep in mind: When using Director you have a choice of importing graphics or sound into the Director file, or linking to those files from an external location on the disk. Video files are always externally linked, meaning that the title loads them from their original location as needed, rather than storing them in the title file.

When distributing Director titles, always remember to include externally linked files with the path to these files updated to reflect their location on the distributed media. When you move the file from inside Director with Save As, links are automatically updated. When creating long titles, one Director title will often consist of many individual Director files that link to one another. The benefit is that you don't have to load the entire title into memory, saving the user from waiting too long for the file to load. But, you'll still need to include drivers for playing video, as well as the Xtras you're using when you distribute your Director title. Since the graphics display and sound playback are contingent on the hardware set up, you can assume that your graphics and sound files will play if the hardware is already configured with the proper drivers. For example, Windows 95 ships with Microsoft Video, so you can assume that it's installed in any Windows title.

> ## Some Key Points to Keep in Mind with Director (continued)
>
> Director also allows you to create self-contained movies that will run on any system, even if that computer does not have Director installed. Director files are cross-platform; you can work on them in either Windows or on a Mac. However, there are inherent differences in the Mac and PC architecture in how they handle text, graphics, sound and video. You may need to make some modifications to your files to assure cross-platform playability. One problem with this all-in-one approach to movie files is that almost all of your Director creations will be too big to fit onto a single floppy disk, which is why most multimedia authors distribute Director movies on CD-ROM. For more information on storage devices, look back at Chapter 5.

Director and the Internet

Another reason to consider using Director is the exciting development Macromedia is undergoing for the Internet. In the scramble to make World Wide Web pages more interesting and interactive, Macromedia has developed *Shockwave* for Director 5.0, a Web browser plug-in that actually plays Director movies on a Web page. As I write this, Shockwave is only compatible with the Netscape Navigator 2.0 browser, but Macromedia has made an announcement that it will work with Microsoft Explorer as well. We'll look at Shockwave and how it's used in Chapter 15.

Macromedia Authorware

Authorware is a full-featured multimedia authoring package for the nonprogrammer and those disinclined to learn programming. Rather than creating movies on a timeline, as you would do with Director, you create your titles using icons on a *flowline,* which is similar to a hierarchical flowchart. Creating titles in Authorware is a process of dragging icons onto the flowline and then defining their content, which controls how objects behave on the stage, for example, when a movie starts and stops. Figure 6.4 shows an example of Authorware's icon-flowline-stage relationship.

How Authorware Works

Authorware is a powerful, sophisticated program. What makes Authorware ideal for the nonprogramming multimedia author is that you can create several types of interactivity

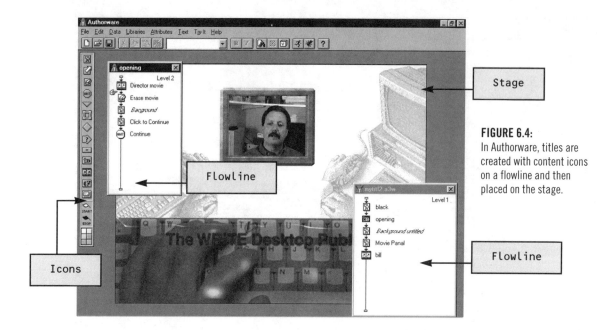

FIGURE 6.4:
In Authorware, titles are created with content icons on a flowline and then placed on the stage.

without having to write computer language scripts—buttons and several common responses are already built-in. There are three primary components of Authorware: icons, the flowline, and the stage (or display). The following describes those components in a bit more detail:

- **Icons**—In Authorware you create titles by dragging icons onto a flowline. Each icon type performs a different function. For example, display icons display an object on the stage. A map icon allows you to setup subflowlines to create branching flowlines. These are used for creating interactivity and alternative paths that the title can take depending on user actions, such as clicking on buttons or other hot links.
- **Flowline**—Flowlines are series of icons arranged along a hierarchical chart, similar to a flow chart. The flowline controls the flow of the titles, and maps, or subflowlines, which allow you to change the direction of the titles based on user input.
- **Stage**—The stage is the area where the title displays, and represents the computer screen from the perspective of users. It represents the part of the Authorware interface that users of your titles will see. Upon it, you can also create simple animations, such as sliding objects across the page, and some pretty slick transitions.

Unlike Director, however, Authorware does not keep all of its supporting files in the same file as the title itself. Instead, the Authorware file acts as shell, maintaining pointers to clips contained in the title. It also contains instructions on when, where, and how the clips and other files are to behave. This makes for smaller multimedia files, but causes a little more work for you when distributing the titles themselves, because you'll often have to include sound and movie drivers, as well as all of the supporting clips. The upside of this approach is that you can create titles that can be distributed on floppy disks, as long as you don't make them over the 1.44MB supported by high density floppy disks. Authorware supports most of the leading file formats, including WAVE, MIDI, Microsoft Video, QuickTime, and others.

Authorware and Interactivity

While Authorware does provide many more built-in routines for creating interactivity, to create sophisticated titles that access databases and return responses and calculations to user responses, you'll still have to get some programming ink stains on your fingers, using Authorware's scripting language. Authorware's scripting language is not an elaborate code like Director's Lingo, it's more of a macro language with one-line commands.

Authorware's built-in interactivity tools work well for initiating user responses inside the title itself, along the flowline. Imagine, for example, that you want to set up a scenario where the title informs a user when he or she has given the right answer to a multiple choice question. Authorware has these relatively simple routines built-in. However, if you want it to be able to create advanced interactivity, such as tallying scores and accessing databases, you'll have to learn more extensive programming. Don't worry, it's not particularly difficult, just a little time-consuming.

Authorware and the Internet

Currently, you can't play Authorware titles on the World Wide Web. However, shortly after this book is released, Macromedia will introduce Shockwave for Authorware. Similar to Shockwave for Director, this Web browser plug-in will allow Authorware titles to play inside the browser. With Shockwave for Authorware, Macromedia will introduce a newer form of technology known as streaming. As it stands now, as with most plug-ins, the browser must first download the file before it is played, causing the viewer (Web-surfer) to sit twiddling his or her thumbs—especially when downloading large files. With streaming, the file will begin to play while downloading, meaning that the viewer will not have to sit through a lot of dead time simply waiting.

According to Macromedia, Shockwave for Authorware will begin playing multimegabyte files within seconds of beginning the download. If you've ever downloaded Shockwave files, movies, or other plug-in files from the World Wide Web, you'll understand how promising the concept of streaming seems.

Asymetrix ToolBook

On the extreme high-end of multimedia programming, you'll find ToolBook. In fact, in ToolBook your multimedia titles are actually *called* books, and each window (or scene) in the book is called a page. While it is a program powerful enough to allow you to create virtually any type of multimedia title, mastering ToolBook requires a strong commitment.

How ToolBook Works

Creating titles, sometimes called *applications*, in ToolBook consists primarily of three components: objects, events, and handlers.

- **Objects**—These can be many things in ToolBook—a text block, graphic, button, movie, sound, and so on. (Even a book itself can be an object.) Somewhat similar to Authorware's icons, objects contain content. You use ToolBook's OpenScript language to control the object's behavior, such as movement, length of play, and colors.
- **Events**—This is what happens while the book is running. An event can be several things: a mouse movement, a mouse click, going to a new page, and so on. You can define your own events and assign them to objects.
- **Handlers**—Handlers are essentially program code, and every handler initiates an event. For example, you can write a handler at the page level to turn to a new page, launch an application, run a movie….You get the picture.

When creating a ToolBook book, you place objects on pages, and then write handlers that correspond to events associated with each object, which in turn are governed by the book's script, or programming language that controls the application. It can get complicated, but the results are very impressive.

Interactivity and ToolBook

While ToolBook allows you to create highly interactive titles, getting there requires you to master the use of handlers and the program's OpenScript. If you've done any programming, you know that this process requires a lot of trial and error, debugging, and patience. Once you learn how to use the program, though, you can create exciting edutainment titles, consumer information materials, courseware—basically anything you can think of.

ToolBook and the Internet

As of this writing, there is no way to utilize your ToolBook applications on the Web. If you plan on distributing your titles via the Internet, this is not the best authoring tool for you. You should consider this solution only if you anticipate distributing your materials other ways.

Other Authoring Solutions

You're certainly not limited to the three authoring programs I've listed here. For example, a few companies, such as MetaTools, offer low-end and intermediate authoring packages that sacrifice power for ease-of-use. With MetaTools Interactive, for instance, you get a simple, icon/flowline-based interface that's great for stringing multimedia clips together, and creating some limited interactivity, such as user-controlled movement from scene to scene. However, there are things you can't do like hook into databases, or program custom dialog boxes.

Another option for programmers is to use Visual Basic programming language to write multimedia titles, much the way you would program a Windows application. (A good book to use if you want to hit the ground running with Visual Basic is Sybex's *Fast Track to Visual Basic 4.*) As you can imagine, this solution is based primarily on your ability to learn and master computer programming. The advantage of this approach is that the sky is limit. If it can be done on a computer, you can program it into your multimedia title.

Media Forum is another interesting solution. Although it's more of a multimedia file manager, Media Forum rounds up all types of multimedia clips, titles, and movies, and plays them based on parameters that you set up. While single-user authors can use Media Forum, its real strength is rounding up multimedia files on a network and arranging them for play back. This program supports a wealth of file formats, including some of the leading presentation programs, such as PowerPoint and Freelance Graphics, as well as Director movies, and standard multimedia clips.

NOTE Because Macromedia Director is leading the pack in multimedia authoring, and the company's aggressive Internet plans seem promising, this book uses it to create a presentation in the Workshop section, which begins with Chapter 8. It's almost time to roll up your sleeves and create your first multimedia title—have fun.

Internet Programming Languages

As the Internet and the World Wide Web become more advanced, we're beginning to see much more interactive multimedia events coming in over phonelines, ISDN lines, and on cable modems. In addition to Shockwave (and some other browser plug-ins) two programming languages, *JAVA* and *VRML* (Virtual Reality Modeling Language), are making inroads into the multimedia authoring world. (We'll look at some World Wide Web multimedia applications in Chapter 15.)

Java

Developed by Sun Microsystems, the people who brought us UNIX (a Web design programming language), Java is a cross-platform language supported by the Netscape Navigator Web browser (and others). It allows Web site designers to program various multimedia events and interactivity into their creations. For example, you can create simple animations, such as scrolling text, moving objects, and so on. You can also create questionnaires, games, and other types of interactivity. At this point, learning Java means learning programming. There are not tools as advanced as Director and Authorware to help you create titles for the Web in Java's language.

VRML

Virtual Reality Modeling Language allows Web site developers to create 3D animation on the Web, similar to the graphics and animations created in 3D modeling programs. As I write this, this application is not widespread, though it has been accepted by the Internet powers that be as *the* standard for 3D applications on the World Wide Web. Like Java, VRML is a programming language requiring some dedication to learn.

CHAPTER 7

Clip Media and Media Editing Software

Featuring

- Audio clips and graphic images
- Video and animation clip media
- Sound, graphics, video, and animation editing software

One of the most useful resources you can have as a multimedia author is a plentiful assortment of *clip media*. Clip media are any ready-to-use audio, video, and animation clips, as well as royalty-free graphics images. In other words, images and sounds you don't have to create yourself because they've been done for you. In this chapter, you'll be introduced to the major categories of clip media, along with the various ways they can be acquired and used.

Once you've located suitable sounds and images, you're bound to run into situations where your video and audio files are far too long. You may also find situations where your images are too large for the allocated screen space, or your animation clip is missing a key element. What are your options? The most common solution is to use editing software. This chapter will provide you with a brief overview of clip media editing software to point you in the right direction, and to help familiarize you with clip media jargon in preparation for the hands-on tutorial in Part Three.

Clip Media

You can acquire clip media—sound, graphics, video, and animation—from a variety of places. The primary sources are CD-ROM collections, floppy disk clip art collections, the Internet, online services such as CompuServe and America Online, and Bulletin Board Services (BBSs). Additionally, most image editing, video editing, and multimedia authoring programs come with collections of clip media. CorelDRAW, for example, ships with about 18,000 drawings, photographs, sound files, and animation files. Of course, you can also create clip media yourself.

WARNING   Not all clip media are free to use. Some clip media are public domain and/or royalty free, while other clip media fall under someone else's copyrighted work. You should determine under which category the clip media you're working with falls "prior" to making a particular clip or image part of your own creation. Should you run across a "to die for" piece of clip media that is indeed copyrighted, do yourself a favor and get permission from the copyright owner. It'll save you a lot of grief in the long run.

TIP To give you a sense of what's out there, you'll find some clip media on the CD-ROM included with this book. You can contact any of the companies listed for information on their wares.

Each category of clip media has its unique role in multimedia, and all four are handled in slightly different ways. The following sections explain the major categories of clip media (sound, graphics, video, and animation), and will introduce you to the similarities and differences among them.

Audio Clip Media (Sound Files)

There are two primary types of audio clip media available today:

- Digital sound files—these are Wave files, stored with the extension **.WAV** on the PC. There are also Aiff (**.aif**), and SoundEdit (**.snd**) formats, which are more common on the Mac.
- MIDI files—this refers to files that carry the extension **.MID**

Let's take a brief look at both types.

Digital Sound Files

Digital sound files, sometimes called Wave files when saved in Wave format, are the most readily available type of audio clip media. Wave files are compatible with most, if not all, sound cards on the market. The wealth of **.WAV** samples available means that you can find anything from a burp to a piano concerto. There are, however, two major drawbacks associated with Wave files: file storage requirements and variable sound quality. They are closely linked to one another, as any decisions you make affecting file size will inevitably impact the quality of the file (sound quality). We'll discuss these concepts, and how they are interlinked, over the next few sections.

The Demands of File Storage: As I said, a primary concern with digital sound files is file size and storage. As with graphics and video, the quality of the sound varies as you manipulate the data to control file size—consider yourself forewarned! Because of this relationship, it's important that you keep sound quality at the forefront of your mind as you plan for, or alter, the size of your files.

A 30 to 60 second **.WAV** file can easily consume anywhere from two to ten megabytes of disk space. The amount of disk space this requires depends on three main factors:

- Sampling frequency
- Bit parameter
- Stereo vs. mono

Sampling Frequency

Digital audio is typically recorded at 44.1kHz, 22.05kHz, and 11.025kHz. The higher the recording frequency, the better the sound quality, and the more disk space it requires. The highest frequency, 44.1kHz, is the quality produced by a stereo compact disc player. You should use 44.1kHz only when you need high-quality stereo sound, such as music.

Voices and sound effects typically don't require a sampling frequency that high. It follows then, that you can save disk space by dropping to a lower sampling frequency, without negatively impacting the sound quality for certain kinds of files. As you'll see in a later section on sound editing software, any sound editor worth its salt will let you resample the frequency.

Bit Parameter

Audio clip media is generally available as both 8-bit and 16-bit samples. The higher the bit parameter, the closer the sample is to approximating the original sound source. You'll have the best luck if you stick with 16-bit samples. As with sampling frequency, you can change the bit rate with sound editing software. However, you gain little or nothing by trying to resample a file upward. Sound editors change frequency sample and bit rates by removing data, but it doesn't work in reverse. In other words, you cannot improve quality by replacing (or inserting) data. Again, the smaller the file (8-bit vs. 16-bit), the more you risk affecting the sound quality.

Stereo vs. Mono

Stereo audio samples demand as much as twice the disk space as a mono audio clip. Again, you need to ask yourself what quality of audio clip you really need. For a clip of a symphony performing Bach's *Passion According to Saint Michael,* stereo may be more appropriate, but for voice or similar sounds, mono should be sufficient.

MIDI Files

MIDI files, while not as versatile as Wave files (i.e., not used for voice recording), also serve as audio clip media solutions. MIDI, which stands for Musical Instrument Digital Interface, was designed to let electronic musical instruments talk to each other. By digitally storing information about the characteristics of a musical note (e.g., loudness, duration, and pitch), rather than the note itself, MIDI files generally use much less disk space than Wave files. For more information on MIDI, refer to Chapter 4.

Graphics Clip Media (Clip Art)

Another common type of clip media is the graphic image, or *clip art*. Clip art runs the spectrum, from simplistic line drawing to multicolored realistic photographs. Issues such as image type, editing obstacles, resolution, file size, and file formats, can make using clip art in multimedia titles a bit tricky. Still, you can't really get by without it.

Generally, there are two types of clip art:

- *Vector images* (draw)
- *Bitmap images* (paint)

In most cases, collections are available in one type or the other. You can buy collections of drawings of just about any thing you can think of, or collections of stock photography with hundreds of pieces. For example, T-Maker, a leading clip drawing vendor, sells small, single-category collections and large multi-category collections. The same is true for stock photography—PhotoDisc, distributors of quality stock photography collections, sells photographs ranging from smiling babies to high-tech industrial images. Then there are blowout collections from companies such as Corel, which contain 20,000 random images, and it just goes on and on.

Shopping for Clip Media

Here you go, off to the computer store, or surfing around the Web, to look for clip media, and you find that the selection is huge! On what basis should you make your decision to buy a particular product? While it's difficult for me to make recommendations (since I don't know what types of titles you're planning to create), I can suggest a few criteria that you should keep in mind:

1. **Appropriateness to task:** Like fonts, clip media can help set the tone of your piece. If you typically create serious business presentations, stay away from silly stuff, such as cartoon characters and burp sounds. Conversely, stodgy business-related images won't work in children's titles. Most importantly, don't use an image just because you like it—make certain it relates to the topic at hand.

Shopping for Clip Media (continued)

2. **Quality:** There are a lot of products to choose from, especially in the clip art category. Beauty is in the eye of the beholder, but you can tell a well-drawn image when you see one. Good stock photography has true-to-life colors, clearly delineated subjects, sharpness, and strong contrast.

3. **How it looks online:** Before you buy anything, go online and look around. AOL, CompuServe, and the Internet contain a wealth of free clip media. Most of the major clip media vendors have Web sites where you can sample their wares—they're worth a visit.

4. **Order samplers:** Almost all clip art vendors will provide free or nominally-priced samplers containing images that give you a good idea of their wares. Often you can find what you need in the sampler, and you're free to use any of the images you find there.

Vector Graphics

Vector graphics, also known as draw-type images, are done mathematically—the computer redraws the shape of an image defined by lines, and then renders the image according to formulas. As a rule, vector graphics are small in file size and easy to edit and resize with little impact on image quality. Figure 7.1 shows an example of a vector image. Typically, draw-type images are used in constructing models in computer aided design (CAD) environments, such as architecture or engineering, and in the development of 3D stills and animation. You can also create them in draw programs, such as CorelDRAW, which is the industry standard for draw-type images, or with programs like Adobe Illustrator, and Macromedia Freehand.

Bitmap Images

Bitmap images, also known as paint-type images, are *pixel-* or dot-based, rather than line-based as is the case with draw-type images. Each pixel contains one bit of color information. Bitmap images can be difficult to edit or resize without using an image editing tool (which we'll discuss a bit further down in *Graphics Editing Software*), and depending on size, resolution, and color depth, bitmap files can be enormous, requiring more storage space than drawn images. Figure 7.2 shows a sample paint-type image, done in Adobe Photoshop, which is one of the most popular programs for this kind of clip art.

FIGURE 7.1:
An example of a vector graphic (draw-type image), rendered through the use of mathematical formulas.

FIGURE 7.2:
An example of a bitmap image (paint-type image), done in Adobe Photoshop.

TIP

The distinctions I'm making between vector graphics and bitmap images are broad. If you plan to create images for your multimedia titles, do yourself a favor and read up on computer graphics formats. There are several good books out there, and it can only help you to be well-informed about the pros and cons of each type of image.

Clip Art Image Formats

Clip art comes in various file formats, and it can be a bit difficult to get a handle on the differences at first. Several of the more popular image file formats are alphabetically listed below:

Bitmap *.BMP

The bitmap file format is used primarily in Windows applications. Images saved in this format consume large amounts of disk space, so if space is a consideration, this format should be avoided. However, bitmapping is widely used in multimedia authoring at lower resolutions.

Computer Graphics Metafile *.CGM

The Computer Graphics Metafile was originally proposed as a graphic file standard. While many software vendors support it, its status as a graphic file standard never lived up to those expectations. The major appeal of this format is its ability to store both vector and bitmap information in the same file.

Encapsulated PostScript *.EPS

The Encapsulated PostScript format is a vector file that uses the PostScript language to draw its image. It is the native format for Adobe Illustrator and is supported by most draw-type programs.

Graphics Interchange Format *.GIF

This high compression rate file format was developed for use by the CompuServe Information Service and is cross-platform compatible, which means that GIF files are recognized on both the Mac and PC platforms. This is the most common format used on the World Wide Web.

Joint Photographic Experts Group *.JPG

The JPEG file format is expected by graphics gurus to become an international standard for encoding digitized photographs. JPEG's major difference from all other current file formats is that it uses the lossy compression scheme (remember this from Chapter 4?). JPEG is also well supported on the World Wide Web.

*.PCX

PCX is the oldest of the file formats. Originally available only on the PC, PCX is a file that is currently gaining support in the Macintosh environment.

Macintosh PICT

PICT is the default file format for images on the Apple Macintosh. It is also widely used in multimedia authoring.

Clip Art Image Formats (continued)

TARGA *.TGA

This file format is used by high-end paint and ray-tracing programs. The TGA format has many variations and supports several types of compression.

Tagged Image File Format *.TIF

The TIFF file format is one of the most common image file formats available. Its compatibility with a multitude of software packages and cross-platform utility make it extremely versatile. It serves as the bitmap format of choice for creating graphics for documents designed for printing on offset presses, as well as the default format for most scanners.

Windows Metafile *.WMF

A Windows Metafile is a vector format popularly supported by the Windows operating system. This format is capable of combining vector and raster images. One benefit of this format is that it maintains file hierarchy when imported into another program, so once it's imported you can still select individual elements of a complex metafile.

Video Clip Media

Video clip media are full-motion video clips you can play on your computer. Unlike clip art collections, there is not currently a wide selection of commercial movie clips available. However, with the explosion of multimedia, more and more are coming on to the scene.

When it comes to video clip media, we're basically talking about two commonly available file types:

- Audio Video Interleaved (AVI), principally supported by Video for Windows.
- Apple QuickTime supported by Macintosh and Windows.

The type you use depends primarily on your application. If you're titles will be used only on Windows machines, AVI is fine. However, if you plan to create cross-platform titles, or have plans for your titles on the World Wide Web, you should use QuickTime—otherwise, some Macintosh users won't be able to see your movies.

AVI

Audio Video Interleaved (AVI) is a type of video that alternates bits of audio and video data one after the other to create a complete digital movie clip on the PC. The AVI process allows video frames to be stored and played back efficiently at speeds supported by hard disk or CD-ROM drives.

QuickTime

QuickTime movies, which are cross-platform compatible, are a type of video clip media that uses a technology known as scaleable compression. Scaleable compression is designed to synchronize audio data with video data using a specialized compression/decompression schedule.

NOTE Another emerging cross-platform standard is MPEG. MPEG is also a compression/decompression standard widely used on the Internet. Many new PC manufacturers are shipping MPEG software with new computers, and Apple is bundling the drivers and viewers with some new Macs. The advantage of this standard is that it allows you to capture and display video at full-screen 640x480 resolution. Since this is primarily a capture and hardware standard, it's difficult to say at this point how widely used it will be. With the advent of DVD (digital video disk), MPEG will become more popular because of its file size capacity—a DVD disk can hold an entire MPEG encoded feature length movie.

Animation Files

Animation files are also considered to be a type of video clip media because they are timed-based files that create motion by displaying still frames in quick succession. Animation files are frame-based and generally run at a rate of approximately 14 fps, although the frame rate varies widely from project to project.

Animation files are typically identified with the extension **.FLI** or **.FLC**, a standard developed by Autodesk for use with Autodesk Animator. However, you may also run across animation files with the extension **.MMM** or **.DIR**, meaning they were created using Macromedia Director. In fact, there are some other programs, such as Gold Disk's Animation Interactive, that have their own proprietary formats, but usually you'll have to export the files to FLC or FLI files to include them in your multimedia titles. You may also run across animation clips in both AVI and QuickTime formats. Depending on the multimedia software you use, it's sometimes necessary to convert animation files to their respective formats. It can get somewhat complicated to sort out which formats work with the various multimedia programs. For instance, Macromedia Director 5.0 does not import FLC or FLI files, but does import AVI or QT files. Once you settle on the software that suits your work best, you'll find that it all starts coming into focus.

TIP If you want more information on video, check out Chapter 4 for a discussion on video capturing hardware, and Chapter 12 for an example of video editing.

Media Editing Software

Media editing programs allow you to create and edit media. The four primary types of media editing software are (you can probably guess by now): sound, graphics, video, and animation (including 3D animation).

Some multimedia programs have their own limited media editing capabilities. Macromedia Director 5.0, for example, has a built-in sound editor, and a 24-bit paint program. However, in addition to their authoring software, most professional multimedia authoring studios come bundled with software for editing the four basic types of clip media.

Sound Editing Software

Sound editors let users improve the sound quality and reduce the size of sound files by sample manipulation. In addition to providing the ability to record and playback sound files, most packages also provide a mechanism for splicing and blending file segments together, and ways of saving files in a variety of audio file formats.

Editing a sound file is a surprisingly simple process. Essentially, you load a sound file into an editing program, such as Macromedia SoundEdit 16 (Mac only) or Sonic Foundry's SoundForge for the PC, and when the sound file is loaded, the sound editor displays a timeline like the one shown in Figure 7.3. This timeline is a graphic representation of the sound file. Once this is displayed, you then use tools to manipulate the file as you desire.

Most sound editing software provides tools to support the following functions:

- **Cut and Paste**—This function lets you change the duration of a sound file by cutting away segments of the file along a time scale, which is usually measured in milliseconds.

- **Echo**—Use this function to give the sampled sound a rich, more robust character, by adding a delay to a sampled sound. Echo adds dimension to the sound, similar to hearing the sound of your voice reflected off the walls of an empty room.
- **Fade**—This allows you to gradually reduce or increase the volume of a sound over time, which is particularly useful when you want to eliminate background noise or static at the beginning or end of a sound sample.
- **Pan**—The pan feature lets you incorporate left-to-right or right-to-left channel stereo as part of your sound file. This feature causes your sound to shift from the left speaker to the right speaker and vice versa in a slow sweeping fashion, creating a sense of dimension to the listening environment.
- **Reverse**—If you've ever heard a recording played backwards, you get the gist of what this feature provides.

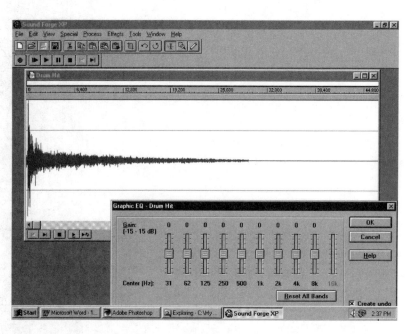

FIGURE 7.3:
An example of a
sound file
being edited in
SoundForge.

Graphics Editing Software

Just like clip art, graphics software comes in two flavors (well really three, but we'll get to that a bit further down): draw and paint, which allow users to load, modify, and save graphic images in a variety of formats. As I mentioned earlier, on Windows machines, the industry standards are Adobe Photoshop and CorelPhoto-Paint for paint-type images, and CorelDRAW for draw-type images. Figure 7.4 shows examples of the two types of graphics applications.

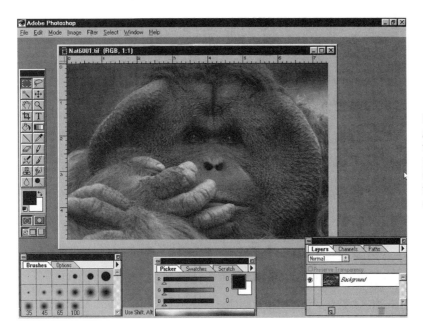

FIGURE 7.4:
Adobe Photoshop (top) is the industry leader in paint-type image editing. CorelDRAW (bottom) set the industry standard in draw-type image editing.

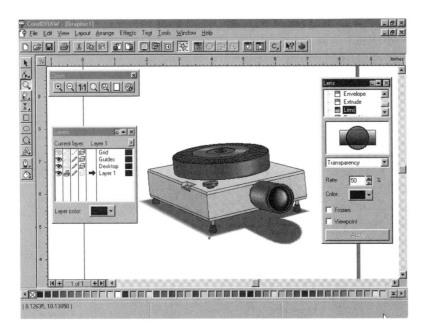

Both are very powerful programs that allow you to perform tasks ranging from simple, such as recoloring images, to complicated special effects, such as creating 3D extrudes and embossing. You should be aware, though, that learning to create artwork in one of these programs is a chore in itself, and usually requires some art background. Often it's easier to rely on clip art as a starting point, and then to use one of the programs mentioned here to edit it.

TIP

If you own or plan to buy CorelDRAW, you don't need an additional paint program for working with photographs. CorelDRAW ships with CorelPhoto-Paint, a nimble and powerful image editing program in itself. CorelDRAW also bundles CorelDream 3D, a respectable 3D modeling package. The advantage of using the programs in the CorelDRAW graphics suite is that they work alike, and in concert, wherever possible.

The third type of graphics software is 3D modeling and rendering, such as Macromedia's Extreme 3D and CorelDream 3D. While these programs are widely used for creating still 3D images, they also allow users to generate 3D animations by setting camera angles and movement over time. Figures 7.5 and 7.6 show before and after shots of a 3D-rendered VW bug.

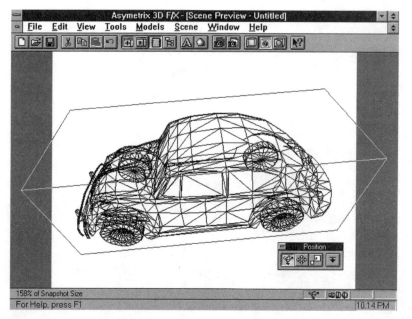

FIGURE 7.5:
Wireframe models are used to create 3D images.

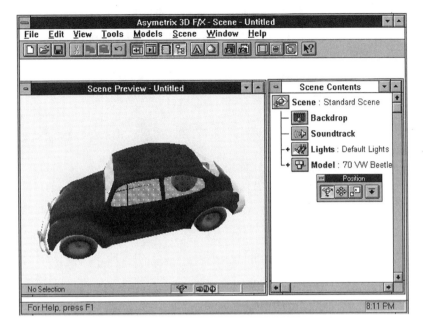

FIGURE 7.6:
This VW Bug was rendered using Asymetrix 3D F/X.

If you own or plan to own Macromedia Director 5.0 or Authorware, both programs ship with Extreme 3D. Be warned though, 3D modeling requires some dedication to learn.

Video Editing Software

Editing video can be as simple as cutting off the first few frames or last few frames of a video clip, or as complex as adding scene transitions and special effects. Probably the most popular all around editing package is Adobe Premiere, with COSA's After Effects leading the way in special effects and image processing of digital video files. Similarly, video editing programs also run the spectrum from simple to complex. With that in mind, look for the following features when evaluating a video editing application:

- **Predefined transitions**—Programs supporting this feature provide a variety of fades, wipes, dissolves, and other effects useful for moving between scenes. This is very easy to do when your source material is digital.
- **Special effects filters**—Look for video editing software that provides and/or supports a variety of integrated or plug-in filters. These filters perform color correction,

adjust brightness, and introduce blurs and warps in frame images. Depending on the sophistication of the software package, the video editor will allow controlled use of many filters over the duration of a video clip.

- **Cel-based Animation**—This is an animation production technique based on the use of celluloid layers to overlay active elements in an animation frame on a static background.
- **Frame-based Animation**—This provides you with an animation production technique approximating digital video.
- **Key frame**—A reference frame in a video clip used by the CODEC (compression/ decompression) scheme to determine the presence of redundant information.
- **Key frame control**—Programs supporting key frame control let you establish different transition settings for a number of places in your video segment. This allows you to maneuver among key frames.

Animation Editing Software

Animation software programs let the user create, edit, and save both frame-based and cel-based animation files. Frame-based animation is the most like digital video. This fact can be illustrated by quickly flipping through the pages of a three-inch thick phone book and observing how the page numbers appear to seamlessly change from one to the next. Cel-based animation, on the other hand, involves overlaying and manipulating a series of differing images as a foreground to a fixed background. Macromedia Director 5.0, for example, is a frame-based animation package (as well as a multimedia authoring program). Autodesk Animator is a cel-based animation program.

Software used to edit animation files must either fully or partially support the following features:

- **Importing**—With this feature, you can work with images created in a variety of draw and paint applications.
- **Tweening**—This is used in the creation of cel-based animation, where the software performs the calculations needed to display movement between two or more slightly different cels. For example, if you created ten cel images of a man with every other image showing the man with his right leg in a different position, the software would make it appear as though the man were moving his right leg.
- **Morphing**—This popular feature lets the user take two images and blend them together, such that the first image appears to transform into the second one. Programs such as MetaTools Digital Morph and Elastic Reality support this feature.

- **3D Rendering**—This feature lets the user create a three-dimensional image from a complex vector graphic called a wireframe model.

3D animation is really a category in its own right so let's examine a bit more closely.

3D Animation Editing Software

Another form of animation often used in multimedia authoring is 3D animation. This type of animation is edited in 3D modeling packages, such as CorelDream 3D, RayDream 3D, and Macromedia Extreme 3D. 3D refers, of course, to graphics that seem to appear three-sided, or, as it is sometimes said, reside in three dimensional space. On the computer screen, the images are flat. The 3D effect is achieved through some fancy shading, and is created in three steps: modeling, rendering, and animating.

- **Modeling**—This is the process of creating the underlying wireframe for the graphic. As you saw earlier in Figure 7.5, you draw a geometric wireframe for the object or multiple objects and scenes, and then cover the object with multishaded planes to give the graphic a 3D effect.
- **Rendering**—Rendering appears at two levels: you can render a single scene to the screen, or you can render an entire animation to disk. Rendering simply refers to the computer calculations done by the 3D software to flesh out the various lighting and shading effects over the wireframe model. When you render an entire animation, each scene is rendered one frame at a time.
- **Animating**—Typically, animation in 3D programs animate from three perspectives: the 3D space (or workspace); a score (similar to the score in Director, which manages objects in the workspace); and the camera. Animating in 3D space entails animating interactively, with various tools. Animating with the score controls the images over a time sequence, and animating the camera changes camera angle and lighting.

While this kind of animation is impressive and can greatly enhance your titles, mastering 3D animation requires some learning and skill. The question is—how much time and dedication can you devote to learning a new program?

Because of the steep learning curves, natural preferences of the multimedia authors, and time required to master, most multimedia firms have several artists, each adept a different aspects of graphic, video, and sound editing.

3

PART

Bringing It All Together

CHAPTER 8

Preparing for the Workshop

Featuring

- The Workshop project
- Working with your mouse, keyboard, and the Windows dialog boxes
- Notes for Windows 3.1 users

Few things are as exciting as beginning a new multimedia project, especially when it includes venturing into new areas. Over the course of the next several chapters, you will be creating a multimedia title for a fictional design firm, called Divine Concepts. Divine Concepts creates advertising material, documentation, Web sites, and other desktop publishing projects for a variety of clients, including a medical firm and a software company. The impetus for creating the title is to showcase Divine Concepts' track record in the hopes of landing new clients.

The company's proprietor has decided that they're more likely to attract bigger clients with advertising material that reflects the high-tech nature of its business. Toward that end, it makes sense to create an electronic brochure (consisting of various multimedia events) to be distributed via CD-ROM.

Does that sound like fun? Good—let's get started.

Overview of the Workshop Project

During the next six chapters, you'll be creating a multimedia brochure designed to run on any Windows computer with a CD-ROM drive.

The title consists of an opening animation segment, a video from the company president introducing the title, and a main menu that branches to sequences highlighting four areas of Divine Concepts' services. While creating the title, you will learn several of the most common procedures comprising the multimedia title creation process:

- Beginning a title in Macromedia's Director
- Editing a sound file and importing it into your Director title
- Creating simple animation in Director
- Editing a digital video clip and importing it into your Director title
- Editing text and graphics and importing them into your Director title
- Creating user navigation features with Director's Lingo scripting language

In addition to Director, you will be using several of the industry-leading production software products including:

- Sound: Sonic Foundry's Sound Forge XP
- Digital Video: Adobe Premiere
- Graphics: Adobe Photoshop

Included on the CD-ROM that came with this book, you'll find demonstration, or *save-disabled*, copies of all of these applications. Save-disabled means that you cannot save your work, so during the course of the Workshop, I'll save the files for you, so that you can use them in the upcoming exercises. Each company has a different name for the demonstration copies of their wares. Adobe, for example, calls their demonstration copies *try-outs*. Macromedia calls theirs save-disabled. For the sake of clarity, from this point forward, they will simply be called *demos*.

> **WARNING**
>
> To run the entire title, your system must have Apple QuickTime for Windows installed. If it's not installed, you can install it by running Adobe Premiere demo Setup.exe, which you'll find in the Adobe\Premiere folder on the CD-ROM included with this book. Also, while creating the CD, it was discovered that a few (very few) computer display systems are not compatible with the 16-bit (MYMOVIE.exe) version of the title. If the title doesn't run on your machine, have no fear. You can still use the Workshop tutorial. The resulting title should run fine on your machine.

At the end of the Workshop you will have created a title called MYMOVIE.exe. To see the title now, you can run it from the *Multimedia Authoring Workshop* CD-ROM by following these steps:

1. Make sure that the *Multimedia Authoring Workshop* CD-ROM is in your CD-ROM drive, then open Windows Explorer from the Programs submenu on the Windows 95 Start menu.
2. In Windows Explorer, scroll in the left list of drives and folders until the icon for your CD-ROM title is displayed.
3. Double-click on CD-ROM drive icon to open the disc.
4. In the list on the right, double-click on the Workshop folder.
5. In the list on the right, double-click on the Final folder.
6. Double-click on the file MYMOVIE.exe, as shown in Figure 8.1.

> **NOTE**
>
> When the title gets to the main menu, you will be provided with four menu choices, as shown in Figure 8.2. This menu is provided as an example. Only the top item, "World Wide Web Page Design," is actually functional. You can click on it to move the movie forward.

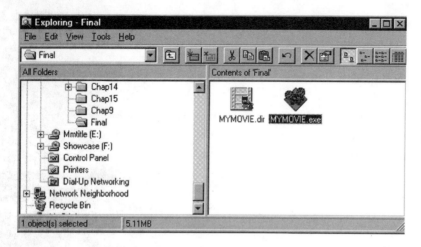

FIGURE 8.1:
Double-click on MYMOVIE.exe to run the title.

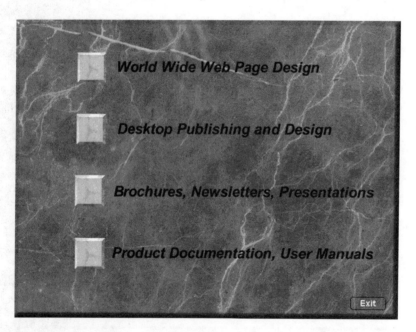

FIGURE 8.2:
On the main menu, only the top item, "World Wide Web Page Design" is functional. Click on it to advance the title.

7. When you've finished viewing the title, click Exit on the main menu to quit.

As you can see, the title contains many of the elements typically found in multimedia productions. You'll learn how to work with them all.

Working with Workshop Files

On the CD-ROM in the Workshop folder, you'll find several Director files, media clips, and image files that you will use to compile your title. Many of them require editing, which I'll walk you through in upcoming chapters. During the Workshop, I will direct you to the various files on the CD-ROM, instructing you to copy them to your hard disk. We will then edit them together in media and graphics editing demo programs. Many of the projects will require you to install the demos (unless, of course, you already own full versions of the software). We'll then import the edited files into your Director title.

As I said, since the demos are save-disabled, you can't save the files after editing them. Therefore, I have included the files in two formats, unedited and edited. You'll find them in separate subfolders in the Workshop folder. Unedited files are in the *Before* folder, and edited files are in the *After* folder. Figure 8.3 shows the contents of Workshop\Chap12\Before, the files you'll use in Chapter 12 to edit a movie.

At the beginning of each chapter, I will instruct you to copy the folders and files to your hard disk so that they will be available during the exercises.

WARNING While creating the title in the Workshop, for the title to run properly, it is necessary that the Workshop folder and file structure remain intact. In other words, do not delete folders at the completion of each chapter. If you find yourself getting short of disk space, as you complete each chapter you can delete the files labeled MYMOVIE.dir and MYMOVIE.exe in any of the folders and, in Chapter 12, you can delete Heidi.avi (after you've finished the chapter). These are the largest files in those folders, so deleting them will save the most space, and won't affect your future work.

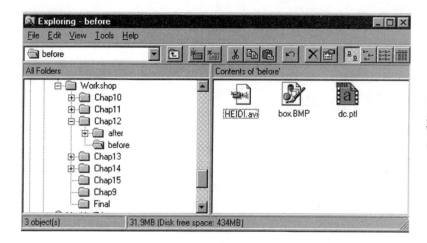

FIGURE 8.3:
An example of the Workshop files you'll use to create your title.

If you have the hard disk space, you can use Windows Explorer to copy all of the Workshop files to your hard disk, skipping this procedure in each of the chapters. The space required for all of the Workshop files is about 100 megabytes. To copy them to your hard disk, click the right mouse button on Workshop folder on the CD-ROM, choose Copy from the pop-up menu, and then click the right mouse button on the drive C: (or desired hard disk) icon and Choose Paste.

Using the Demo Software

The applications that you will use during the tutorial to edit and put together your title are also located on the CD-ROM. The purpose of these demos are, of course, to allow you to see how the programs work. They were selected because they are leading, industry-standard multimedia applications.

Information for contacting each of the vendors is included on the Readme.doc files contained in the setup program folder for each application.

The applications are organized by vendor. Macromedia Director, for instance, is in the MMedia folder; Photoshop and Premiere are in the Adobe folder, and so on. We will use these applications to develop the Divine Concepts title and supporting files. You will then use the saved versions of the edited clips supplied on the CD-ROM to continue compiling the title.

Table 8.1 lists the demos and in which chapters you will use them.

Table 8.1: Workshop applications and where they are used		
Chapter	**Element Type**	**Applications Used**
Chapter 9	beginning the title	Macromedia Director
Chapter 10	sound	Sonic Foundry Sound Forge XP Macromedia Director
Chapter 11	animation	Macromedia Director
Chapter 12	digital video	Adobe Premiere Macromedia Director
Chapter 13	text and graphics	Adobe Photoshop Macromedia Director
Chapter 14	creating interactivity	Macromedia Director
Chapter 15	finishing the title and preparing Internet titles	Macromedia Director Macromedia Shockwave* Macromedia Afterburner** Netscape Navigator***

*Macromedia Shockwave is not on the CD-ROM. You can download it for free from the Macromedia Web site at http:\\www.macromedia.com.

**Macromedia Afterburner is not on the CD-ROM. You can also download it from the Macromedia Web site. However, it is restricted to licensed Director users. You cannot use it with the save-disabled demo because you must be able to save your Director files to use Afterburner on them.

***Netscape Navigator is not on the CD-ROM. However, you can download it from the World Wide Web at: http:\\www.netscape.com.

TIP Each chapter begins with instructions for installing the demo programs. If you're curious and want to install any or all of the demos now, feel free to do so. Simply find the Setup.exe file in the folder for the program you want to install and double-click on it. Then follow the directions on screen.

To save disk space, you can delete the demo application used in a specific chapter at the completion of the chapter. The only program you'll use in every chapter is Director, so *do not* delete it until you've gone through the entire Workshop.

The way in which you should delete each program depends on the program itself. All of the demos, except for Director, are not full-fledged Windows 95 applications. They can be deleted with Windows Explorer. Director is a full-fledged Windows 95 application (if you're on Windows 3.1, see *For Windows 3.1 Users* below) and should be deleted with the Windows 95 Add/Remove Programs control panel. This evokes Windows 95's uninstall program, which removes all the application files and completely uninstalls the program. To uninstall Director and Sound Forge XP, follow these steps:

1. On the Windows 95 Start menu, scroll up to Settings.
2. Choose Control Panel from the submenu.
3. In the Control Panels window, double-click on Add/Remove Programs. This displays the Add/Remove Programs dialog box shown in Figure 8.4. This dialog box allows you to remove programs from your system or add components to them.
4. Click the Add/Remove button.
5. Follow the directions on your screen to delete the application.

NOTE Windows 95 versions of both Photoshop and Premiere are available. As of this writing, Adobe had not yet released Windows 95 demo versions.

Photoshop and Premiere are deleted by following these steps:

1. Open Windows Explorer from the Start/Programs menu.
2. Find the folder containing the program files (WinApp32/for Photoshop, Premiere for Premiere) in the list on the left.
3. Click the right mouse button on the folder.
4. Choose Delete from the pop-up menu, as shown in Figure 8.5.

5. Click Yes in the Confirm Folder Delete dialog box.

6. In the Confirm File Delete dialog box, click Yes to All.

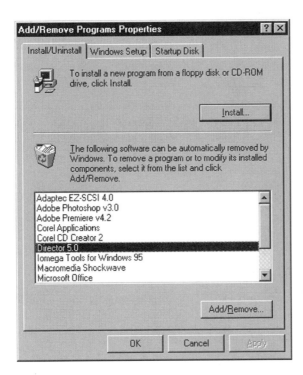

FIGURE 8.4:
Use the Add/Remove
Programs dialog box
to remove programs
from your system.

FIGURE 8.5:
Choose Delete
from the pop-up
menu to delete
the folder and files.

Using Windows in the Workshop

Chances are that you already know how to use Windows, and this book follows standard Windows conventions and terminology. Just in case, though, this section provides you with an overview of some of the conventions and terms used in the remainder of the Workshop.

Mousing around in Windows

So you already know how to point and click? Let's make sure you know what I'm talking about when I use other mousy terms.

- **choose:** I use this term when you have a list of choices, such as a menu or in a dialog box. It is used interchangeably with *select*. For example: If I say, "Choose Save As from the File menu", you would click on the File menu and then click on Save As from the list of options on the menu.

- **double-click:** Place your mouse on the object I tell you to "double-click on," and click the left mouse button very fast. Double-clicking is usually used to open a program, a file folder, or a dialog box.

- **drag:** Click and hold the left mouse button on the object I tell you to "drag," and hold the mouse button down until the mouse is in the position I tell you to drag to. Dragging is used to move objects across your monitor, such as a graphic from one place to another.

- **select:** Similar to *choose*, I use this option to tell you to click on a command or another option to turn it on, or to open a dialog box. Another way in which *select* is used is to tell you to make an object active, such as "Click on the text block to select it." When an object is selected it's active. Depending on the program and the object selected, selected objects are highlighted in some manner. In Figure 8.6, for example, the letter "i" is highlighted by the bounding box and small square handles around it.

- **Shift-click:** Hold the Shift key while clicking on the object indicated. This is used most often for selecting multiple objects.

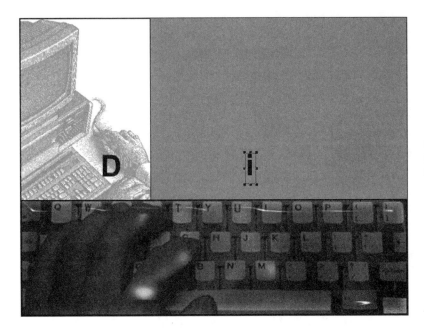

FIGURE 8.6:
An example of a selected object.

Keyboard Conventions

About the only keyboard term I use in this book is *type*, which is simple enough. All you do is type the character string that follows the word *type*. The characters will appear in bold letters. For example:

Type **Divine Concepts**.

All you would do is type the letters in *Divine Concepts* where I instruct you.

I did, however, want to make you aware of *keyboard shortcuts*. Most windows programs allow you to evoke commands and perform certain functions by holding either the Shift, Ctrl, or Alt keys (or combinations) while pressing a letter, number, or function key. In most programs, for example, Ctrl+A is the same as choosing Select All from the File menu. To see keyboard shortcuts for the commands on menus, simply open the menus. If a command has a corresponding keyboard shortcut, it is displayed to the right of the command, as shown in Figure 8.7.

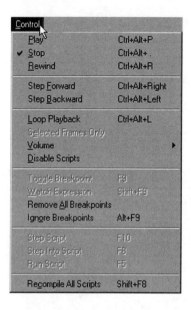

FIGURE 8.7:
Keyboard shortcuts are listed to the right of the menu commands.

Windows Dialog Boxes

I just want to make you aware of how to navigate your system from the Open, Save As, and Import dialog boxes you'll use in the various programs. Rather than repeating this process in the Workshop, I simply tell you to "go to" certain directories. In Director, for example, if I say, "Go to Workshop\Chap9\Before" you would do this:

1. Choose your drive from the Look In drop-down list, as shown in Figure 8.8.
2. Find the Workshop folder in the list of folders and files, then double-click on it.
3. Find the Chap9 folder in the list of folders and files, then double-click on it.
4. Find the Before folder in the list of folders and files, then double click on it.

Simple enough, right? The Open, Save As, and Import dialog boxes in all of these programs work similarly.

For Windows 3.1 Users

Here's some good news for Windows 3.1 users: This book and the demo programs on the CD-ROM are totally compatible with your operating system. While the instruction and screen shots are all done for Windows 95, you should have no problem following along.

Many of the dialog boxes will look different, and some of the procedures. For example,

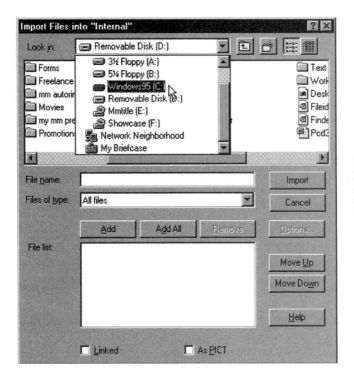

FIGURE 8.8:
Use the Look In list to choose the drive where the files are located.

when I instruct you to perform functions in Windows Explorer, you will instead use File Manager. Rather than using the Start menu to launch programs, you'll double-click on program icons in Program Manager—but if you're using Windows 3.1, you've probably had your computer for at least a year now and know how to use Windows with no problem.

When you install the demo programs, the setup programs determine which version of Windows you are using and install the appropriate files. It doesn't get much easier than that!

TIP

In addition to the workshop files, you'll also find several other media clips and clip art files you can experiment with or use in future titles. Also included is information from the vendors on purchasing collections.

CHAPTER 9

Creating the Introduction

Featuring

- Preparing your display system
- Working with the tutorial files
- Setting up Director
- Importing cast members
- Using Director's Score window
- Viewing your movie

This is it! If you've read this book chapter by chapter, you're probably eager to start creating your first title. This chapter walks you through creating the Introduction to the overall piece. As will be the case with each of the chapters in the Workshop section, you'll begin by installing the program(s) you'll be using in this chapter, and then copying (onto your hard drive) the supporting files from the CD-ROM that is included with this book. In addition to installing those files, since this is the first chapter in the Workshop portion of the book, you'll also set up Windows 95 to work optimally for the title you are about to create. This will ensure that your new title will display properly on all Windows computers.

Getting Windows Ready

You'll remember from Chapter 3 that when you are creating a multimedia title for other computers—especially systems unfamiliar to you, such as those of prospective clients—you should create the title to work on a minimum configuration. In other words, the title should run well on a relatively slow computer with standard VGA display capabilities (640x480/256 colors).

Setting the title to standard VGA display capabilities doesn't mean that most computers can't display at higher settings, it's simply not polite to expect people to reconfigure their systems just to run *your* title. Besides, many computers users have never learned how to change their display settings.

> **NOTE**
>
> **You may think I'm kidding about the resolution and color depth settings, but I can't tell you how many times I've gone into a client's office only find brand new, powerful Pentiums running with minimal display settings. More often than not, the user doesn't know that the settings can be changed. It's better to err on the side of safety and convenience.**

It follows then, that when beginning a title, your main consideration should be setting the proper display system color depth since many of the systems out there are set to 256 colors, or 8-bit color depth. Using low color depth also creates smaller file sizes, allowing the title and supporting media clips to run faster. For example, images consisting of 256 colors can be as much as ten times (or more) smaller than images with 16.7 million colors. Nothing hinders the performance of your title (and the experience for the user) more than sluggish file loads and screen redraws.

> **TIP**
>
> Adjusting display settings is not the only way to optimize the speed of your title, there are a number of other steps you can take. Video clips, for example, can be altered to run optimally from CD-ROM discs by changing the frame rate and other settings, as discussed in Chapter 12. As these issues arise throughout this tutorial, I'll show you ways to keep your titles from getting too large and sluggish.

Finding the Windows 95 Display Control Panel

All of Windows 95 configuration options are located on the *Control Panels*, which are small utilities that allow you to change your system settings. Display system resolution and color depth are among the many settings you can alter from the display Control Panel.

To change display settings, follow these steps:

1. Click the Start button in the lower-left corner of the screen.
2. Scroll up to Settings, and then select Control Panel from the submenu.
3. In the Control Panels window, double-click on Display Properties dialog box.

This opens the Display Properties dialog box, shown in Figure 9.1. From here you can change several aspects of your monitor and graphics card's performance. (As with so many of the dialog boxes throughout the Workshop section, it's far beyond the scope of this book to explain all of the settings in detail. For additional information on the display Control Panels and other Windows configuration options, I suggest you refer to Sybex's *Mastering Windows 95*.)

Changing Color Depth and Resolution

To create a comfortable working space for yourself, you can set the resolution of your screen to 1024x768 if your monitor and graphics card allows. I recommend a 1024x768 resolution setting for your computer for two reasons: First, it allows you to see more of the Stage area while working in Director's windows. Second, you can see more of the Stage area while you create your title. If you have a small monitor (14 or 15 inches), this setting

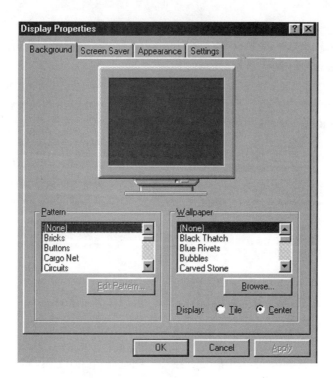

FIGURE 9.1:
The Windows 95 Display Properties dialog box; use it to set display resolution, color depth, and many other options.

may not be comfortable—objects might be too small to see. If so, feel free to choose a lower setting, like 800x600 or 640x480. Remember though, if you do, your screens will look slightly different from mine. Just a caution.

Also, some older computers do not come with display adapters that support 1024x768 resolutions. If yours does not, don't worry, you really don't need that ability to create great multimedia titles.

To change the color depth and resolution, follow these four steps:

1. Click on the Settings tab of the Display Properties dialog box, as shown in Figure 9.2.
2. From the Color Window drop-down list, choose 256 Color.
3. Use the slider in the Desktop Area to select 1024x768.
4. Click OK to close the Display Properties dialog box.

Once you've finished these four steps, and depending on your previous settings, one of two things will happen: Windows will either display a dialog box informing you that it's about to resize your desktop, or it will offer to restart your system. If the first scenario occurs, simply click OK in both ensuing dialog boxes. If the second scenario occurs, click OK to allow Windows to restart your computer. If you have any programs open, you will be given a chance to save your documents. In either case, once you have finished, close the Control Panels window.

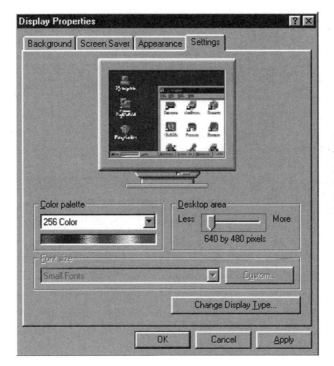

FIGURE 9.2:
On the Settings tab, use the Color Window to control color depth, and the Desktop Area for resolution.

If you choose 800x600 or a higher setting, the dialog box also provides a Font Size option with two choices: *Small fonts* and *Large fonts*. Choosing small fonts causes menus and dialog boxes to consume less monitor real estate, but can be hard to read on small monitors. As a rule of thumb, use small fonts on large monitors, and large fonts on small monitors. The best way to choose is to try Small fonts first—if you can't see your menus comfortably, change to Large fonts.

Your system is now ready to start multimedia authoring.

Preparing the Workshop Files

As I mentioned in Chapter 8, each chapter in the Workshop requires a tryout version of one or more software titles and some media clips. In this chapter, for example, you'll use the Macromedia Director 5.0 tryout and several graphics files I've prepared for you in Photoshop. The tryout application needs to be installed and the graphics should be copied to your hard disk, which I'll explain in more detail over the next couple of sections.

TIP

If you already have Director 5.0, by all means, use it rather than the tryout. You can also use Director 4.0, though your screens will look a little different from mine.

Installing the Director Demos

On the CD-ROM that came with this book, in the Macromed\Director\Evalcopy folder, is a save-disabled copy of Director 5.0. To install it on your system:

1. Place the *Multimedia Authoring Workshop* CD-ROM in your CD-ROM drive.
2. Using the Windows Explorer (Start\Programs), find the Setup.exe in the Macromed\Win-Dir directory, and then double-click on it.
3. In the Welcome dialog box, click Next.
4. In the Select Components dialog box, select your version of Windows (3.1 or Windows 95 and NT).
5. Continue following the directions, accepting the defaults, until the installation is complete.

Copying the Workshop Files

In the previous chapter, we created a new folder on your hard disk called Workshop. If you haven't done that yet, please return to Chapter 8 and follow the directions for creating the new folder. In this, and the remaining Workshop chapters, you will copy folders and files to the Workshop folder for use in your title. Once the Workshop folder is created, follow these steps for copying the Chapter 9 files:

1. From the Start button, open Windows Explorer, which is under Programs.
2. Find your CD-ROM drive in the left list of drives and folders.
3. Click on the CD-ROM drive icon to open the disk.
4. Find the Workshop folder in the right list of folders and files in Windows Explorer, then double-click on it.
5. Find the Chap9 folder, then click the right mouse button on it.
6. Choose Copy from the pop-up menu.
7. In the left list in Windows Explorer, find the Workshop folder you created on your hard disk.
8. Click the right mouse button on the Workshop folder, and then select Paste from the pop-up menu.

Windows will create a Chap9 folder inside the Workshop folder. Once this happens, copy the three graphics files into the Chap9 folder. You are now ready to begin your title.

Beginning Your Title

Now that Director is installed and you've copied the graphics files for this part of the Workshop, you will set up Director by configuring the application and creating the Stage on which your title will play.

NOTE While your working on your title in this chapter, and during the rest of the Workshop, remember that since you are working with save-disabled versions of the software, you'll need to complete each chapter before stopping and closing the application. You can't close the application and come back to it without relaunching and starting over unless you own a full-featured version of the software (and saved the project where you left off, of course).

To open Director, follow these steps:
1. Click the Start button in the lower-left corner of the screen.
2. Scroll up to the Programs section of the menu, then to the Macromedia submenu.
3. From the Macromedia submenu click on Director 5.0 Demo.

This is the only time I'll provide you with instructions for opening Director—from now on I'll assume you know how to launch the application.

Arranging the Director Desktop

Macromedia and other software vendors try to provide you with the optimal work environment by default. However, since people have different preferences for this sort of thing, the first thing we'll do is arrange the Director desktop the way I do for my titles. As you get more proficient in Director, you may choose to setup your screen differently than mine.

For our title (and most others), you'll use three Director windows: *Score*, *Cast*, and *Control Panel*. I'll describe each window and its function the first time you use it. In the meantime, let's make sure all three are open and placed in workable positions on the screen. (By default, Director calls the *Cast window*, "Internal," meaning that the objects are imported and maintained within the movie file. However, you can name the Cast window anything you want.)

In Director, you open all windows from the Window menu, shown in Figure 9.3. In most instances, you can tell if a window is open by the presence of a checkmark beside its name, or command. However, the Cast window does not display a checkmark when it's open, and the Stage command (from the menu) hides all of the windows, and displays only the Stage. (The reason for this is to allow you to see just the Stage, without all of the other windows cluttering up the screen, which is a great feature when using a small monitor set at a low resolution.)

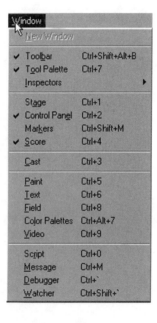

FIGURE 9.3:
The Window menu: from here you open Director's various windows.

Follow these steps to make sure the necessary windows are open:

1. Click on the Window menu, then make sure there are checkmarks beside the Score and Control Panel.

2. If neither the Score nor the Control Panel have checkmarks, scroll down and select the command, after which a checkmark should appear. If neither have checkmarks, repeat this procedure for each command. Each time you select a command, the window should appear (or disappear if it is already displayed).

3. Arrange the windows as shown in Figure 9.4. To move windows, click in the *title bar* (the solid-colored bar at the top of the window with the window name in it), hold the

mouse down, drag it to the place you want, and let go of the mouse. To resize windows, hover the mouse cursor over a lower-corner of the window until it turns into an arrow pointing in both directions, click, and then drag the edge to desired size, and let go.

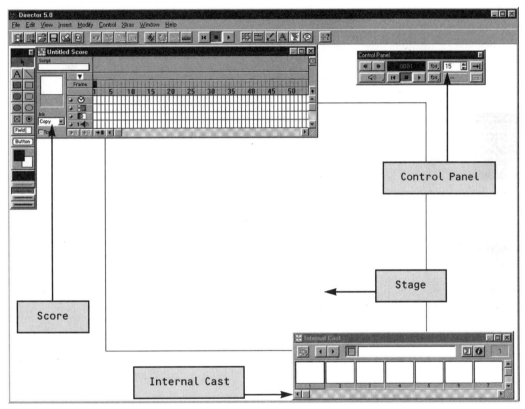

FIGURE 9.4:
Arranging your windows in this manner will allow you to see most of your Stage.

TIP

In addition to using your mouse to open windows and execute commands, you can also use the keyboard shortcuts displayed to the right of the commands on the menus. For example, Ctrl+1 is the equivalent to the Stage command, and Ctrl+2 toggles the Control Panel on and off.

Setting the Stage

In Director, the files you create are called *movies*. This can be confusing, because no matter what kind of title you create—games, interactive presentations, edutainment—they're all movies, as depicted by the next dialog box that you work in: Movie Properties.

In this section you will set your movie's *color window*, Stage size, and the color of the Stage itself. Remember from Chapter 6 that the Stage is the area in which you create the movie, and, when the final title is played back, the Stage is all that's displayed, where the entire presentation takes place.

NOTE By default, Director comes configured for making the size movies you will be creating. The purpose of this exercise is to show you how to change these parameters. Not all of your Director creations will necessarily be 640x480. Shockwave titles bound for the World Wide Web, for instance, are usually much smaller so they download quickly.

To set up your movie's stage size and color, follow these steps:

1. From the Modify menu in the Director 5.0 dialog box, select the Movie command, then select Properties. The Movie Properties dialog box is displayed, as shown in Figure 9.5. From here you control screen size, movie's color palette, and several other options. As you can see, the Stage Size is already 640x480. You can change it by selecting an option from the drop-down list, or by creating a custom size by typing values into the fields to the right of the Stage Size drop-down list—but for our purposes, leave it as it is.

   The Stage Location drop-down box has a default setting of Centered, which places the Stage in the middle of the monitor. You can change where the Stage is located by selecting a different setting from the drop-down list. The Default Palette tells Director which color system to use. In Director for Windows, the default is the Windows system (System - Win), *or* the color palette Windows is currently using. This tells Director to use the current system palette, which, if you'll recall, you set earlier to 256 colors.

2. Click on the Stage Color swatch (box) to open the Color window.

3. Select the second in the top row.

4. Click OK to close the dialog box.

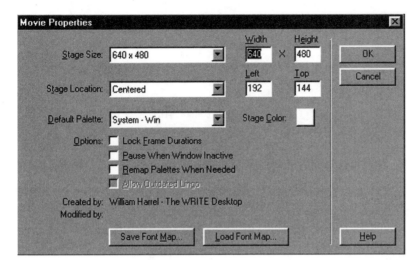

FIGURE 9.5:
The Movie Properties dialog box is used to set many options, including Stage size, location, and color properties.

As you can see, most of the default settings in this dialog box are very suitable for your new movie. All that you changed was the Stage color (which was optional—and can be changed again at any time). You'll see as we move on that this color will be the back drop for the introduction portion of the title, so pick something you like, the introduction is the first thing users will see. (Remember though, that whatever you pick for this movie will be lost, but I'll have a second color chosen in the version of the movie we use from here on out.) OK, it's now time to start bringing in your graphics.

Working with Cast Members

In Director, *cast members* are the *elements*—graphics, sound, animation, etc.—that make up your title. Cast members can either be elements you create in other programs— such as Photoshop graphics, Premiere movies, or Sound Forge sound files—and import into the title, or they can be elements you create in Director, such as text, shapes made with the drawing tools, or images you draw in the Paint window. Throughout the Workshop, you will use both methods, importing elements and creating them in Director.

In this section you will import three images created in Photoshop. As you import them, Director will query you about what color palette to use. I've already saved them as 256 color (or less) images, making this step easy for you. I'll show you how to change an image's color depth, and address some other color issues, in Chapter 13.

It's time to import images as cast members into your title, as shown in Figure 9.6. To do so, follow these steps:

1. From the File menu, choose Import.
2. In the Import Files Into "Internal" dialog box, go to the Look In drop-down box and choose the Workshop\Chap9\Before folder.
3. Double-click on the first filename in the list (Compsml2.bmp) to add it to the File List box at the bottom of the dialog box (a File List is a list of files to import).
4. Double-click on the second filename in the list (Compsml3.bmp).
5. Double-click on the third filename in the list (Keyboard.bmp).

FIGURE 9.6:
You can use the Import Files Into "Internal" dialog box to import one file at a time, or several files at once.

The files you imported in steps 3–5 are the three files you want. However, these files are not in the order in which we want them to appear in the Internal Cast window; we want the keyboard to appear first. To move it to the top of the list, you should follow these easy steps:

1. Select the third file in the File list (Keyboard.bmp).
2. Click Move Up twice to move the file to the top of the list.
3. Click Import to import the images.

TIP
You can save a couple of steps by adding each cast member to the list in the order you want them. Director will list them in the order they are added.

As Director begins the import, it displays the Import Files Into "Internal" dialog box shown in Figure 9.7. From here you tell the program how to color the image. If you choose Image (8 bits), for Color Depth, Director will use the image's Color window. If you choose Stage (8 bit), Director will apply the color palette you assigned to the title earlier in this chapter. Since I have already assigned these images the system color palette in Photoshop (which, again, you'll learn about in Chapter 13), they already use the same color palette as the title.

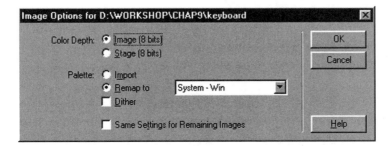

FIGURE 9.7:
Use the Image Options for D:Workshop\Chap9\keyboard dialog box to tell Director how to color your images.

For this title, all the images will use the Windows system palette, which is System - Win in the drop-down list. (Using individual palettes for separate images allows you display colors not available in the system palette currently used by the title.) Tell Director to use the Windows system palette, using these steps:

1. In the Image Options for D:\Workshop\Chap9\keyboard dialog box, make sure that for Color Depth, Image (8 bits) is selected.
2. If it is not selected, select Remap To under Window, then make sure System - Win is displayed in the drop-down list.
3. Select Same Settings for Remaining Images.
4. Click OK.

When the files finish importing, they wind up in the Internal Cast window, as shown in Figure 9.8. Each file is now a cast member of the title, ready for placement on the Stage, which is the topic of the next few sections. You'll see as we progress through the Workshop, that the Cast window can hold many objects. Each element is numbered in the order they are imported. These numbers are important in the creation of the title, as you'll see in the next section.

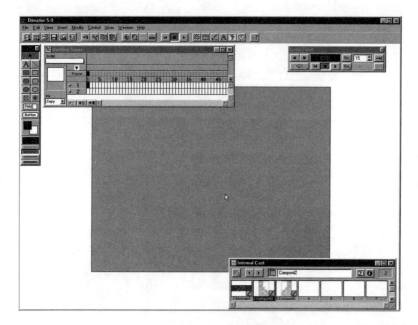

FIGURE 9.8:
When the figures finish importing, they appear in the Internal Cast window.

Working with the Score and the Stage

Within the Score, you can define when an element appears on the Stage and many aspects of its behavior, such as timing and transitions between scenes. Basically, the Score is a long sheet of frames that will make up a movie sequence. Each frame represents a small measure of time.

Frames are numbered by column across the top and by row on the left side. The top identifies each frame sequentially. The numbers on the left side identify each row, known as a *channel*. Again, the columns of frames represent small measurements of time, and channels are where you place the elements that make up your title. For each additional frame (or period of time) that an element (cast member) appears in the Score, the longer that element appears in the movie.

As shown in Figure 9.9, the Score also contains channels for transitions, sounds, color palettes, setting the movie's tempo (in fps), and scripts. Basically, the general flow of the movie is controlled by the Score.

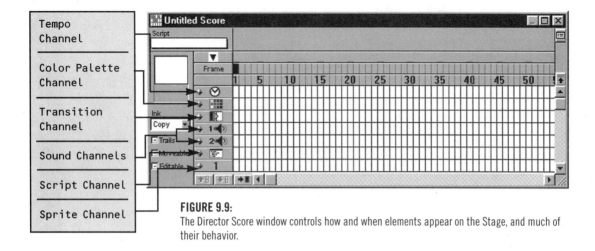

FIGURE 9.9:
The Director Score window controls how and when elements appear on the Stage, and much of their behavior.

Placing the First Element in the Score

In this section you'll place the first graphics cast member in the Score, and control when it appears and for how long. When you move a cast member to the Score, it becomes a sprite, which is an object that appears on the Stage and is controlled by the Score. As we move through the Workshop, you'll learn how to use the Score to control the behavior of not only sprites, but also the other elements of your title.

There are two ways to place an object in the Score:

- Select a cast member and move it to the frame representing the point in the Score when you want it to appear on the Stage.
- Select the frame(s) in the Score where you want the cast member to appear, and then move the cast member to the Stage.

In this section you'll get to try both methods. Let's start with the first one:

1. Select the first cast member (the keyboard) and drag it from the Cast window to frame 8 in channel 1, as shown in Figure 9.10. (We're putting it in frame 8, as opposed to frame 1 or 2, because this is where we want this cast member to make its first appearance.)

2. When the correct frame is highlighted, release the mouse button.

The sprite appears on the Stage and the number 01 appears in the frame, because it is cast member number one, and the 01 entry is called a cell. A *cell* is a unit of information about the sprite, such as size and position on the stage. As is, the sprite will appear on the Stage for only a split second because it only appears in one frame. We want this sprite to remain on the Stage for the entirety of the Introduction, which means that this cast member should appear in frames until the end of this section of the movie.

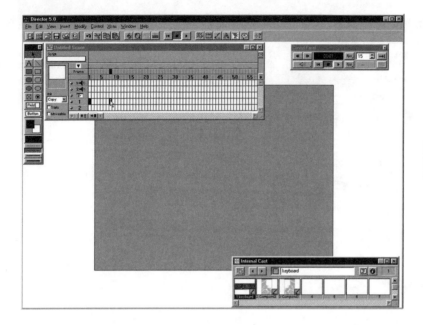

FIGURE 9.10:
Dragging a cast member from the Cast to the Score.

There are a number of shortcuts for accomplishing this, and you will be exposed to various ways to do this throughout the Workshop. But before filling in the rest of the frames, let's decide where we want the graphic to appear on the Stage, and then go ahead and place it there. It's important that you do this *before* you fill in additional cells, otherwise, as you'll see, the object will appear in the correct place only during the selected frame.

Arranging Sprites on the Stage

Arranging sprites on the Stage is similar to placing elements in a page layout or presentation program. You simply select the object with the mouse and move it to the place you want it.

Keep in mind that any changes you make to a sprite—moving, resizing, and so on—impacts the display of the object only during the frame selected in the Score. You can affect several, or all, frames in a channel by selecting them before making a change on the Stage. I'll show you how to do that later in the Workshop.

To arrange sprites (or elements) on the Stage, follow these steps:

1. Select the keyboard image from the Internal Cast window with your mouse.

2. Drag it to the center of the Stage, as shown in Figure 9.11

Also, note that the image of the keyboard has a thin black border around it. You should place the image so that the border appears at the bottom and on both the left and right sides.

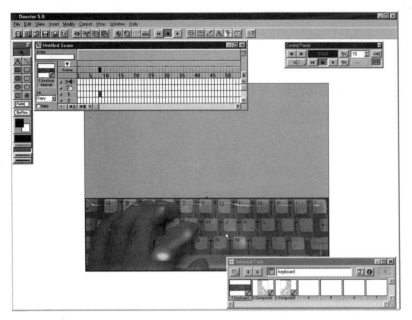

FIGURE 9.11:
Place the image as shown here; you'll see the number 01 in frame 8.

TIP

When moving a sprite into a tight place, or to place it precisely, you can use the Up, Down, Left, and Right arrow keys to nudge it small distances.

As I mentioned above, we want the sprite (keyboard graphic) to remain on Stage for the entire Introduction, rather than appearing for only the duration of the single frame we placed it in (frame 8). Here's how to do it:

1. Click on frame 8 in channel 1 to select it.

2. Using the scroll bar at the bottom of the Score window, press the arrow pointing right to scroll until frame 200 is visible.

3. Shift-click (by holding down the Shift key, while clicking on the frame) on frame 200 in channel 1. This selects the entire channel to this point (from frame 8 through frame 200), as shown in Figure 9.12.

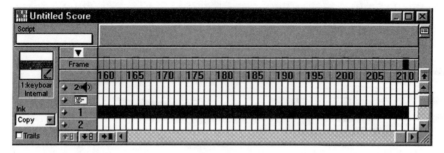

FIGURE 9.12:
Use the Shift-click method to select all of the frames between two points.

4. From the Modify menu, select In Between (or press Ctrl+B). All of the frames from 8 through 200 are filled, and the keyboard sprite should reappear on the Stage. At this point, Director also adds another couple of hundred frames to the Score. This sprite should appear until at least frame 600, so you'll need to repeat this process a couple of times to fill in the desired frames (from frame 8 through frame 600).

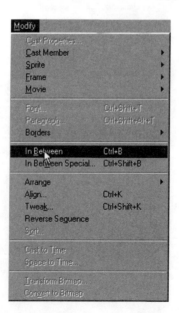

NOTE Placing sprites and filling in the frames is usually a trial and error process, requiring you to judge timing and a few other variables as you construct the movie. As you'll see later in the Workshop, it's often necessary to stretch the original distance (or increase the length of time) that a sprite appears, and move channels around.

5. Repeat steps 2 through 4, for all of the frames between 8 and 600.

Now that frames 8 through 600 have been selected, the sprite will be on stage considerably longer. You can move on to set a transition to determine how the object makes its appearance onto the Stage.

TIP You can also use Cut and Paste to fill in frames by selecting a block of frames, copying it with the standard Windows Copy command (Edit/Copy) and then using Paste (Edit/Paste) to place the copy in another section of the Score.

Creating Transitions

Transitions refer to the manner in which sprites appear on (and disappear from) the Stage. If you don't tell Director to do it differently, new sprites simply appear. By applying transition effects—fade, dissolve, wipe—you can make objects appear and disappear with a little more pizzazz.

In Director, you apply transitions in the Transition channel of the Score. In this section you will apply a transition that causes the keyboard to dissolve (which in this case, means fade in) onto the screen, rather than simply appearing when the movie plays to frame 8. Here's how to apply this transition:

1. Using the scroll bar at the bottom of the Score window, use the left arrow to scroll to the beginning of the movie.
2. Using the scroll bar on the right side of the Score window, use the up arrow to scroll to the top of the Score.
3. Double-click on frame 8 in the Transition channel, which is the third channel in the Score window (third from the top). This displays the Frame Properties: Transitions

dialog box, shown in Figure 9.13. From here you apply a transition effect and control the duration and smoothness of the transition. As you can see from the list in the Transitions box, Director supports several different transition types.

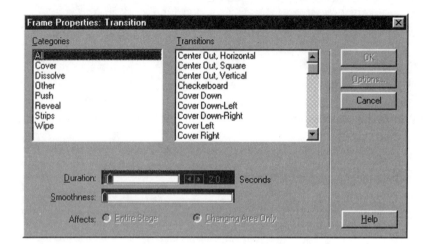

FIGURE 9.13:
Use this dialog box to apply and control transition effects.

4. In the Categories box of the Frame Properties: Transition dialog box, select Dissolve.
5. In the Transitions box, scroll through the alphabetical list of transitions and select Dissolve, Pixels.
6. Go to the Duration slider and make sure it's set at 2 seconds (this should be the default).
7. Click OK.

When we run the movie a little later in this chapter, the keyboard will dissolve onto the Stage. Notice that cell 04 appears in frame 8 in the Transition channel of the Score, and that you have a new cast member in the Internal Cast. This cast member represents the transition cell you just created. Again, *all* elements of your movie are cast members, including the color palettes, tempo settings, scripts, and other elements that actually control the behavior of sprites, sounds, animations. A transition, then, is a cast member as well.

So far, you haven't really done a lot of fancy stuff to your new movie, but let's rewind and play it just to get a feel for what's happened so far. (I'll go further into the concepts of rewind and play in the "Trying Out Your Movie with Control Panel" section later in this chapter.) To see what we've done so far, follow these steps:

8. Press Ctrl+Alt+R to rewind the movie.
9. Press Ctrl+Alt+P to play the movie.

Watch as the keyboard dissolves onto the stage.

Placing the Remaining Graphics

So far you've learned how to place a sprite in the Score, arrange the sprite on the Stage, fill frames to extend the duration of how long a sprite remains displayed, and apply transitions. This is a lot of ground to cover in a short period of time. So let's place a couple of more sprites and apply transitions for practice (besides, you've got two more cast members to place, right?).

You will begin by placing cast member 2. This time, though, you'll use a slightly different method. Here we go:

1. In the Score window, use the scroll bar to display frame 22 in channel 2.
2. Select frame 22 in channel 2.
3. Drag cast member 2 (the computer) onto the Stage.

Essentially, this method produces the same result as the method we used to place the first cast member onto the Stage: we have a sprite on the Stage and a cell number in the selected frame in the Score. Now that the sprite is on the Stage, we need to resize it. To do that, follow these steps:

1. Use your mouse to drag the sprite downward until the top of the image is visible, as shown in Figure 9.14

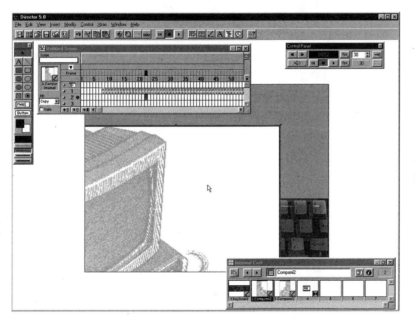

FIGURE 9.14:
Use your mouse to drag the sprite downward until you can see the top of the image.

2. Hold the Shift key down and drag downward on the upper-right corner of the image to resize it, as shown in Figure 9.15.

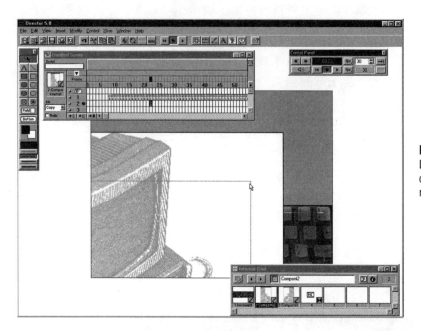

FIGURE 9.15:
Drag on the upper-right corner of the image to resize it.

Holding Shift while resizing constrains the action proportionally, causing both sides to resize evenly. Be sure to use this method so the image does not get distorted.

3. Continue resizing and moving the image until it is approximately the same size, and has the same location as the one in Figure 9.16. (I moved the Score window to better see my work, you might want to do the same.) This sprite has a border around it, so make sure that the border is visible along the upper-left corner edges of the Stage.

When you move a cast member to the stage, you are actually placing a copy of the cast member. Changes you make, such as resizing and placement, are saved in the cell inside the frame(s) in the Score where the sprite is located. The cast member in the Cast is not changed. With this method, you can use the cast member over and over without actually changing the original source.

FIGURE 9.16:
Resize and move the sprite until is looks as close as possible to this one.

4. Click on frame 22 in channel 2.
5. Use the scroll bar on the Score window to get to frame 600.
6. Shift-click in frame 600.
7. Choose In Between from the Modify menu. All of the frames from 22 through 600 should be filled.

Now let's apply a transition to this sprite:

1. Scroll to frame 22 on the Score window, then scroll up to see the Transition channel.
2. Double-click in frame 22 in the Transition channel.
3. In the Categories box of the Frame Properties: Transitions dialog box, select Other.

4. In the Transition box of the dialog box, choose Random Rows. Random Rows is a transition effect, like Dissolve, which you'll see the next time you play the movie. Also, you can place as many elements in the same the channel as you like, as long as they are at different places along the channel (e.g., one ends at frame 250, the next begins at frame 251).

5. Click OK.

You've got one last sprite to place. Repeat steps 1 through 3 you used to place the second cast member, but this time select frame 200 in channel 3 and end in frame 600 (rather than frame 22 in channel 2, as you did with cast member 2 of the computer) to place cast member 3. Go ahead and move and resize this sprite once you've placed it, as you did with the others. When you finish, your Stage should look like Figure 9.17.

FIGURE 9.17:
Your Stage should look like this after you place and arrange the second and third sprite.

Adjusting Entire Channels

As you can see, the two computer sprites are overlapping the keyboard, which is not the effect we want. What should we do? We could go to each of the 600 frames and move the keyboard forward, but that would be an excruciating process. You've probably guessed that Director provides a method to move and adjust entire channels in the Score.

The sprites on your screen go from the top of the Score downward. In other words, sprites 2 and 3 are now sitting on top of sprite 1. To remedy this problem, sprite 1 needs to move below the others. To do this, follow these two simple steps:

1. Double-click on frame 8 in channel 1, selecting all the contiguous frames of the sprite (up through frame 600), or use the shortcut you learned above.

2. At the bottom of the Score window, to the left of the scroll bar, there are three buttons. The two left ones, icons of frames and up and down arrows, allow you to move selected frames up and down in the Score. Click twice on the button with down-arrow. Did you notice that each time you clicked one of the computers moved behind the keyboard? Good. You're done placing these sprites.

NOTE No matter how much planning you do, you can't really avoid moving and changing elements in the Score. That's why I had you do these last couple of steps. This is an important part of authoring—trial and error, and rearranging. You'll get a chance to do more of it as we move along, I think it will help you troubleshoot when you work on your own titles.

You've done a lot of work so far. If you are *not* working with a save-disabled version of Director, you should save your work. Simply choose Save As from the File menu, select a folder in which to save the file, and name the file. If you *are* working with a save-disabled version, we're almost done with this chapter, at which point I'll save the movie for you, so you can pick up from where we've left off when you begin the next chapter.

Working with Markers

As you place several sprites, the Score gets bigger and longer, making it difficult to determine where objects begin and end. Director lets you apply markers along the Score to help you navigate your way through long, cluttered Scores. The marker icon is the small upside down triangle near the upper-left corner of the Score window. To place a marker, follow these steps.

1. Drag the new marker from the marker icon over to the eighth column. This will mark where the first sprite begins (in frame 8 channel 2).

2. Type Begin Keyboard to label which sprite begins here. As long as you do nothing else between dragging the marker and typing the label, the text will display directly

beside the marker, as shown in Figure 9.18. You can now easily find the beginning point for this sprite by choosing Markers from the View menu, and then selecting the marker you want to go to from the submenu, as shown in Figure 9.19.

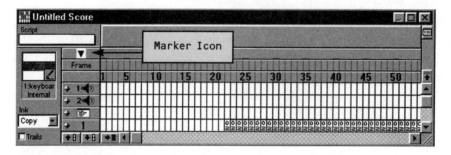

FIGURE 9.18:
Placing the first marker to show where the keyboard sprite begins.

3. Use steps 1 and 2 to place markers for the other two sprites at frame 22 and frame 200. Name the markers 1st computer and 2nd computer, respectively.

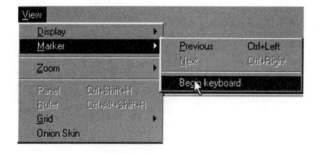

FIGURE 9.19:
Use the Marker submenu to go to the desired marker.

Trying Out Your Movie with the Control Panel

As you go about creating your movie, placing sprites, using transitions, and so on, you'll undoubtedly need to see how your changes look when the movie runs. I, for example, run the movie each time I make a change to see how my change was implemented, and whether I'm satisfied with it. Director's Control Panel (not to be confused with Windows' Control Panels), shown in Figure 9.20, allows you to run all, or portions of, your movie.

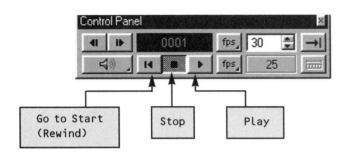

FIGURE 9.20:
Use the Control Panel to try out your work.

The Control Panel provides extensive control over how the movie plays back, including changing frames per second (fps), volume, and several other options. However, in this section, we're mainly concerned with playing your work from beginning to end to see how your movie plays out so far. To do this, you use the Rewind and Play buttons. You'll use other Control Panel options in later chapters.

To play your movie, follow these steps:

1. Once you're in the Control Panel, click the Go to Start button.
2. Click the Play button.

The movie should begin playing, and you'll see the transitions we selected earlier on. Notice that the number of the frame currently playing, is displayed in the Control Panel's LCD. Remember, you can stop the movie at any time by clicking on Stop, and you can play it back as many times as you like.

WARNING If only a portion of your movie plays, make sure the Selected Frames Only button in Control Panel is not depressed.

TIP Curious about the other buttons in the Control Panel? Simply hover your mouse cursor over them and a description of each option will pop up. This also works with the buttons across the top of the Director window.

OK. Granted, your title isn't very exciting so far, but trust me, it will get better as you import additional objects. Hang in there.

Saving Your Movie

If you're working with a save-disabled version of Director, you can't, of course, save your new movie. Have no fear, I've saved a copy of the work we've done so far in Workshop\ Chap10 folder on the CD-ROM disc. You'll be using it in the next chapter.

If you are using a full version of Director, create a folder in the Workshop folder on your hard disk called Chap10, and save this movie as MYMOVIE. Director will automatically add the .dir extension. Director movies are saved as you would any other document in a Windows application.

TIP

If for some reason you ran into trouble with any of the processes or steps we've covered in this chapter, you can load up the movie file I've provided and play it to get a better idea of what we are trying to accomplish. Having a visual may help you get through any tricky parts.

Now that we've got the basic structure of the Introduction laid out, we're ready to create some new sprites and animate them. It's this kind of effect that makes multimedia authoring so much fun.

CHAPTER 10

Working with Sound

Featuring

- Installing the workshop files
- A brief look at Sound Forge XP
- Opening, playing, and editing sounds
- Applying sound effects
- Placing sounds in your Director movie

What's a multimedia title without sound? Silent and boring, mostly—so in this chapter we take a quick look at the sound editing process. While there are, literally, hundreds of ways to alter sounds with a computer, sound editing programs can make the process fun and painless.

In this chapter, we'll cover the basics of sound editing: you'll take a brief look at the anatomy of a sound editing program; and then learn how to cut a sound; apply echoes and other sound effects; and finally how to mix two sounds together. After editing your sounds, you will then import them into the Director movie you began in the previous chapter.

This book relies on Sound Forge XP, but there are several perfectly suitable applications for altering sound files. For novices, sometimes you'll find all you need with the free applets that ship with some of today's popular sound cards. Nevertheless, you'll be able to have more control over the sounds you use once you learn to work with a sound editing program like the one in this chapter. As always, if you get stumped at any point, feel free go directly to the file MYMOVIE.dir in the Chap10 folder, and take a look at where we're heading, it may help to clarify the process.

Installing the Workshop Files

At the risk of seeming redundant, this is a reminder that each of the chapters in the workshop section use tryout applications and media clips from the CD-ROM disc included with this book. In this chapter, in addition to Macromedia Director (which you installed in the previous chapter), you'll also use Sound Foundry's Sound Forge XP and two sound clips (Blues2.wav, Keyboard.wav). You'll find Sound Forge in the SF folder; Blues.wav is in Workshop\Chap10\Before; and Blues2.wav and keyboard.wav are in Workshop\Chap10\After folder.

Installing Sound Forge XP

To install Sound Forge XP, place the *Multimedia Authoring Workshop* CD-ROM in your CD-ROM drive (you should remember which drive it was from the last chapter), and then follow these steps:

1. From the Windows 95 Start menu, select Run.
2. In the Open drop-down box, type: **d:\sf\setup**.
3. Click OK.
4. Follow the directions on the screen for installing the program.

When you finish installing Sound Forge XP, a new menu item will show up on the Start menu.

 **NOTE** Almost any sound editing program, including the ones that come with popular sound cards (such as SoundBlaster), will perform most, or all, of the functions we cover in this chapter. Each program may work a little differently, but most sound editors are straightforward and easy to use. For the purposes of this Workshop, however, I suggest you use the version of Sound Forge XP provided on the CD-ROM, just so you can learn the basics. Everything you do here will undoubtedly be useful with whatever sound editing program you ultimately decide to use. Once you get the gist of things, it may save you money to use what you already have.

Copying the Workshop Files

To copy the workshop files to your hard disk, you'll use Windows Explorer. Follow these steps:

1. From the Start button, go to Programs, and then open Windows Explorer.
2. Find your CD-ROM drive in the left list of drives and folders.
3. Click the CD-ROM drive icon to open the disk.
4. Find the Workshop folder in the right list of folders and files in Windows Explorer, then double-click on it.
5. Find the Chap10 folder, then click the right mouse button on it.
6. Choose Copy from the Edit pop-up menu.
7. In the left list in Windows Explorer, find the Workshop folder you created on your hard drive.
8. Click the right mouse button on this Workshop folder (on your hard drive), and then select Paste from the Edit pop-up menu.

Windows will create a Chap10 folder inside Workshop and then copy the files for this chapter into the new folder. You are now ready to begin. Included in the folder is the Director movie you created in the previous chapter, as well as a *Before* folder that contains the file you'll be editing, and an *After* folder that contains the two completed sound files for your title (we're using two sound files in our movie, but we're only editing one of them in this chapter; the other I've provided already edited).

Getting to Know Sound Forge

When you installed Sound Forge, the setup program should have created a Sound Forge XP DEMO entry on your Windows 95 Start/Programs menu. To start the program, click the Start menu, scroll up to Sound Forge XP, and then choose Sound Forge XP 3.0 DEMO.

Before you open a sound, the application is quite sparse, as shown in Figure 10.1. Right now, only a bare minimum of menus and buttons are displayed—you can't really do much until you open or record a sound.

FIGURE 10.1:
The Sound Forge XP application—ready and waiting for you to open and edit a sound.

There are three ways to get sounds into this application: open an existing sound, record a sound from either an audio CD or a microphone, or copy and paste a sound from another application. In this chapter, you do not record a sound because to do so would assume that you have a microphone. However, (just so you'll know) sounds are recorded in this program by selecting Record from the Special menu.

Opening and Playing Sounds

You open sounds in Sound Forge XP just as you would text or graphics in a Windows application. Perhaps surprisingly, you'll see that you edit sounds in a similar manner as well. To open a sound, follow these steps:

1. Choose Open from the File menu.
2. Go to the Workshop\Chap10\Before folder.
3. Double-click on Blues.wav.

Your screen should look like Figure 10.2. The graph in the window marked Blues.wav is graphic representation of the sound, with the wide portions of the chart indicating loud sounds and the narrow portions representing quieter sounds. Notice that several menus have been added, including Effects and Process, and if you open these menus, you'll see that several new commands are now available. Sound Forge is a powerful program, allowing you to control and change many aspects of a sound file. For example, you can add special effects, such as echo and reverb, you can cut sounds, and you can increase the tempo.

Now that the sound is open, you can play it by simply clicking the Play button.

Notice as the file plays that a hairline crosses over the graphic of the sound. The sound gets louder in wider areas, and quieter in narrow areas. You'll also see a smaller hairline sliding slowly across the top of the window—the numbers below this line depict filesize bytes (you can change this to show a time scale, by choosing Seconds from the View menu). Based on this indicator, as the sound plays, you know how many bytes have played and how many are left to play. This, in conjunction with the sound graphic, allows you to determine where to cut or enlarge sounds. In the case of *this* sound, it is too long for our purposes, and some of the music at the end isn't necessary for this title. To address this, we'll use a process sometimes called *tops and tails.*

Cutting Tops and Tails

Tops and tails actually refers to cutting a file at the beginning *and* at the end. In this example, however, you will cut away only the end of the file, making it shorter (smaller in filesize) and eliminating the portion of the clip we don't want.

In a moment, you'll be instructed to play the sound file again. After clicking Play, watch both the hairline on the graphic and the filesize byte indicator. After the hairline crosses close to the 300,000 byte marker, the harmonica sound changes dramatically—you want to cut from this point on. To do so:

1. Click the Play button to play the sound.
2. Note that around the 300,000 byte mark, the sound changes (the tune and tempo slows down).

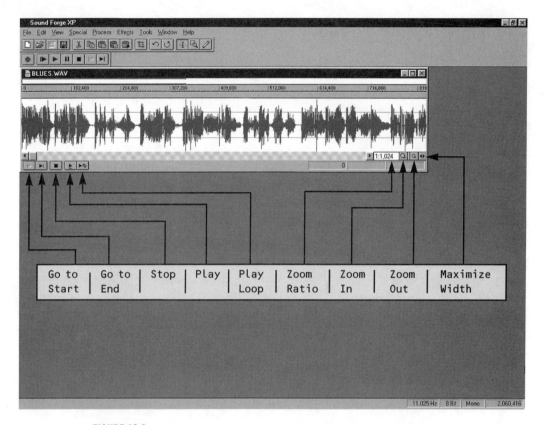

FIGURE 10.2:
The Sound Forge desktop after you open a sound. The program is now ready to perform its magic.

3. Click in the graphic as shown in Figure 10.3.
4. Click the Stop button. The hairline should return to the point where you clicked. You can tell exactly where the cursor is in the file by the Section Left indicator near the bottom-left of the window. In Figure 10.3, the indicator reads 327,681, indicating that there are that many bytes to the left of the hairline. (Some cut jobs require precise measurements. You can use this indicator and the graphic when you need to be exacting, or when working from a time scale, you can measure precisely by seconds.) Perhaps you noticed while playing the sound that not all of it is displayed in the window—well, this is where the Zoom In and Zoom Out buttons come in. You use them to compress and expand the graphic of the sound.

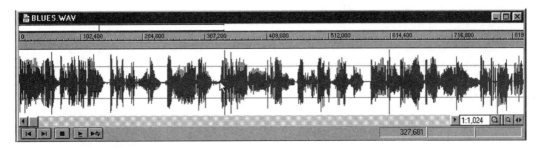

FIGURE 10.3:
Click here to mark the portion of the sound where you want to begin your cut.

5. If your Blues.wav window does not stretch from one side of the Sound Forge application window to the other, click the Maximize Width button. (It's the button in the
lower-right corner of the window with two arrows on it.)

6. Click the Zoom Out button.

 Depending on the resolution of your monitor, more or less of the
sound is displayed in the window. You can tell that all of the sound
is displayed when the graphic runs out and a thin blue line is displayed at the far right end. If all of the sound is not displayed on
your screen, repeat Step 6.

7. Beginning at the hairline, drag your cursor to the right to select the segment of the
sound you want to cut, as shown in Figure 10.4.

8. Select Clear from the Edit menu.

The end of the sound has been removed. Now let's add a special effect.

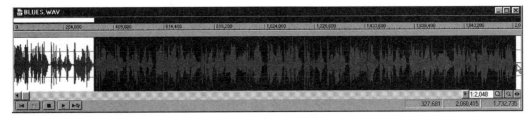

FIGURE 10.4:
Select the portion of the sound to be deleted.

Creating an Echo

Sound Forge, and programs like it, support several types of special effects (ways to change the sound). You can apply an effect to an entire sound file, or to only a selected portion of the sound. One of the most common effects is echo, which is what we will be applying to our sound file. To apply an echo to Blues.wav:

1. Click the Go to Start button to rewind the sound.
2. Click Play to play the sound again. This time, watch the hairline. You'll want to add the echo from about the 65,000 mark on.
3. Click at about the 65,000 mark on the graphic, as shown in Figure 10.5.

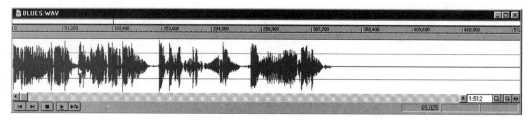

FIGURE 10.5:
Click here to mark where the echo begins.

4. Shift-click at the end of the sound graphic to select the sound all the way to the end.
5. Select Delay/Echo from the Effects menu.

NOTE You can also control the intensity of the change (in this case, echo effect) that you make to the sound by adjusting the Dry Out and Delay Out sliders, and you have the choice of applying multiple echoes (which we will not be doing). However, excessive effects can distort the sound too much. As with many aspects of multimedia authoring, getting just the right effect is a matter of trial and error. As you get more familiar with the program, you'll have a better idea how each effect changes the sound.

6. Move the Dry out slider up to 60%. This determines how much of the sound is processed with the effect. In this case, 60 percent of the sound is effected and 40 percent left intact.

7. Click OK.

8. Click Go to Start and play the sound.

If you watched the graphic after clicking OK, you might have noticed that it changed slightly while the effect was applied, depicting the modified levels of intensity. Now you have an echo in part of your sound file. Let's save the file and place it in the movie.

Saving Your Sound File

Sounds are saved similarly to other Windows documents, using the Save As command on the File menu. However, when saving a sound file, you should be mindful of where it will be played back. This file, for instance, is destined for a multimedia title designed to play from a CD-ROM, hence, we want it to be good quality and play quickly, so that the processing of the file doesn't interfere with the animation and other aspects of the title.

NOTE   Since you're working from a demo version of Sound Forge XP, you can't save the file you've edited in this chapter. However, I've saved it for you in the Workshop\Chap10\After folder on the CD-ROM disc. If you followed the directions at the beginning of this chapter, the file now resides on your hard disk and is ready for placement in your Director movie. This chapter is primarily for future reference, when you begin preparing your own files on complete (non save-disabled) versions of sound editing software.

Remember from Chapter 4 that sound files play at various kilohertz and bit-rates, up to 44kHz and 16-bit stereo, which is the highest quality. The file you started with in this chapter is 11kHz and 8 bits. You may remember from the several discussions about computer files in Part One, that you can successfully resample data downward (by eliminating extraneous information), but you can't really resample them upward (by adding nonexistent data).

That's why you should capture and record media clips at the highest rate—then you can resample them as desired. For this type of sound file—one that contains only one instrument and few other effects and noises, the highest rate would be overkill. You'd stand to gain little, and run the risk of the slowing down your title on low-speed CD-ROM drives.

In this situation, you'd get by with an 11kHz, 8-bit sound, which is the attribute of this file. To change the sound to stereo (you don't have to change this from mono to stereo, I'm just showing you how it's done so you'll know how to do it for other titles) and save it, you would follow these steps:

1. Choose Save As from the File menu.
2. This brings up the Save As dialog box shown in Figure 10.6. From here you save the file. Notice, though, that you have several options not available in standard Windows Save As dialog boxes. From here you control the sound attributes.

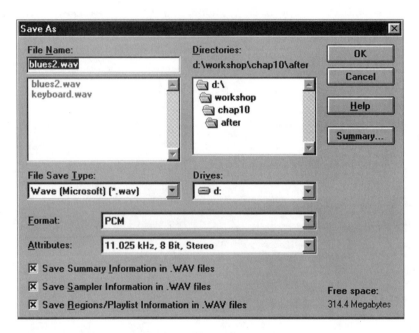

FIGURE 10.6:
The SoundForge Save As dialog box—use it, not only to save sounds, but also to designate sound attributes.

3. For Attributes, select 11.025kHz, 8 bit, Stereo from the pull-down list.

NOTE If the original sound was sampled at a higher rate (in kHz), you would have more options in the Attribute list. In other words, were this a 44kHz, 16 bit, Stereo file, you would be able to save it as any number of lower quality formats, e.g., 22kHz, 16 bit, Stereo; or 11kHz, 8 bit, Mono.

4. Go to the Workshop\Chap10\After folder on your hard disk.

5. Save the file as Blues2.wav.

6. Close Sound Forge.

If you changed the file from mono to stereo, you're now ready to place the file in your Director movie. If you left it in mono, that file is also ready to be placed.

Placing Sounds in Director

Director has two sound channels, allowing you to play two sounds at once, which, as you'll soon see, lets you create some rather impressive soundtracks. In this section, you'll import Blues2.wav. Once you've imported it, you'll fill in frames in the score to play out the sound, and then import an additional sound to play simultaneously with the first one.

Begin by opening the MYMOVIE.dir, the saved version of the title you started in the previous chapter. You'll find it the Workshop\Chap10 folder.

Importing Sound Files into Director

Remember from Chapter 9 that Director cast members are either created inside Director, or created in other applications and imported into the Cast window. Both of the sounds used in this section are Sound Forge WAV files, and you can find them in the Workshop\Chap10\After folder. Once you locate these two sound files (WAV), follow these steps to import them into your Director movie:

1. In Director's Cast window, select the first empty cast member box, number 7.

2. Choose Import from the file menu.

This opens the Import dialog box shown in Figure 10.7, which you may remember from the previous chapter. From here you bring cast members into your movie.

1. Go to the Workshop\Chap10\After folder on your hard disk.

2. Double-click on Blues2.wav to add it to the import list.

3. Double-click on Keyboard.wav to add it to the import list.

4. Click the Import button.

The two files are added to the cast, as cast members 7 and 8. You can now place them in the score.

FIGURE 10.7:
Use the Import dialog box to bring sounds into the movie cast.

Placing Sounds in Director's Score

Sounds are placed similarly to other cast members, the main difference being that they are placed in the sound channels. To place the first sound file, follow these steps:

1. Drag the cast member Blues2 (cast member 7) from the Cast window to frame 1 in the sound channel in the Score window marked **1**.
2. Scroll to right in the score until frame 610 is displayed.
3. Shift-click in sound channel 1, frame 610, to select the entire row of frames, as shown in Figure 10.8.
4. From the Modify menu, select In Between. The cell 07 fills the selected rows.
5. You can now check your work by rewinding and playing the movie. Click the Go to Start button on the Control Panel.
6. Click Play.

Now your movie has a little sound. Let's place the second file (cast member 8). This time you'll place it a little later in the score, so that it starts playing after the music starts. Actually the next sound, which is a sound effect of a computer keyboard, should start at about the same point as the echo in Blues2 begins, so you should play the movie again to determine where that point is.

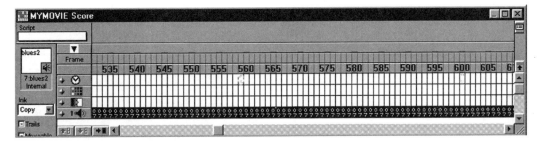

FIGURE 10.8:
Place the sound file from frame 1 to frame 610

NOTE A drawback to multimedia authoring for different types of computers with different processor speeds and CD-ROM drives is that it's difficult to time sounds exactly. What we're shooting for here is to get the keyboard to start at "about" the same time as the echo.

To place second sound file:

1. Rewind the movie, by pressing Go to Start.
2. Scroll to the beginning of the score.
3. Play the movie (as many times as necessary), watching to see at what frame (approximately) the echo in the music begins, it should be around frame 63.

You might have to run the movie a few times to actually see where the echo begins. You can also try stopping the movie, and then using the Step Backward and Step Ahead buttons—in conjunction with Play—in the upper-left corner of the Control Panel to zero in on the exact frame. Because I already did this when I prepared the movie, the next step tells you where to place the next cast member.

1. Drag cast member 8 (Keyboard.wav) from the Cast window to frame 63 in the second sound channel.
2. Scroll to frame 610, as shown in Figure 10.9.
3. Shift-click on frame 610 in sound channel 2 to select the frames.
4. Choose In Between from the Modify menu.

The keyboard sound effect is much shorter than the blues track. Whenever you need to extend a sound, you can *loop* it to make it run over and over again. Files can be looped in sound editing programs, or you can loop them in Director.

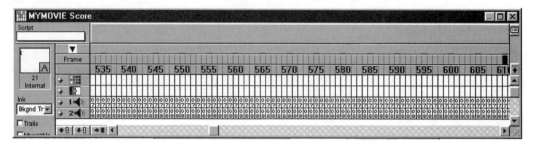

FIGURE 10.9:
Fill the second sound channel as shown here.

For our movie, you should loop cast member 8, by following these steps:

1. Double-click the keyboard cast member (number 8) in the Cast window. This brings up the Sound Cast Member Properties dialog box shown in Figure 10.10. From here we can loop a sound clip so that it plays continually, or until it runs to the end of the score.

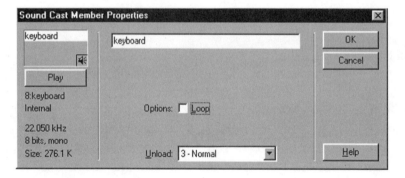

FIGURE 10.10:
Use the Sound Cast Member Properties dialog box to tell Director to loop a clip.

2. For Options, click Loop.
3. Click OK.
4. Rewind and play the movie.

Your movie is starting to come together. Did you notice that the graphics disappear toward the end of the sound clips? We need to do a quick fix to make them appear for the whole movie. Remember, part of this process is making everything happen when it's supposed to. We've got one more little maintenance step to perform, and then we can move on to the next chapter, *Working with Animation*.

Movie Maintenance

Now that the sound clips run past the graphics, to frame 610, you also want your images to extend that far, so that they'll display until the sound stops. To do so, follow these steps.

1. In the Score window, scroll right and down so channels 1, 2, and 3, are visible at frame 610.
2. Click the cell labeled 02 in channel 1, frame 610, then shift-click on channel 3, frame 610.
3. Scroll to frame 660.
4. Shift-click on frame 660 in channel 1, 2, or 3. All three channels should be selected, as shown in Figure 10.11. With this method you can fill all the selected frames at once.

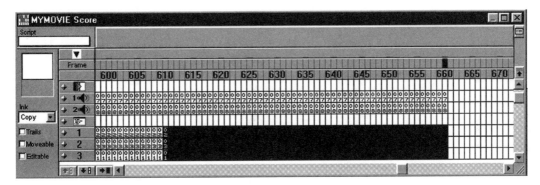

FIGURE 10.11:
You can select several channels and fill them all at once.

5. Choose In Between from the Modify menu.
6. Press Go to Start and play the movie.

Saving the File

Once you've added the sound files, you can save the whole file as explained in the last chapter. If you don't have a full version of Director, I've saved the file for you on the CD-ROM in the Workshop\Chap11 folder. It's ready to go for the next chapter.

CHAPTER 11

Working with Animation

Featuring

- Installing the Workshop files
- Setting up a grid
- Animating Director sprites
- Tweening

Animation brings your multimedia titles to life. As you saw in Chapter 7, there are several ways to create animated text and graphics: you can create them in dedicated animation programs, such as Autodesk Animator; you can use Macromedia Extreme 3D and import them from the one of many clip media collections available; or you can download images from the Internet and online services.

One benefit of Director is that you can create several types of 2D animation without having to use an additional program. Not only does this save you from the time-consuming process of learning a separate application, but you also have fewer files to manage, since the animated objects are internal cast members. In addition, the animations are much smaller than those imported from other applications, saving memory and load times.

Simple animation (moving sprites around on the stage) in Director is easy, as you'll soon see. In this chapter, after installing Workshop files, you'll turn on Director's grid, which establishes reference points on the stage where you place sprites precisely—then you'll create several animated sprites from text objects. By the end of this chapter, you should understand the basics of animation, and your title will have come a long way toward a full-fledged multimedia work of art.

Installing the Workshop Files

If you've been working through the Workshop portion of this book, Director should already be installed on your system. (If not, go back to Chapter 9 and follow the steps for installing Director, you'll need it for doing these animation exercises.) All you need to do is copy the Chapter 11 files to the Workshop folder on your hard disk. To do that, follow these steps:

1. Open Windows Explorer from the Start menu, under Programs.
2. Make sure that the *Multimedia Authoring Workshop* CD-ROM is in your CD-ROM drive, and then find the CD-ROM disc icon in the list of folders and drives in the list to the left.
3. Click the CD-ROM icon to open the drive.
4. In the list of folders on the right, double-click on the Workshop folder to open it.
5. Click the Chap11 folder to select it.
6. Click the right mouse button on the Chap11 folder, then choose Copy from the pop-up menu.
7. In the list of drives and folders on the left, find the Workshop folder.

8. Click the right mouse button on the Workshop folder, then select Paste from the pop-up menu. Windows will copy the contents of Chap11 to your hard disk, creating the Chap11 folder. This folder should contain the Before and After folders, which house the Director files you'll need to complete this chapter.

Setting Up a Grid

A *grid* is a set of intersecting lines that act as guides to help you place sprites on the stage. (Figure 11.1 shows a stage with a grid.) Later in this chapter, you'll create several animated sprites that require exact arrangement in relation to one another. You'll use the grid to align the sprites.

FIGURE 11.1:
An example of a grid on the Director stage—use it to help align objects precisely. When you run the completed title, the gridlines will not display.

Before beginning this exercise, launch Director, and open MYMOVIE.dir, which you'll find in the Workshop\Chap11 folder you copied to your hard disk in the previous section. Now, follow these steps to turn on Director's grid:

1. Click on the View menu, and then select Grid.
2. Select Show from the Grid submenu.

You now have a grid on your stage. Before leaving this section, you should become familiar with the other two options—Snap To and Settings—on the Grid submenu. The first, Snap To, gives the gridlines a magnet-like quality. When placing sprites on the stage, if you get close to a gridline (within a few pixels), Director assumes that you are trying to place the object *on* the line, and the sprite "snaps" to the gridline. This allows for the greatest precision, but can be a nuisance when you *don't* want objects to sit precisely on the grid (as is the case with our title).

Settings allows you to change the size and color of the grid. In this chapter, for size, you use the default settings, which is 64x64 pixels. In some titles, though, you may want a tighter (smaller squares) or looser (larger squares) grid. Changing the grid color, of course, makes it easier to see the grid when it's on colored backgrounds. For example, by default the gridlines are red—if your background is red, you could see the grid more easily by changing it to yellow.

To change the grid size or color:

1. Choose Settings from the Grid submenu, which displays the Grid Settings dialog box shown in Figure 11.2.
2. Adjust the size of the grid by changing the values in the spacing fields. Change the color by clicking on the Color swatch and choosing a new color from the pop-up palette.

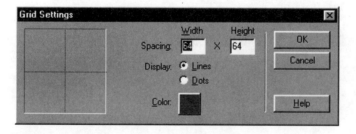

FIGURE 11.2:
The Grid Settings dialog box—use it to change the size and color of your grid.

Adding Animation to Your Movie

We want to include the name of the company in this title somewhere, right? That calls for the placement of several letters—D-i-v-i-n-e C-o-n-c-e-p-t-s. One possible design is to have the letters slide onto the screen from the right, as though they are being typed in real time. The procedure for creating this type of animation is remarkably easy. I'll go into it in much more detail below, but for now, here is a quick overview of the process.

First, you select the position in the score (the beginning frame) where you want the sprite to appear, and place the sprite at its beginning position. Then you go to the point in the score (the ending frame) where you want the sprite to stop moving, and place the sprite again. Then use In Between (which you learned how to use in the two preceding chapters) to fill in the frames between those two positions in the score. (You can also cause the sprite to move along a curve, or a *multi-direction* path, with In Between Special, which we'll look at briefly later in this chapter.)

This type of animation is known as *cell animation*. In each cell (frame), the sprite moves a small amount, creating the illusion of movement. This method is similar to the flip-book animation, where an object is drawn in various, slightly different positions on several sheets of paper. When you stack the sheets on top of each other, and flip through them quickly, the object appears to move.

NOTE While this type of animation is fun, it can also be tedious. Director provides several ways to speed up the process, which, unfortunately, I don't have the space to show you in this brief tutorial. If you're serious about multimedia, you really should invest in a book specifically about Director. You'll also find a lot of useful information in Director's Help index under "Animation."

Creating a New Sprite

Remember from Chapter 9 that a cast member becomes a sprite when you move it from the Cast window to the Stage. As you know, you can import sprites from graphics applications or create them inside Director, in the program's Paint window, or from the Text window. In this section, you will create several sprites using the Text window, animating each one as you go.

Let's begin:

1. Scroll downward in the Internal Cast window until the first empty cast position is displayed (position 9).
2. Select position 9.
3. From the Window menu, select Text.

This displays the Text window shown in Figure 11.3. If you've worked much with a word processor, this palette probably appears straightforward. In this section you'll use it to create a few characters (letters) to use as sprites in your animation. We'll look at this palette more closely in Chapter 13, in the meantime, you'll make three simple changes to this window's settings before using it—typeface, text size, and style.

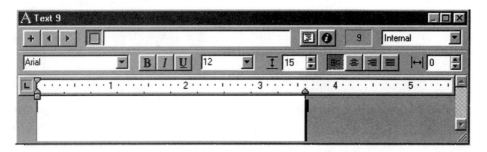

FIGURE 11.3:
Use Director's Text window to create text cast members.

4. If Arial is not the typeface shown in the first drop-down list in the second row of options, select Arial from the list of fonts on your system.
5. Click on the B (Bold) next to the list of typefaces to turn it on.
6. From the point size drop-down list, select 48. Your Text window should look like Figure 11.4.
7. Type the letter **D**.
8. Close the Text window.

The D is added to the Cast in position 9. You can now place it in the desired position on the stage and in the score.

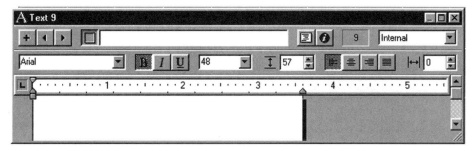

FIGURE 11.4:
Set the typeface to Arial, the type style to Bold, and the point size to 48.

Animating Sprites

1. In the Score palette, scroll downward and to the right, until frame 85 in channel 4 is displayed.
2. Select frame 85 in channel 4.
3. Drag cast member 9 to the stage, as shown in Figure 11.5.

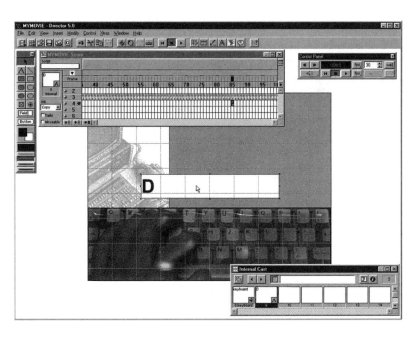

FIGURE 11.5:
Place the sprite as shown here.

Right now, there are a couple of problems with your sprite. The text box, or area, containing the letter is too long, and the background is white, blocking out the objects behind the box. Follow these steps to remedy this.

4. Using the middle control point at the far right end of the text bounding box, resize the box as shown in Figure 11.6.

FIGURE 11.6:
Drag on the middle-right control point to resize the text box.

5. In the Score window, click on the Ink (lower-left of palette) drop-down list, and then select Bkgrnd Transparent. This makes the text box background transparent, so that it does not blot out the other objects on the stage. You can now place the spite in its beginning position.

NOTE The last three procedures—creating the sprite, resizing the text box, and changing the background—are tedious, but crucial steps. Director provides several shortcuts to take some of the tedium out of this process, which I'll show in the "Adding More Letters" section below. I did it this way first to acquaint you with these functions and what they do.

6. Move the sprite to the position shown in Figure 11.7, using the grid for guidance.
7. In the Score window, scroll to the right until frame 125 is displayed.
8. Select frame 125 in channel 4.
9. Drag cast member 9 onto the stage as shown in Figure 11.8 (use the grid to place it precisely).
10. Use Ink in the Score window to change the background to transparent (for now you have to do it each time you add a copy of the sprite to the stage—I'll show you how to avoid this a little later).

FIGURE 11.7:
Using the grid as a reference, place the sprite as shown here.

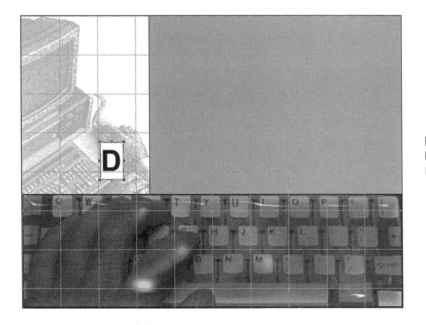

FIGURE 11.8:
Place a copy of cast member 9 in this position.

Tweening

The controlling of a sprite from frame to frame is called *tweening.* In the animation you are creating, for instance, Director calculates the total distance between the sprites in the selected frames, and then moves the sprite across the stage a fraction of that distance for each frame. Director can also tween size, color, background color, and a couple of other options. When tweening size, for example, you start with one-sized object and end with a different-sized object. Tweening calculates the increment sizes that should fall between the beginning and ending frames to make the progression look seamless. If you had to approach this using traditional cell-based animation techniques, (as is the case with most Disney features and Saturday morning cartoons) it would be very laborious, and require lots of trial and error. Director helps speed things up.

To animate the letters in your animation, you need to fill in the frames between 85 and 125, and then *tween* the position of the sprite as it crosses the stage, *and* adjust the speed at which it comes onto the stage and eases into its final position. This makes the movement seem a little more natural, rather than simply sliding the sprite from one place to another. Here's how to do it:

1. Click on the cell in frame 125 in channel 4.
2. Scroll left, and then shift click on frame 85 in channel 4.
3. Choose In Between Special from the Modify menu. This displays In Between Special dialog box shown in Figure 11.9. You should use this when you want to control various aspects of cells within a selected block of frames, or when you want to create curved or multi-direction animation. In this situation, you're animation moves across a straight line, not in multiple directions, but you still want to modify the movement slightly to make it look more natural.

TIP

While we don't animate any objects on a curved or multi-direction path in the Workshop, it's easy to do, requiring just a few more steps. To animate an object on an arc, for example, you would place a sprite in a frame at the beginning of the path, in the middle, at the top of the arc, and at the end of the path. Director's tweening will do the rest. For multi-direction paths, simply place the sprite at each point where the direction changes.

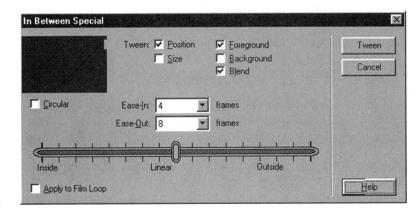

FIGURE 11.9:
Use the In Between Special dialog box to tween sprites during animation.

4. In the Tween portion of the dialog box, click on Position to select it.
5. To slow the speed at which the sprite enters the stage, under Ease-in, select 4 frames.
6. To slow the speed at which the sprite comes into its final position, select 8 frames under Ease-out.
7. Click Tween to close the dialog box.
8. Rewind (Go to Start) and play the movie.

Looks pretty good, right? The only problem is that the "D" disappears too quickly. To fix this, you want to slide it into place and hold it there while the other letters slide in beside it. I'll bet you've already figured out how to do this, but I'll show you just in case:

9. Click on frame 125 in channel 4 to select.
10. Scroll right and Shift-click on frame 660 in channel 4 to select the cells between.
11. Choose In Between from the Modify menu.
12. Rewind and play the movie.

That's more like it. Now let's add some other characters.

Enhancing the Illusion of Movement

The animation technique highlighted in this section is fairly simple. However, it is same process you would use for creating animated graphics that *seem* more sophisticated. For example, to create a flying bird, a running animal, and other forms of action, you would use the same kind of tweening. The difference is in the sprites.

Remember the earlier analogy to simulating animation with a clip book by using graphics in incremental stages of movement? This works the same in cell animation. Check out the three images of the bird in Figure 11.10. To create the illusion of movement with these images (sometimes called *actors)* in Director, you would place them in frames along the path, one after the other, to make the bird fly. You would then use In Between Special to control the speed and other aspects of the animation.

FIGURE 11.10:
Actors used to create an animation of a flying bird.

Adding More Letters

In this section, I'll help you place and animate a few more of the letters in your animation. But don't worry, I won't have you do them all (although you may if you want to). I completed the sequence and saved it for you in the Workshop\Chap11 directory you copied to your hard disk at the beginning of this chapter.

During the following exercise, in some places, you'll take a couple of different approaches to creating and placing the sprites. For example, I'll show you how to resize the text before placing it in the cast, and how to change the background in your sprites all at once, rather than having to do it each time you place a copy on the stage. Let's start with this:

1. Select Text from the Window Menu.
2. Click on the plus (+) button in the upper-left corner of the Text window. This adds the current character or string of characters to the cast, and provides you with a clean page for creating a new text cast member. Notice that the Text window title bar now reads Text 10. Notice also that position 10 is now active in the Cast window. You are about to create cast member 10.
3. Type the letter **i**.
4. Drag the thick black bar at the right end of the text block to the left to make it fit the character, as shown in Figure 11.11. This step shortens the text box, so that you won't have to resize it on the stage when you place the sprite.
5. Close the Text window.

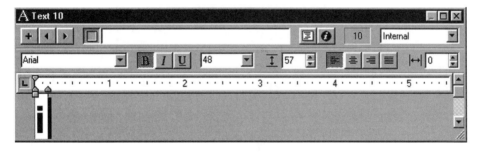

FIGURE 11.11:
Drag on this black bar to shorten the space containing the text.

What *I* did when originally creating this section of the title was use the above method to create all the letters in the Divine Concepts sequence, one after the other. But I won't make you place and animate all those characters now. Let's do a couple more, though, just for practice.

When placing the next **i** in the following steps, you want it to enter the stage just as the **D** finishes its placement. To accomplish this, you will overlap the placement of cast member 10 by five frames in relation to cast member 9.

1. In the Score window, scroll until frame 120 in channel 5 is displayed.
2. Click on frame 120 in channel 5 to select it.
3. Drag cast member 10 to the stage and place it as shown in Figure 11.12.

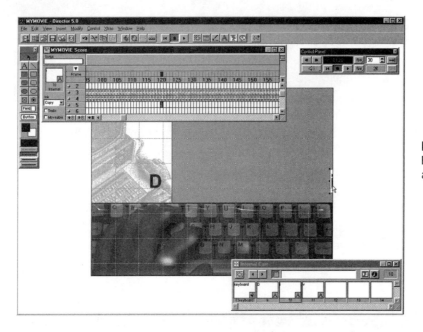

FIGURE 11.12:
Place cast member 10 as shown here.

4. Scroll the score to the right, until frame 165 in channel 5 is displayed.
5. Click on frame 165 in channel 5 to select it.
6. Drag cast member 10 to the stage and place it as shown in Figure 11.13.

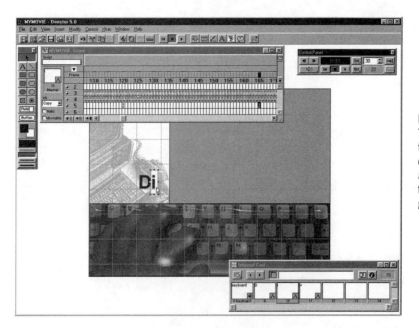

FIGURE 11.13:
Then move forward in the score and place cast member 10 again, as shown here. (Remember to use the grid for guidance.)

7. Click on frame 165 in channel 5 to select it.

8. Scroll left, and then Shift-click on frame 120 in channel 5 to select it and the frames in between.

9. From the Score window Ink drop-down list, select Bkgrnd Transparent. This step changes the background to transparent in all the cells, saving you a few steps from the previous method. In the next step, when you choose In Between Special, the dialog box will open with the same settings you used on the previous sprite. These are the settings you want, so you don't have to change anything.

10. Select In Between Special from the Modify menu.

11. Click on Tween.

12. Click on frame 165 in channel 5 to select it.

13. Scroll right to frame 660 in channel 5 and then Shift-click on that frame.

14. Choose In Between from the Modify menu.

15. Rewind and play the movie.

NOTE If you played the movie to the end, you might have noticed that the music ends before the movie. I'll show you how to fix this a little later in the "Behind the Scenes Authoring" sidebar.

Getting the idea? Now you'll place the **v**. In placing this sprite, you'll run into a slight problem. If you place the **v** as you did with the previous letter—the animation portion occupying 40 frames to the right—it comes on to the stage at the same time the second computer makes its transitioned display. This will cause the letter to also take on the transition effect you assigned to the computer sprite in Chapter 9, which is not the effect you want. So, this time you'll place the sprite so that the animation sequence ends five frames before the cell in frame 200 in the transition channel. The next sprite, the second *i* in *Divine* will also need to start five frames after the transition cell.

Now let's place the **v** sprite. To do so,

1. Click the plus (+) symbol to add a new sprite.

2. Type the letter **v**.

3. Using the same method from Step 4, shorten the text box.

4. Repeat steps 1 through 15 to place cast member 11 (the **v**). You will begin in frame 160 in channel 6, and end the animation at frame 195.

When you finish, the **v** should finish its animation at the position shown in Figure 11.15.

Behind the Scenes Authoring

By now you may be wondering how I came up with the positions and frame placement of the sprites used in this animation. For example, it's not really practical to just start placing sprites on the stage, hoping that when you're finished that they'll wind up exactly where you want them. In this case, the letters will be lined up and spaced so that when the animation is finished, *Divine Concepts* will be exactly in the center of the stage.

To accomplish this, I typed out all the characters in *Divine Concepts* in the Text window, adding the text string to the Cast window far down in the window (number 40), so that it would be well out of the way of my ongoing work. Then, again scrolling way down in the score (channel 40), I placed it on the stage directly above where the animation would stop, in all of the frames between 1 and 660, so that it displayed during the entire movie. Figure 11.14 shows this technique. When I finished the animation sequence, I deleted cast member 40 and all of the cells in channel 40.

Another way to do this is with Director 5's new Onion Skin (View menu) feature. This feature works similarly to the technique used in hand-drawn animation. The artist draws figures in the animation sequence of clear sheets of paper, stacking one over the other, so that he or she can see the position of preceding figures in relation to previously drawn ones. Onion Skin works inside Director's Paint window, and works best when using figures in various stages of action, such as animals or people running or walking. Look in Director's Help system under "Onion Skin" for a description of this feature.

To figure out which frames to use, I calculated how many frames are between the first frame in which the sprite enters the stage and the (current) end of the move, and then divided that number by the number of sprites—575 frames, divided by 14 sprites equals approximately 40 frames per sprite.

As I said earlier in this chapter, there are several ways to accomplish the same task in Director. The above method is slow, tedious and methodical. I included it to provide you with a better understanding of how the Score palette works.

However, the fastest, easiest way to create this animation is:

1) Create a template image of the finished text (as described above) in a low channel, say 40.

2) Go to the final frame, create and place all the letters at their end positions, in that one frame.

Behind the Scenes Authoring (continued)

3) Select all of the letters in this frame, copy them, and place them in the first frame (85); drag them all off-screen, to the right.

4) In Between Special them all at once.

5) Manually, offset the time of each letter (row) by the 35 (or so) frames you choose.

6) Delete the template member from score.

Done. No time or frame calculations.

FIGURE 11.14:
This is the technique used to place all of the characters of Divine Concepts.

Animating Several Sprites at Once

So far you've learned how to animate one sprite at a time. Sometimes your titles may call for more than one animation on the stage at the same time. You may, for instance, want to have two figures enter the stage from different directions, or have them move at the same time in response to some stimulus or user response.

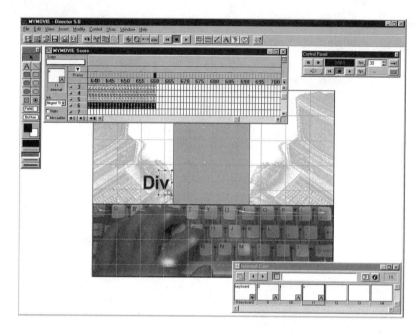

FIGURE 11.15:
The sprite will stop at this position.

In this exercise, you'll take the name *Divine Concepts* and move it from its current position to the top of the stage. In effect, you'll be moving 14 sprites at the same time. Though in this situation the sprites will move in unison, at the same time in the same direction, you would use a similar method to move sprites in different directions. You can have as many animated sprites on the stage as you need. The trick is to use the Score and separate channels for each sprite during the same columns of frames.

TIP If you want to complete the animation sequence yourself, simply print the Score (choose Score in the Print dialog box). Then place the sprites in the frames shown in the printout and animate them as you did in the previous section of this chapter.

To begin this exercise, you should close the movie you worked on in the previous section and then open the copy of MYMOVIE.dir I saved for you in the Workshop\Chap11\After folder. It contains the completed animation sequence you were working on earlier in this chapter. Once you've opened the movie, rewind it and play it.

As you will see when you finish playing the movie, the animation sequence is completed, but you are going to move all of the sprites at once to the top of the stage. Let's begin:

1. In the Score window, scroll to the right until frame 660 is displayed.
2. Resize the Score window as shown in Figure 11.16, so that you can see all of the channels containing all of the current sprites.

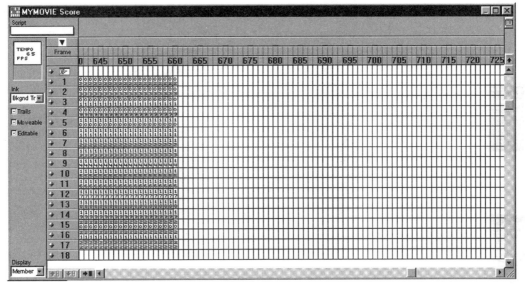

FIGURE 11.16:
Resize the Score window so you can see more channels and rows.

3. Click on frame 660 in channel 1 to select it.
4. Shift-click on frame 660 in channel 17 to select it and the frames in between.
5. Scroll right, if necessary, and then Shift-click on frame 685 in channel 17. This selects all the frames in all the selected channels between frame 660 and 685— a quick way to extend the display of several sprites at once.
6. Choose In Between from the Modify menu.
7. Click on frame 685 in channel 4 to select it.
8. Shift-click on frame 685 in channel 17 to select the frames in column 660 between channels 4–17.
9. Move or resize the Score window so that you can see the stage.
10. Hold the Shift key and drag all of the selected sprites upward, as shown in Figure 11.17. Holding the Shift key constrains the mouse so that you can move it only in one

direction, which prevents you from wavering. In other words, you can't move it both horizontally and vertically.

FIGURE 11.17:
Drag the sprites upward until the top gridline on the stage intersects the center of the letters.

11. Shift-click on frame 660 in any of the channels between 4 and 17 to select all the frames in between.
12. Choose In Between Special from the Modify menu.
13. Click on Tween.
14. Rewind and play the movie.

The last animation uses the same settings as those discussed previously, so you don't need to change the settings in In Between Special.

OK, you're now ready to move on to the next chapter to edit some digital video.

Saving Your Title

Normally, at this point, I would advise you to save your work if you were using a full version of Director. However, I've made some other changes to the movie, in addition to those you've done in this chapter. They are saved in the Workshop\Chap11\After\MYMOVIE2.dir file. You should open the movie now and rewind and play it to see what I've done. Also, there is a projector, or self-running version of the work we've done so far, in the same folder. You can see how far you've progressed by running it. To run the projector, simply double-click on the MYMOVIE2.exe file from Windows Explorer.

To complete the movie, I extended the display of all the sprites and added a new sound file at the end. If you would rather complete the title yourself, instead of using mine, print the score for MYMOVIE2.dir and place the sprites and sound file exactly as shown in the printout.

CHAPTER 12

Working with Digital Video

Featuring

- Installing the Adobe Premiere demo and Workshop files
- Getting to know Premiere
- Importing and editing a video clip
- Creating a video title and adding transitions
- Editing a video's sound track
- Placing a video in your Director title

One of the coolest aspects of multimedia authoring is working with digital video, sometimes called full-motion video. Whether you use a video camera to record your own videos, or glean from the thousands of clips available, movies are a dynamic way to spruce up your titles.

In this chapter you'll learn how to open an AVI file in Adobe Premiere, one of the leading video editing programs. You'll then place the strip on a timeline, remove extraneous footage from the beginning and end, add an introductory title, and then use transitions to switch between the title and the action contained within the clip.

Once the video is completed, you will prepare it to run from a CD-ROM within your Director movie, and then save the file and place it in your Workshop title. While this overview of the video editing process is by no means comprehensive, it will give you an understanding of how straight-forward film editing can be, and prepare you to move on to your own video editing projects with confidence.

Installing Adobe Premiere and the Workshop Files

In this chapter you'll use the Adobe Premiere demo provided on the CD-ROM that came with this book. Premiere is a full-featured video editing application with which you can alter and enhance digital video clips in numerous ways; you can also use it to capture video from various sources, including camcorders, VCRs, and laser discs. (To capture video, though, you'll need more than software—you'll need to install a capture card in your computer.) To install Premiere:

1. Insert the *Multimedia Authoring Workshop* CD-ROM into your CD-ROM drive.
2. In Windows Explorer, find the CD-ROM in the left list, then click on it to open the disc.
3. In the right list in Windows Explorer, double-click on the Adobe folder to open it.
4. Double-click on the Premiere folder to open it.
5. Double-click on the Disk1 folder to open it.
6. Double-click on Setup.

This displays the Adobe Premiere Tryout Installer dialog box shown in Figure 12.1, which allows you to install the demo version of the software. Notice that there are four options. If Microsoft Video and QuickTime are already installed on your system, the two corresponding options are dimmed. If not, you'll need to install all four options onto your system to work through this chapter.

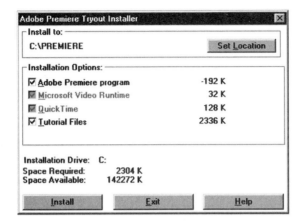

FIGURE 12.1:
Use this dialog box to install the desired Premiere demo options.

7. Make your selections and then click Install. When the installation is finished, you'll be asked to restart Windows.
8. Click Restart Now to restart Windows.

The Premiere demo is now installed. To copy the Chapter 12 Workshop files, follow these steps:

1. In the left list of files and folders on the CD-ROM, double-click on the Workshop folder.
2. Select the folder entitled Chap12, and then click the right mouse button on it.
3. Choose copy from the pop-up menu.
4. Find your hard disk in the list on the left.
5. Click the right mouse button on the hard disk icon.
6. Choose Paste from the pop-up menu.

Windows will copy the Chap12 folder and its contents to your hard disk. You are now ready to begin editing your first video.

Getting to Know Adobe Premiere

When you installed the Adobe Premiere demo, the setup program should have created an Adobe menu item in the Programs menu, and placed a Premiere 4.0 Tryout icon on the submenu. In this section you'll use that icon to launch Premiere so you can take a look at the program's interface.

To launch Premiere:

1. Click the Windows Start menu, scroll to Programs, then click Adobe.
2. Select Premiere 4.0 Tryout on the submenu.

3. Make sure Presentation - 160x120 (the default) is selected, then click OK.

The program displays the New Projects Presets dialog box shown in Figure 12.2. From here you select the type of project you'll be working on. The selection you make depends on what you intend to do with the video you'll be editing or capturing. As you select items in the list on the right, a description of the setting's uses is displayed. In this case, you'll use Presentation - 160x120, which is a general purpose setting.

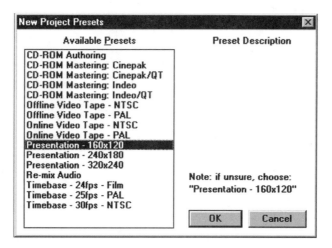

FIGURE 12.2:
Select the Presentations—160x120 in the New Projects Presets dialog box.

The three listings beginning with "Presentation" represent the three most common video sizes, with 160x120 being the smallest. The largest setting, 320x240 is half the size of a 640x480 monitor screen. Keep in mind that the larger the video viewing area, the larger the movie file—the more space on your disk it consumes and the harder your computer works to process it. A problem with using a large setting on a video you'll run from a CD-ROM is that they tend to run much slower, causing a jerky playback—especially on slower CD-ROM drives.

The first time you open Premiere, several windows—Transitions, Preview, Project, and Construction—are displayed. So many windows are open, in fact, that the screen seems quite cluttered. As with Director, Premiere allows you to open and close windows at will (from the Windows menu), as well as move them around within the Premiere interface. In Figure 12.3, I have closed the Transitions window to get it out of the way, and moved the other three around to make them all easier to see.

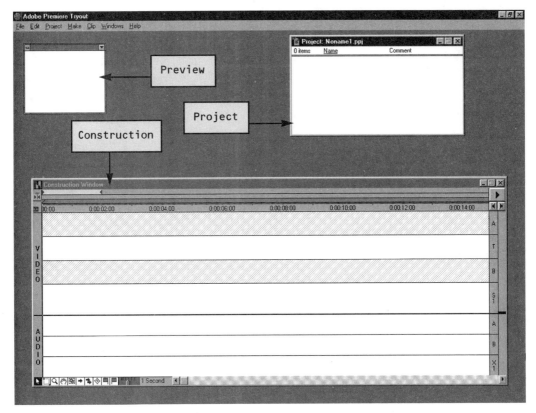

FIGURE 12.3:
The Premiere interface, waiting for you to begin a project.

In Premiere, an editing session is called a *project*. Perhaps you've noticed that the Premiere screen looks similar to Director; for instance, Premiere's Project window works like Director's Cast window. This is where the video clips and other elements of your project are housed. The *Construction window* resembles Director's Score, in that it is the timeline on which you layout the project. The *Preview window* is where you see the results of your work, similar to Director's Stage.

During the first portion of this chapter, you'll use these three windows to edit and construct your video. A little later, under *Working with Transitions*, you'll learn how to use the

Transitions window. I'll give you more details about each window when we reach the point in the tutorial where they come into play.

Importing and Editing a Video Clip

In Premiere, you usually start with an existing video clip or capture one from an external source. In this case, you'll start with AVI file saved in Workshop\Chap12\Before. As with the sound file you edited in Chapter 10, you'll trim away some extraneous material at the beginning and end of the clip. The typical procedure consists of four steps, as follows:

1. Import the clip into the Project window.
2. Play the clip to see what you want to trim.
3. Mark the place you want the clip to begin and end.
4. Move the clip to the Construction window.

Using this four-step process, you can edit and combine several clips into one project, or simply edit one clip to make it more appropriate for your multimedia title.

Importing a Video Clip

As with Director, clips, graphics, and other elements are brought into a Premiere project with the Import command on the File menu. Premiere places the clip in the Project window, which works as a holding area until you edit the clip and place it in the Construction window.

To import a clip into Premiere:

1. From the File menu, choose Import File...
2. Go to the Workshop\Chap12\Before folder on your hard disk.
3. Double-click on Heidi.avi.

Premiere places the clip in the Construction window, as shown in Figure 12.4. Notice that there are two boxes: one contains a picture of the *first frame* in the clip; the other contains *information* about the clip, such as duration (length), size, and the sample rate of the audio *track*. As you edit various aspects of the clip, the information in this box will reflect any changes you make.

FIGURE 12.4:
A new clip in the
Construction Window.

Playing a Video Clip

Individual clips are played from the Clip window, which is a VCR-like controller that allows you to play, stop, and rewind the clip at will. As you'll soon see, you can also use the Clip window to tell Premiere where to begin playing a clip and where to stop playing it.

To open Heidi.avi in the Clip window and play the video:

1. Double-click on the Heidi.avi clip in the Project window. This opens the Clip window, shown in Figure 12.5, displaying the first frame in the video. Use it to play the movie.

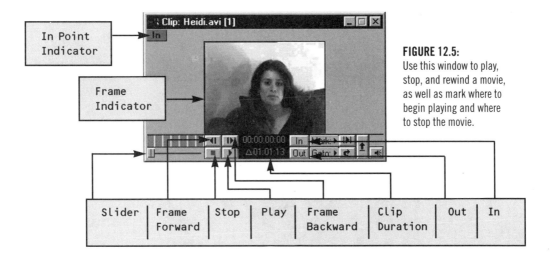

FIGURE 12.5:
Use this window to play, stop, and rewind a movie, as well as mark where to begin playing and where to stop the movie.

2. Click the Play button.

As the video plays, you'll notice that there's a spot where Heidi goofs up near the beginning, and a few frames of snow at the end—these are the places you will want to trim the video.

Behind the Scenes Authoring

By now you may be wondering where this video came from. Heidi and I filmed it in my office with a camcorder. As you can probably tell from the video, it took several attempts (over 30) to finally get it right, which is not uncommon. I captured the video with my capture card at the highest possible quality—30 frames per second, 16.7 million colors. Then I opened the clip in Premiere and saved it as a Microsoft Video (AVI) file, the one you are now working with.

Trimming a Video Clip

Premiere lets you trim off the tops and tails of a clip, cut material out of the middle, splice clips together—you name it. In this section you will use the program's In/Out function to tell Premiere where to begin playing the movie and where to end. This simple procedure is performed in the Clip window. If you were you trimming in the middle or making several cuts, you would use the Trimming window.

To trim Heidi.avi, follow these steps:

1. Using the slider in the Clip window, drag left to rewind the clip.
2. Play the clip until Heidi says, "Introduction, Take 31," then click the Stop button.
3. Using the slider again, scroll the clip until the Frame indicator reads 00:00:16:00, as shown in Figure 12.6.

FIGURE 12.6:
Using the slider, place the Frame indicator at frame 16:00.

4. Click the In button. Notice that the In Point Indicator appears in the upper-left corner of Clip. This tells Premiere to begin playing the clip here, after you place it in the Construction window. Now let's clip out that little bit of snow at the end of the clip.

5. Play the movie to the end.
6. Using the Frame Backward button, jog the clip back until the frame in which Heidi's face first appears (00:01:00:23).
7. Click on the Out button. Notice that the Out Point Indicator appears in the upper-left corner of Clip. This tells Premiere to end playing the clip here, after you place it in the Construction window.
8. Click on the X in upper-right corner of the Clip window to close it.

Adding a Clip to the Construction Window

The Construction window, shown in Figure 12.7, allows you to combine clips, still images, transitions, and sounds. Clips and still images are placed in the A and B *tracks* in the Video portion of the Construction window. Transitions are placed in the Transition (T) channel, and sounds are placed in the A and B tracks of the Audio portion of the window.

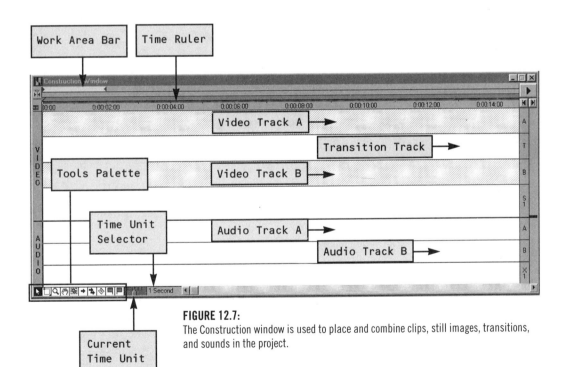

FIGURE 12.7:
The Construction window is used to place and combine clips, still images, transitions, and sounds in the project.

To place a clip in the Construction window, follow these steps:

1. If it is not already selected, click on Heidi.avi in the Project window to select it.
2. Drag the clip to the Construction window as shown in Figure 12.8.

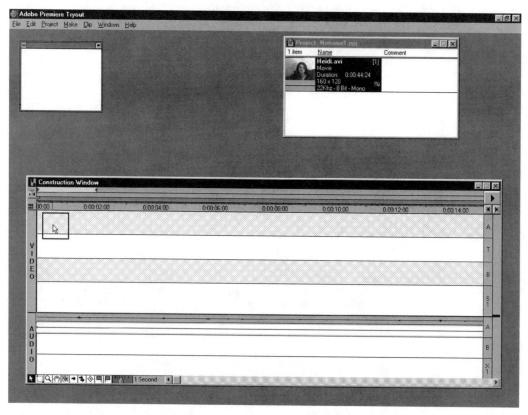

FIGURE 12.8:
Drag the clip from the Project window to the Construction window.

The clip and its sound track fills the Video Track A and Audio Track A. At this point, the video spans to the end of the Construction window and beyond. You can see the entire clip by adjusting the Time Unit Selector. To adjust the time scale of the Construction window, drag the slider in the Time Unit Selector to the right until Current Time Unit reads 4 seconds, as shown in Figure 12.9.

FIGURE 12.9:
Drag the Time Unit
Selector to the right,
as shown here.

NOTE

If you are using a 640x480 or 800x600 display setting, you should drag the Time Unit Selector a little further to the right, so the Current Time Unit reads 10 seconds. Otherwise, all of your clip may not fit in the displayed portion of the Construction window.

The clip shortens to fit in the window. Now look to the upper-left portion of the Construction window. Notice the yellow bar with red arrows at each end—this is the Work Area Bar. It determines how much of the Construction window plays when you preview your work. Only the area within the yellow bar plays, so currently, just the first few seconds of the clip plays. To stretch the Work area, drag the Work Area Bar to the right, as shown in Figure 12.10.

FIGURE 12.10:
Drag the Work Area Bar to expand the work area to include the entire clip.

TIP

You can shorten the construction bar to preview selected areas of your work, which is helpful when editing long clips.

To expand the work area:

1. Drag the right arrow on the Work Area Bar to the right until it reaches the end of the clip. When you reach the end of the clip, the bar will snap into place. We are now ready to create a still image—a title—in Video Track B. To view the clip, complete with your In/Out edits, you would choose Preview from the Project menu. You now control the play of the entire project with the *Controller window*, which you'll use in a minute.

2. Select Preview from the Project menu.

3. Let the clip play until the end.

4. Choose Controller from the Window menu.

Similar to the Clip window, the Controller, shown in Figure 12.11, allows you to play, rewind, and mark your movie. The difference is that the entire project now plays in the Preview window.

FIGURE 12.11:
Use the Controller window to play and control the contents of the Construction window.

Adding a Title to Your Movie

Premiere allows you to add still images to your movies from a graphics program, such as Photoshop, or you can create your own simple graphics with Premiere's Title window. To create a title for your project with Title, follow these steps:

1. Select New from the File menu, and then select Title.

This opens the Title window, which is a very simple graphics application, shown in Figure 12.12. This window contains tools for creating text and simple shapes, such as squares, rectangles, and circles. Notice that the shape tools are shaded on one side and clear on the other. To draw a box with a color fill, you select the right side of the tool, to draw a box with no fill, you select the left side of the tool.

2. Click on the right side of the Rectangle Tool (third tool in left column) to select it.

3. Beginning in the upper-right corner of the Canvas, draw a box covering the entire canvas area, as shown in Figure 12.13.

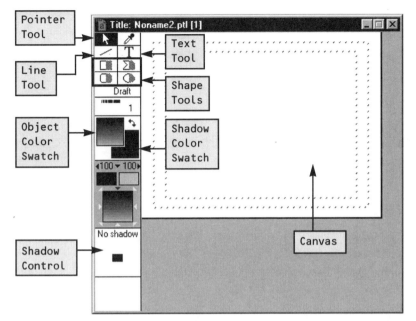

FIGURE 12.12:
Use the Title window to create titles for your movies and simple graphics.

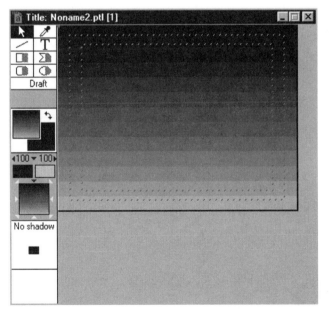

FIGURE 12.13:
Draw a square over the entire canvas area.

NOTE Depending on the version of the software—you may or may not get a gradient fill for the background. At this point it makes no difference, since you'll be changing the color of this box right away.

4. Click on the Object Color Swatch. This opens the Color Picker, which is a relatively standard dialog box for choosing colors in Windows. From here you can choose a new color for the fill in the box you just drew. You can either click on the color you want, or create a color precisely by defining red, green, and blue values in the text fields in the lower-left corner of the dialog box. Usually, when working with clips and images that will be displayed on a monitor, you can choose your colors by sight. But I want to be sure that you are using the same colors I am, so you'll use the text fields.
5. Make sure the value in the Red text field is **0**.
6. Click in the Green text field, then type **235**.
7. Click in the Blue text field, then type **251**.
8. Click OK to close Color Picker.

The box you drew changes to the color you defined in Color Picker. Now let's create some text:

9. Click on the Text Tool.
10. Click in middle of the Canvas.
11. Type **Divine Concepts**, as shown in Figure 12.14.

NOTE If your text is larger or smaller than shown here, don't worry, you'll be changing the type size soon.

12. Drag the mouse cursor over the text to select it.
13. Click on the Object Color Swatch.
14. In Color Picker, change the Red, Green, and Blue text fields to **0**. This makes the object black.
15. Click OK.

The text is now black. In the next few steps, you'll use commands on the Title menu to change the size, style, and alignment of the text:

1. Select Font from the Title menu.
2. In the Font dialog box, make sure that Font is set to Arial, set the Font Style to Italic, and set the Size to 36. When you finish, your Font dialog box should look like Figure 12.15.

FIGURE 12.14:
Type the text as
shown here.

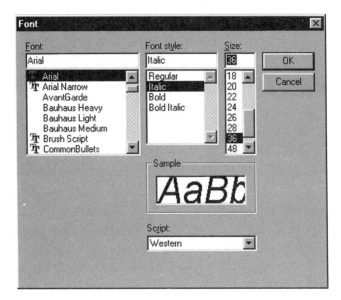

FIGURE 12.15:
Set the Font to Arial,
the Font Style to Italic,
and the Size to 36.

3. Click OK.

4. Drag the upper-right handle (the small gray box on the text bounding box) to the right until all of the text fits on two lines.

5. From the Title menu, select Justify, then select Center from the submenu.
6. From the Title menu, select Center Horizontally.
7. From the Title menu, select Center Vertically.

The Title window also allows you to create shadows easily, from the Shadow Control portion of the window in the lower-left corner. In the Shadow Control box in the Title window, drag the T upwards and to the left until the settings above the T read -3 x -3. When you finish, your Title window should look like Figure 12.16.

FIGURE 12.16:
When you finish, your title should look like this.

You're finished with the title of your movie. All that's left to do is save it and import it into the project. When you save a title, Premiere gives it a .ptl extention. Since the tryout version of the software doesn't let you save titles, go ahead and close the Title window by clicking on the X in the upper-left corner of the window.

You'll find a saved version of the title in the Workshop\Chap12\Before folder on your hard disk. Now lets bring the title into your project:

1. Choose Import from the File menu, and then choose File from the submenu.
2. Double-click on dc.ptl to import it.
3. Drag Dc.ptl from the Project window to Video Track B in the Construction window, as shown in Figure 12.17.

FIGURE 12.17:
Place the title as shown here.

As is, the title does not start at the beginning of the track, nor does it end in the desired place in relation to the clip in Video Track A. We want to fix that, so in order to make this adjustment, you need to expand the Construction window time scale so that you can see more of the area in the Construction window that you're working on.

4. Using the Time Unit Selector slider, slide the slider to the left until the Current Unit Time Indicator reads 1 Second.

You can resize an object in a track by dragging on either end of it. In this case, you want to stretch the title both left and right, as shown in Figure 12.17.

5. Drag on the left edge of the title until it fills the blank area of Video Track B.
6. Drag on the right edge of the title until it fills the area up to 00:01:12 frames.

TIP Above the Time Ruler you'll find a blue downward-pointing arrow—this is called the Playback Head and you can use it to place and resize objects precisely. In Figure 12.18, I dragged the Playback Head into the position where I wanted the title to end, using the Controller window to gauge my progress, and then stretched the "Divine Concepts" title to the Playback Head.

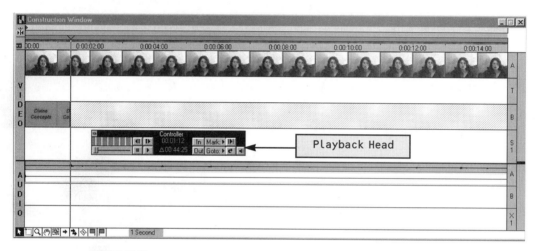

FIGURE 12.18:
Use the Playback Head to align objects precisely.

Adding a Transition to Your Video

Remember from Chapter 9 that transitions are special effects that create a fancy way to move from one scene to another, or to introduce a new element. Similar to Director transitions, Premiere allows you to transition between Video Track A and Video Track B. Transitions are chosen and controlled in Premiere from the Transition window.

To add a transition to your project:

1. Choose Transitions from the Windows menu.

This brings up Premiere's Transition window shown in Figure 12.19. As you can see, when this window is active, animations show you how each transition works—with Track B transitioning over Track A. To choose a transition, find the effect you want, and then drag it to the Transition track in the Construction window.

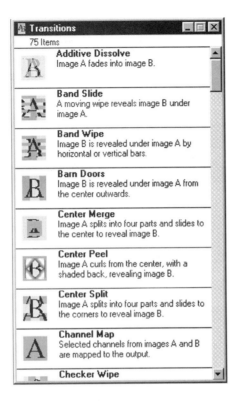

FIGURE 12.19:
Premiere's Transitions window—use it to choose and place transitions between video clips.

2. Scroll downward in the list of transitions until Flip Over is displayed.
3. Drag Flip Over to the Transition Track in the Construction window.
4. Place and resize it as shown in Figure 12.20.

You can control various aspects of how a transition works, such as which track displays first and the speed at which it occurs, depending on the transition effect itself. In this case, by default, the transition flips Track A over Track B, which is exactly the opposite from what we want. The effect we want is for the title to display first and then for Heidi.avi to flip in over it, instead of vice versa. It makes more sense when you see it:

5. Double-click on the transition you just placed in the Construction Window. This brings up the Flip Over Settings dialog box, shown in Figure 12.21. If you were using a different transition, this box would have the title of that transition. As you can see by the Start and Finish thumbnails, right now the transition starts with A and ends with B. If you drag on the slider beneath Start, you can see how the transition works.

FIGURE 12.20:
Place and resize the transition as shown here.

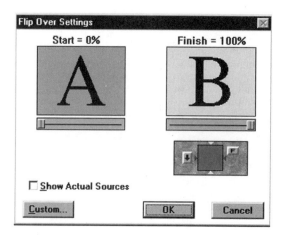

FIGURE 12.21:
Use this transition settings dialog box to control the behavior of your transition.

6. To change the Start and Finish order, click on the downward-pointing arrow beside the animation of the transition.

TIP If this were the only aspect of the transition you were changing, you could make this change by clicking on the same arrow in the transition marker in the Construction window. Also, if you'd rather see the actual clips in the Start and Finish thumbnails, you can select Show Actual Sources. Figure 12.22 shows how the thumbnails look when you use this setting.

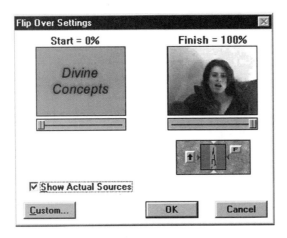

FIGURE 12.22:
Use Show Actual Sources to show the actual clips in the Start and Finish thumbnails.

If you played with the Start and Finish sliders, you've seen that the Flip Over transition consists of Video Track A flipping over to replace Video Track B, all in a single pane, or *band*. This is a nice effect, but we can make it more interesting by increasing the number of bands, which gives us a shutter effect. To do so:

1. Click on the Custom button.
2. In the ensuing dialog box, change the number of Bands to 2.
3. Click OK.
4. Slide the Start slider back and forth to see how the change affects your transition.
5. Click OK to close Flip over settings.
6. Select Preview from the Project menu to see your work so far.

Looks pretty good, don't you think? Now all that's left to do is adjust the sound track so that it begins with Heidi saying, "Hi."

Editing Your Video's Audio Track

Premiere lets you edit sound in many ways, similar to SoundForge and other Sound editing packages. However, all we're interested in doing in this section is trimming away the beginning of the sound track, so that the "Take 31" portion is not heard. There are a number of ways to do this; for this exercise, I've chosen one of the simplest methods. Keep in mind, as you perform these next few steps, that I've already done all the playing, rewinding, starting, and stopping necessary to figure out where to make this change. If you were starting from scratch, it would require a little more trial and error on your part.

To edit the beginning of the audio portion of the video, we'll work directly in Audio Track A in the Construction window following these steps:

1. Using the Controller for guidance, drag the Playback Head to the 00:01:00 frame position.
2. In Audio Track A, click the mouse cursor directly on the point where the Playback Head and the Volume Control Line intersect, as shown in Figure 12.23. This adds a control point to the Volume Control Line. You'll use it, and a couple of others, to turn the volume off for the front portion of the video.

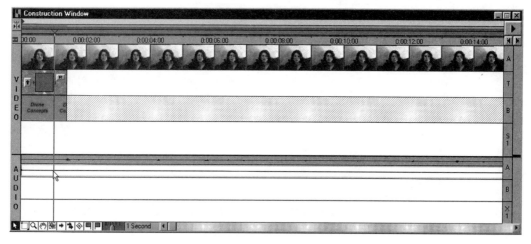

FIGURE 12.23:
Click here to add a control point to the Volume Control Line.

3. Click on the line again, directly in front of the Playback Head.
4. Drag down the second control point you created and drag it slightly to the right, as shown here.

5. Drag down the control point at the extreme left end of the line, as shown here.

In effect, what you've done is turned off the volume for this portion of the video. Adjusting this line up increases the volume.

6. Choose Preview from the Project menu to review your work so far.

Saving Your New Video

As with Director, in Premiere you typically create your movie in one file—the project—and save it to another—the movie. Since you are working with a save-disabled version of Premiere, you can't do either. Saving the project file is easy, you simply save it in the desired folder on hard disk as you would any other Windows file. You'll find a saved version of the current project in the Workshop\Chap12\Before folder.

Saving or making a movie in Premiere is another story. It is at this point that you must be mindful of where the movie will be played. In this case, it will be played inside your Director title from a CD-ROM, which means it must be saved with the optimal settings for running from a CD-ROM drive.

While you can't save the project file or make a movie with the demo version of Premiere, this is an important aspect of editing video. I'll go over the process with you in the following section, showing the settings I've used and why I chose them.

Running Heidi.ppj

Let's begin by opening the finished version in the Premiere project (.ppj) file. To open and play the file:

1. Choose Exit from the File menu to close Premiere and clear the existing project.
2. Launch the Premiere 4.0 Tryout from the Start menu.
3. Choose Open from the File menu.
4. Go to the Workshop\Chap12\After folder and double-click on Heidi.ppj to open the file.
5. Choose Preview from the Project menu.

Behind the Scenes Authoring

As the movie runs, you'll see that I've made some changes at the end, adding another transition (Tumble Away) and a copy of Dc.ptl. I also stretched the Work Area Bar slightly to accommodate longer play of the title. Then I used the method in the previous section to turn off a portion of the audio at the end of the clip. Figure 12.24 shows how the end of the movie is constructed in the Construction window. If you want to practice, you can construct the movie again, using Figure 12.24 as a guide for finishing the project.

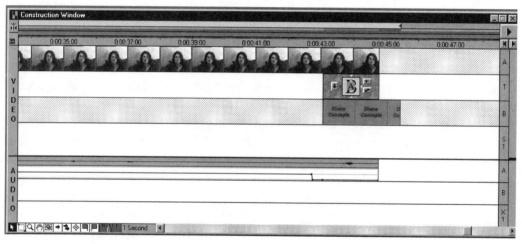

FIGURE 12.24:
How the tail of Heidi.avi was finished.

Making a Movie

One of the biggest benefits of using Director to create multimedia titles is that the files are compatible with the Macintosh version, so it can run on a Mac as long as all of your supported (*linked*) files—such as video clips—are cross-platform compatible. Premiere allows you to make movies in both of the popular desktop computer formats, Microsoft Video (AVI) and Apple QuickTime (MOV). In this exercise, you'll save your video in QuickTime (.mov) format.

When creating a movie for a CD-ROM, it's important to keep in mind that getting optimal performance is a trade-off between quality and speed. Remember that just because you might have a super-fast 6x or 8x CD-ROM drive, your prospective audience may not. Some of them may still be limping along with 2x drives.

To get optimal performance from a CD-ROM, your videos should be compressed to about 15 fps. This is about the speed at which many CD-ROM drives can run a movie without dropping frames. In addition, you will also want to adjust image quality and the color palette. To maintain sharpness of an image during video playback requires a lot of data, and you can speed up the rate at which the movie plays by decreasing image quality slightly.

Seldom will you want to try to create True Color (16.7 million color) movies for playback from a CD-ROM drive. It takes an incredible amount of data to recreate all of those colors frame after frame. *Your* video will be running inside a 256-color multimedia title. However, resampling to 256 colors could cause a new set of problems. First, when Premiere resamples a movie palette, it creates a color based on the movie, not the Windows system palette, which will not import properly into a Director movie set at 256 colors. Also, a movie resampled to the Windows system palette will not look right when running on a Mac.

One further consideration is that the movie may look different when running under Windows 95 than under Windows 3.1. Given all of this, the safest palette to go with is thousands of colors. It will look a little snowy running on a system set to 256 colors, but not impassibly so. Ideally, digital video works best at thousands of colors, and any time you can control the environment the video runs in, you should set the Windows Display Control Panel settings (as described in Chapter 9) to 16 bit (thousands) of colors. Whenever I distribute a title containing video to customers, I suggest that they make sure their systems are set to a minimum of 16 bit color.

 **TIP**

To see the video Heidi.avi at optimal settings, you can change your display system to 16 bit color to view the movie, and then change it back before going back to work in Director.

In Premiere, movies are made with the Make Movie command on the Make menu, which displays the Make Movie dialog box shown in Figure 12.25. From here you would save the movie and use the Output Options and Compression to adjust image quality, color depth, and frames per second.

NOTE When preparing movies that will run only in Windows 95 (or Windows 3.1), you can use Premiere's Capture Palette option during the capture process. With Capture Palette, Premiere allows you to allocate up to 20 colors to the Windows system palette, which will give you a closer match and be more likely to import without palette conflicts into Director. This procedure is described in Premiere's Help system under Capture Palette Command.

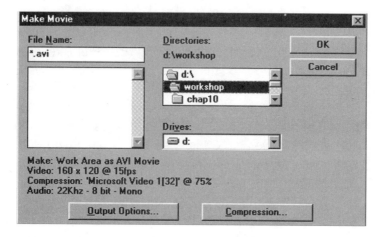

FIGURE 12.25:
Use the Make Movie dialog box to create movies from Premiere projects.

Let's look at Output Options first. Click on the Output Options dialog box to open the Project Output Options dialog box shown in Figure 12.26. From here you would set the type of movie, frame size, and the audio settings. For Heidi.ppj, the settings are as shown in Figure 12.26—AVI movie type, a size of 160x120, and sound settings of 22kHz at 8 bit mono.

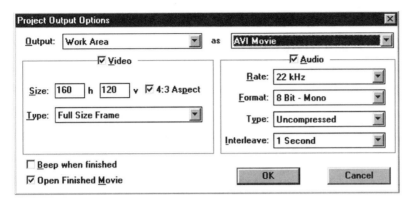

FIGURE 12.26:
Heidi.ppj's output options are set as shown here.

TIP
Sound quality can also affect how well a movie plays back from a CD-ROM. Unless your video contains movies or sound effects that require CD-quality (44.1kHz, 16 bit stereo), you should use low settings. If you need CD-quality sound, you'll have to make frames per second and image quality adjustments to compensate.

Now let's look at Compression. Clicking on the Compression button in Make Movie displays the Compression Settings dialog box. From here you would set the compression method (see Chapter 4), the color depth, and fps. Figure 12.27 shows the settings I used when creating Heidi.avi.

TIP
When creating movies for playback from a hard disk, and certain types of removable media (such as Zip or Jaz disks), compression settings are not as crucial, since these devices are much faster than CD-ROM drives. Your only real consideration in these instances is file size. For example, a one-minute clip of Heidi.avi at 16.7million colors, 30 fps, with optimal image quality would range between 60 and 80MB. However, if you've got the space, go for it. Your movies will look, run, and sound much nicer.

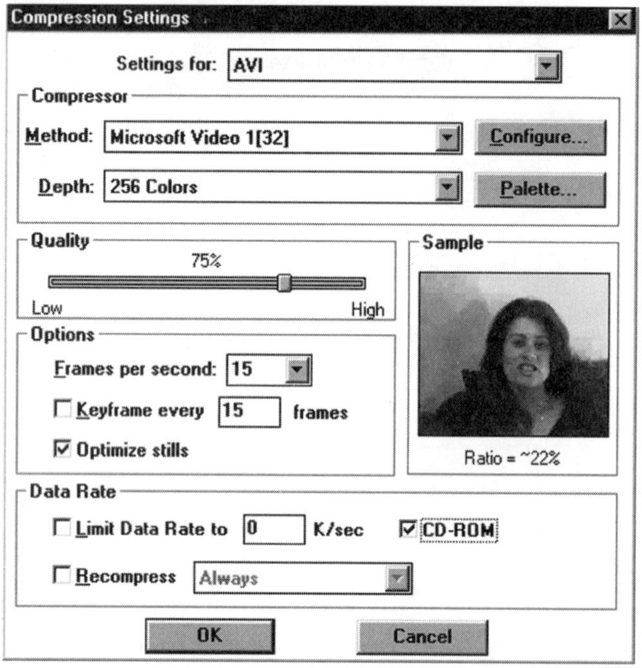

FIGURE 12.27:
These settings were used for making Heidi.avi.

After choosing these settings, you would simply name the file and click OK in Make Movie. Premiere will do the rest.

Placing a Video in a Director Movie

Placing video clips in a Director movie is a lot like placing any other file—you simply use the Import command to bring the clip in to the Cast, choose the place in the Score where you want it to begin, and then place the video on the screen. The are two important differences, though, when working with video files: One, rather than filling the frames in the Score where you want the movie to appear, you instead pause the Director movie while the video plays. Two, when importing videos—because of their large file sizes—it's usually a good idea to link the clip to the Director movie, rather than import it as an internal cast member. You may want to make some changes to the video's fps rate, and other options that Director supports, to help you control how the movie plays back. You'll learn how to pause the Score for videos, link a video (and why), and to control how it plays back in this section.

To begin:

1. If you haven't already done so, close Premiere and open Director; then open MYMOVIE.dir (you'll find it in the Workshop\Chap12 folder on your hard disk).

Behind the Scenes Authoring

Since you last saw this file in the preceding chapter, I made a couple of behind the scenes changes. First, I placed a graphic of a gray box that will provide a screen for your new video to play on. Then I stretched sprites 1, 2, and 3 in the Score to frame 850. You'll use these extra frames when placing some interactivity controls in Chapter 14.

Then I added two transition cells in the Transition channel. The first one dissolves the video screen onto the stage, and the second dissolves the text *Divine Concepts* from the screen. All that's left for you to do is to place the video clip.

If you are working with a full version of Director and would rather make these changes yourself, simply print the Score to use as a reference (or scroll through and note where the new elements are placed). You'll find the gray box (Box.bmp) in the Workshop\Chap12\Before folder on your hard disk. You can see which transitions I used (at which settings) by double-clicking on them in the Transition channel in score. The graphic of the box is cast member 24; the transition is cast member 25. To see how the box is placed on the stage, simply play the movie.

---

2. Rewind and play the movie.
3. In the Cast palette, scroll to position 26 and select it.
4. To import Heidi.mov, choose Import from the File menu.
5. Go to the Workshop\Chap12\After folder on your hard disk.
6. Double click on Heidi.mov to add it to the Import list.
7. At the bottom of the dialog box, click on Linked, as shown in Figure 12.28.

Linking a file tells Director not to import the clip directly into the movie file. Instead, the program creates and maintains a "pointer" to the file, which means that Director remembers the location of the file and loads it when needed. This serves two purposes: It keeps Director movie file small and manageable, thereby requiring less time to load; and it allows you to change or update the digital movie at will. Each time you make a change, Director will use the updated version of the clip, keeping your title current. You can also use this method to link spreadsheet data, and charts and graphs that are subject to frequent changes.

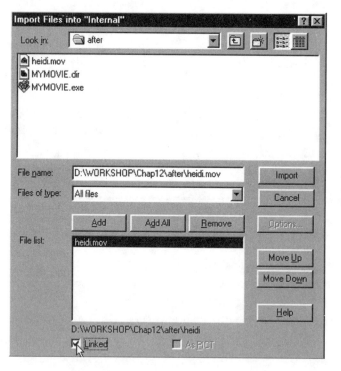

FIGURE 12.28:
Use the Linked option to tell Director keep the video clip separate from the movie file.

8. Click Import.
9. In the Cast palette, double-click on cast member 26. This displays the Video dialog box, shown in Figure 12.29. From here you can play the movie or control various aspects of the video playback.

FIGURE 12.29:
The Video dialog box—use it to play the movie or to control various aspects of how the movie plays back.

10. Click on the icon on of an *I* in the upper-middle of the dialog box. This displays the Digital Video Cast Member Properties dialog box shown in Figure 12.30. From here you control how the movie plays, including fps rate, disabling the sound track, disabling the video track, looping the video, pausing it, and so on. In this dialog box, we want to increase the default fps and tell Director to preload the video. This last option tells Director to load the clip ahead of time, so that there is no lag time before it plays.

11. In the Rate section of the dialog box, change the fps setting to 15.

12. Click on Enable Preload.

13. Click on OK to close the dialog box and save the settings.

14. In the Score palette, scroll until frame 840 in channel 19 is visible.

15. Click on frame 840 in channel 19.

16. Drag cast member 26 and place it in the gray box as shown in Figure 12.31.

17. Scroll in the Score until the frame 844 in the Tempo channel is visible.

18. Double-click on frame 840 in the Tempo channel. This displays the Frame Properties: Tempo dialog box, shown in Figure 12.32. The primary function of this dialog box is to control the speed, or tempo of the movie. You can use it to increase the fps rate, as discussed in Chapter 11, or you can use to pause the movie to play a sound or video clip. With either option, the movie pauses while the clip plays.

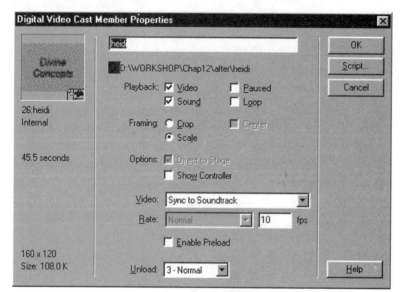

FIGURE 12.30:
The Digital Video Cast Member Properties dialog box—use it to control how the video plays inside your Director movie.

FIGURE 12.31:
Place cast member 26 as shown here.

FIGURE 12.32:
Use the Frame Properties: Tempo dialog box to pause a movie while a video clip plays.

19. Select Wait for End of Digital Video in Channel at the bottom of the dialog box.
20. In the field to the right of the Wait for End of Digital Video in Channel option, type **19**.
    This tells Director to play the video in channel 19 before advancing to the next frame.
21. Rewind and play the movie.

Great! The movie is placed and plays to the end. In the next chapter you'll learn how to create graphics and text for your title.

Saving the Movie File

As in previous chapters, to save this file, choose Save from the file menu, or choose Save As to save the file to another name or to another folder. There's a saved version of the work we've done so far in Workshop\Chap12\After on your hard disk. Feel free to open and run it anytime.

CHAPTER 13

Working with Graphics and Text

Featuring

- Getting to know Adobe Photoshop
- Defining color palettes in Photoshop
- Placing graphics in Director
- Editing cast members in Director's Paint window
- Working with text

Virtually every multimedia title you create will contain some text and graphics—the staples of computer documents. There are a couple of ways to generate text and graphics for Director movies: For less-sophisticated graphics needs, you can use Director's Paint window, or a similar graphics application, such as Adobe Photoshop or Corel Photo-Paint. As graphics editors go, Director's Paint window is rudimentary: It allows you to create simple bitmap cast members from its collection of shape, text, and paint tools, and you can also use it for simple editing of existing graphics, such as erasing a portion or changing colors within an image. However, when it comes to resampling an image's resolution or color depth—you'll need a full-fledged image editor for that. The enhancing and special effects plug-ins supported by Photoshop, and other programs like it, can sharpen images, emboss for a 3D effect, bevel edges, create drop shadows—just about anything.

You can create text inside the authoring program from the Text window, or with a word processor, such as Microsoft Word or Corel WordPerfect. The method you choose depends primarily on how much text you need. It makes more sense to use the Text window when all your work calls for is a couple of words, a title, or a phrase. If it gets more complicated than a few words, it's easier and faster to use a word processor.

We'll be looking at the various methods for graphics and text creation in this chapter. Bear in mind that the programs you'll be using have capabilities far beyond the ways in which we'll be using them. However, after completing this section of the Workshop, you'll have a good sense of the potential of these applications.

Installing the Workshop Files

If you've been working through the Workshop chapters to this point, this section may seem redundant. To complete the exercises in this chapter you use the Adobe Photoshop demo (located in the Adobe\Photoshp folder on the *Multimedia Authoring Workshop* CD-ROM), your word processor, and the tutorial files (located on CD-ROM in the Workshop\Chap13 folder). You'll also use the Director demo you installed in Chapter 9.

Installing the Adobe Photoshop Demo

While you can use virtually any image editing program to complete the graphics editing portions of this chapter (including Macromedia xRes, which comes with Director Studio suite), we'll be using Adobe Photoshop. Photoshop is the indisputable industry leader in image editing software. It was the first of its kind, and each new version sets improved standards for software of this type.

The demo used in this chapter is version 3.04, a Windows 95 program, though you can also elect to install it for Windows 3.1. The setup program recognizes which version of Windows your running and installs the appropriate files.

NOTE If you have the full version of Director Studio, feel free to use xRes to perform the editing functions in this chapter. The commands, and where you find them in the program, are slightly different, but you should have no trouble finding them. Also, if you have Corel Photo-Paint or CorelDRAW (which includes Corel Photo-Paint), you can use it for these exercises.

To install the Photoshop demo, follow these steps:

1. Place the *Multimedia Authoring Workshop* CD in your CD-ROM drive.
2. In Window Explorer (found under Programs on the Start menu), find the CD-ROM drive icon in the list of drives and folders on the left.
3. Click on the CD-ROM icon to open the drive.
4. In the right list of folders, double-click on the Adobe folder to open it.
5. Double-click on the Photoshp folder to open it.
6. Double-click on the Disks35 folder to open it.
7. Double-click on the Disk1 folder to open it.
8. Double-click on the Setup icon.

This launches the Photoshop setup application. The first screen displays the Set Location dialog box shown in Figure 13.1. From here you choose where on your system the demo will be installed. You can either select the default (C:\WINAPP32\PHOTOSHP) or change the location.

9. If desired, change the location of the demo installation.
10. Click on Continue.

When the setup application has finished installing the program, it will add a Photoshop 3.04 Tryout icon to the Adobe submenu under Programs in the Windows 95 Start menu. You are now ready to run the demo.

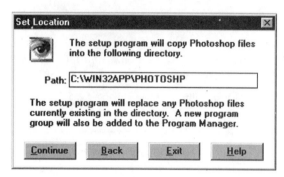

FIGURE 13.1:
Use the Set Location
dialog box to determine
where to install the
demo files.

Installing the Workshop Files

The Chapter 13 Workshop files consist of several graphics images and a text file saved in Rich Text Format (RTF) format. We'll look at RTF a little more closely in *Creating Text in Your Word Processor* later in the chapter. The files are located in the Before and After folders in the Workshop\Chap13 folder on the CD.

If you already know how to copy them to your hard disk, do so. If you don't remember, follow these steps:

1. Making sure that the *Multimedia Authoring Workshop* CD is still in your CD-ROM drive, find the Workshop folder in Windows Explorer and double-click on it to open it.
2. Select the Chap13 folder.
3. Click the right mouse button on the Chap13 folder, the choose Copy from the pop-up menu.
4. In the list of folders and drives in the left list in Windows Explorer, find the Workshop folder on your hard disk, and click the right mouse button on it.
5. Choose Paste from the pop-up menu.

When all of the files are copied, you are ready to begin preparing graphics and text.

Getting to Know Adobe Photoshop

As mentioned, Photoshop is a powerful image editing package. It's used (especially on the Mac) for a wide range of graphics creation and enhancements, including hard copy printed material, presentations, and multimedia authoring. In fact, this program is so widely used among graphics artists that many desktop computers are configured to run this application. For our needs—creating images for a multimedia title—the configuration requirements are not too exacting. In other words, the image files are small enough to run on any Windows machine. Some applications, such as full-color image editing for magazines and posters, require a fast computer and lots of memory. Keep in mind during this section that the following exercises will just scratch the surface of what you can do with this program. Hopefully, you'll be inspired to play around with it on your own.

To launch Photoshop, follow these steps:

1. From the Windows 95 Start menu, select Adobe from the Programs menu.

2. Select Photoshop 3.04 Tryout from the Adobe submenu.

Once the program has completed launching, it will look like Figure 13.2. While this relatively clean, streamlined interface may not look all that foreboding, there's a lot of hidden muscle behind the scenes.

The Photoshop interface consists of several floating palettes, and the bulk of the actual image editing is performed with the tools in the Toolbox palette. They consist of paint brushes, erasers, pencils, airbrushes, shape tools, and a host of others.

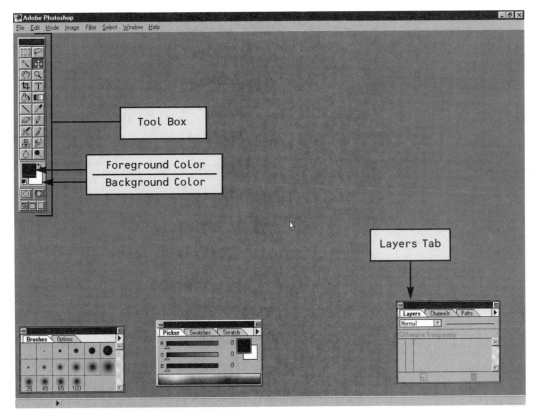

FIGURE 13.2:
The Adobe Photoshop interface, ready to begin work on an image.

In Photoshop, you can either begin with an existing image—a scanned graphic, clip art, or stock photography—or you can use the New command on the File menu to start with a blank canvas. Most often, people who use this program begin with existing images. One of the more common procedures is to combine several existing images to create an entirely new picture, as you'll do in the following steps:

1. Choose Open from the File menu.
2. Go to the Workshop\Chap13\Before folder on your hard disk.
3. Double-click on the file name Paper.tif to open it.

The image shown in Figure 13.3 opens. This will serve as a background for the collage of images you are about to create. As is, it is too large and of too high a resolution for your Director movie stage. To address this, you need to resize it to 640x480 pixels. Images are resized in Photoshop with the Image Size command on the Image menu.

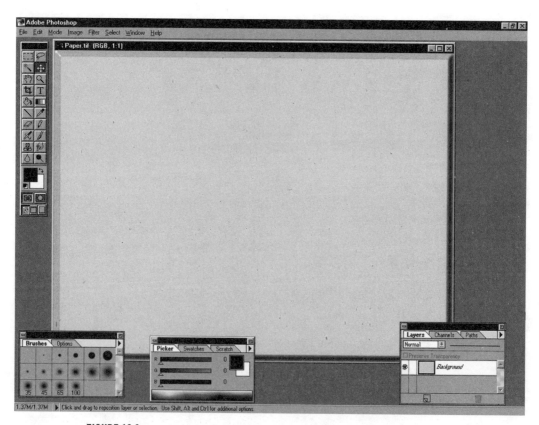

FIGURE 13.3:
This image will serve as a background for your completed collage of graphics.

TIP If you are using a 1024x768 display setting (or larger) and can't see all of your image, you can resize the canvas window by dragging on its edges. Dragging at the corner will resize in two directions. If you are using an 800x600 (or smaller) setting, to see all of the image, you should select the Zoom tool (the magnifying glass): hold the Alt key and click on the image to zoom out on it. Then, if necessary, you can resize the canvas window.

To resize Paper.tif:

4. Select Image Size from the Image menu.

This displays the Image Size dialog box shown in Figure 13.4. From here you adjust the image's physical size, or dimensions, as well as its resolution—all of which affect the image's file size. Notice that, by default, Photoshop displays dimensions in *inches*. Since we are designing for the computer screen, we want to see the image size in *pixels*.

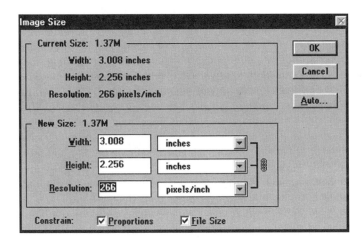

FIGURE 13.4:
Use the Image Size dialog box to adjust dimensions and resolution.

To change the unit of measurement, follow these steps:

5. In the New Size section of the Image Size dialog box, click on the Width drop-down list, and select Pixels from the list.

6. Click on the Height drop-down list, and select Pixels from the list.

As you can see, the image is currently 800x600 pixels. We want it to be 640x480. However, before we can change the image size, we must first turn off the File Size option in the Constrain section of the dialog box. Here's why: If the File Size option is on when you resize an image, Photoshop keeps all the data contained within the image. To accomplish this, the program adjusts the image resolution. Since we are decreasing the size of the image, the resolution of the image would increase. Were we increasing the size of the image, the resolution would decrease.

Typically, computer monitors display images at 72 dpi. Anything larger wastes disk space and causes the computer to work too hard to display the image, often slowing down the pace of your multimedia title. It is counter-productive to increase the resolution of an image.

> **TIP** If you are scanning an image that you plan to enlarge by a factor of two, scan the image at twice the resolution required for the target media. For an image designed to display at 75 dpi on a monitor, then, you would scan it at 150 dpi. This would allow you to double the dimensions of the image without degrading the quality.

7. Click on File Size to deselect it.
8. Select the text in the Resolution text field and change it to **72**.
9. Select the text in the Width text field and type **640**.

Notice that the Height field automatically changed to 480. This is because the Proportions box is checked at the bottom of the dialog box, telling Photoshop to resize the image equally horizontally and vertically. If you turned Proportions off, you would have to enter each dimension separately. A drawback to that method is that if your numbers are not precise, you will distort the image. Your dialog box should look like Figure 13.5.

10. Click OK to resize the image.

The image should now match the measurements of your Director movie stage.

Combining Images

Now that the background is the right size, you can place some other graphics on top of it. In this exercise you'll use one of Photoshop's most helpful features: *layering*. In image editing software such as Photoshop, when you use Layers, each layer remains separate until you flatten the layers into one composite image.

The reason for this is that image editing software uses a paint and canvas metaphor. Once you paint an object on the canvas, it dries and becomes part of the painting. The only way to change it is to paint over it—here's where layering comes in. Layers act as

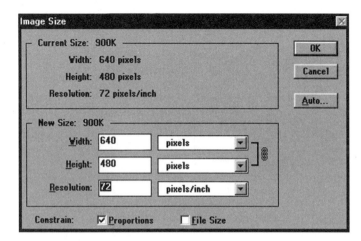

FIGURE 13.5:
Make these changes
to Image Size:
Width = 640 pixels,
Height = 480 pixels,
Resolution = 72,
File Size = off.

clear overlays, similar to acetone sheets, where you place objects such as text and other elements. While on the layer, the objects retain their autonomy, allowing you to edit and move them separately as needed.

As we move through this section, the concept of layering will become clear. Start by looking at the Layers tab in the lower-right portion of the screen. Notice in Figure 13.3 that right now there is only one layer—Background—which is the image displayed in the Paper.tif window. To place another image on top of the Background on a separate layer, follow these steps:

1. From the File menu, select Open.
2. In the Workshop\Chap13\Before folder, double-click on Globe.psd (.psd is the extension for Photoshop documents) to open it.

Globe.psd opens in its own window, as shown in Figure 13.6. Notice that this window has a checkerboard background behind the globe. What this means is that the globe is sitting on a transparent canvas, or background. The reason I saved these images in Photoshop's native format is that it supports transparent backgrounds. Other graphics file formats, such as .tif, .pcx, or .bmp, do not. They must have a solid background, either white or some other color. As you'll see in a moment, the transparent background allows you to place only the globe, without anything behind it to blot out the texture in Paper.tif.

3. Using the Globe.psd title bar, move the window containing the globe to right, so that the upper left corner of Paper.tif is visible, as shown in Figure 13.7.

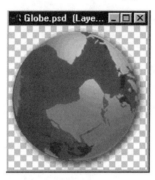

FIGURE 13.6:
Globe.psd in its
own window with a
transparent background.

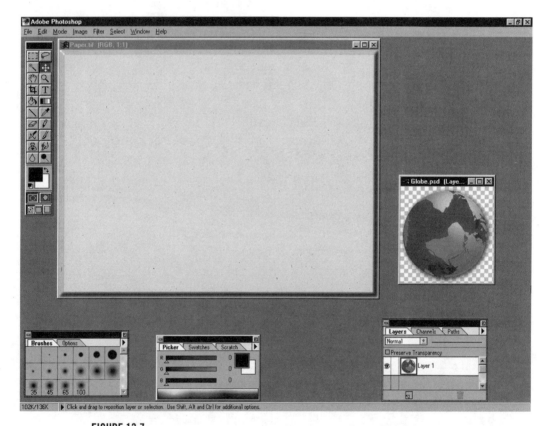

FIGURE 13.7:
Place Globe.psd so that you can see Paper.tif.

4. Select the Move tool from the Toolbox (second tool in second column, the one with the four arrows).

5. Click in the middle of the globe in Globe.psd and drag it onto Paper.tif, as shown in Figure 13.8. When you are close to the position shown in the figure, release the mouse button.

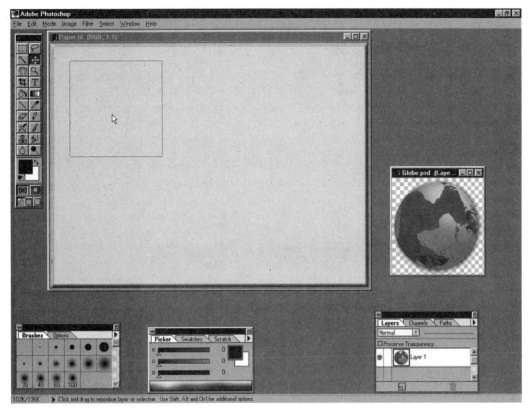

FIGURE 13.8:
Drag from window to Paper.tif as shown here.

Two things should happen: First, the globe should now be on the texture in Paper.tif. Second, there is a new layer in the Layers palette, Layer 1. Photoshop allows you to give layers distinctive names, to make them easier to identify.

6. Double click on the word Layer 1 in the Layers tab.

This displays the Layer Options dialog box, which provides extensive controls over this layer that are far beyond the scope of this introduction. All we want to do is rename the layer.

To get a description of this dialog box, look in Photoshop Help under Layer Options (after the dialog box is closed). To do so, select Search for Help On from the Help menu and then type Layer Options in the Help Topics dialog box.

7. Type **Globe** in the Name field.

8. Click OK to close the dialog box.

9. Click on the X in the upper-right corner of the Globe.psd window to close it.

The globe now sits on Paper.tif on its own layer. You can move it around and edit it without affecting the texture underneath.

10. Choose Show Rulers from the Windows menu to turn on Photoshop's rulers.

11. Using the Move tool, align the globe so that it is about .5 inches away from the top and left edges of the Background layer, as shown in Figure 13.9 (don't worry about being exact).

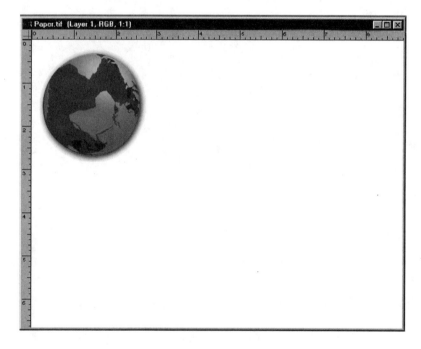

FIGURE 13.9:
Place the globe as shown here.

Now let's place one more layer:

12. Choose Open from the File menu.

13. In the Workshop\Chap13\Before folder, double-click on WWWpage.psd to open it.

14. Drag the text in the WWWpage.psd window and place it as shown in Figure 13.10 (use the figure for guidance and again, don't worry about being too precise).

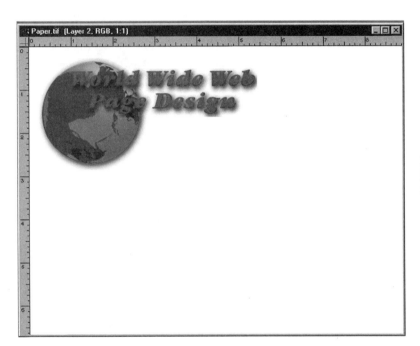

FIGURE 13.10:
Place the text as shown here.

Behind the Scenes Authoring

Where did these graphics came from? The first two, Paper.tif and Globe.psd, came from stock photography collections. Paper.tif is a background texture I cropped to the right shape, and then I used Inner Bevel, a Photoshop plug-in from Alien Skien's Black Box collection, to create the beveled edge—a feat I don't have the artistic skill to accomplish on my own.

Behind the Scenes Authoring (continued)

The globe was cut from a larger image; then I used the Drop Shadow, another Black Box plug-in, to create the shadow behind the globe. The text was created in Photoshop with the Text tool. Then I used Inner Bevel and Drop Shadow to give it a 3D effect. Both the globe and text were placed on a new Photoshop canvas with transparent backgrounds, which is one of the background options available when you use the New command on the File menu.

---

15. Double-click on the Layer 1 text in the Layers palette.
16. Type **WWW Text** for Name in the Layer Options dialog box.
17. Click OK to close the dialog box.

Defining Color Palettes in Photoshop

Remember from Chapter 9 that when creating multimedia titles, you typically design for the lowest common denominator—a display system set at 640x480 with 256 colors. The graphics you are working with in this chapter are 16.7 million, or TrueColor, images.

If you were to use them as is, Windows would have to dither them to display the 256 colors defined in your Director movie, causing an unclear, improperly colored image. The alternative is to resample the colors in the image so that they match the color palette used in your movie.

A Word about Color Palettes

This stuff about color palettes can get pretty confusing. Basically, the way it works is that when you save an image or digital movie, information about the colors in the image are saved with the file. This color-defining data is called the palette. The palette can contain between 2 (black and white) and 16.7 million colors. As you learned earlier in Chapter 3, the number of colors a system can display, its *color depth*, is defined in terms of bits-per-pixel: 4 bit, 8 bit, 24 bit, and so on.

A Word about Color Palettes (continued)

Computer image files define colors in a similar manner. However, images containing less than 16.7 million colors are not confined to using the system palette. For example, programs like Photoshop let you *map* any colors to the image you choose. Programs like Director can read and use the color palette to adjust the stage colors to match.

Granted, this can be a complicated process requiring a sophisticated knowledge of how computers use color. Usually, though, when designing for multimedia titles, you resample to the system palette for the type of computer the title is designed to run on—in this case, Windows. However, sometimes it's important that your images maintain palettes closer to their original colors. In these cases, you would adapt the color palette to the image. Director would then use that color palette when it displayed the image in a movie.

Note, too, that color palettes are also important when working with graphics designed for the World Wide Web. The GIF image format used for much of the graphics on the Web are resampled to 256 colors or less.

In Photoshop, an image's color *mode* is adjusted from the Mode menu, shown in Figure 13.11. Most of the commands on this menu are for dealing with images destined for printed material. To reasample an image's color depth you would use the *Indexed Color* command.

FIGURE 13.11:
The commands on the Mode menu allow you to adjust color depth and mode.

To adjust your image's color mode, follow these steps:

1. Choose Indexed Color from the Mode menu.

A dialog box opens asking if you want to flatten the image or combine the layers into one. Only the Photoshop .psd in TrueColor mode format supports layers. In order to index the colors, Photoshop must flatten the layers. Note, though, that this is a one-way street—you cannot unflatten the layers.

> **TIP**
> At this point, before flattening the layers, I usually save the image as a Photoshop.psd file in case I need to go back and change the image.

2. Click OK.

This displays the Indexed Color dialog box shown in Figure 13.12. As you can see, the options for creating a color palette are extensive—far beyond the scope of this book. You'll find a description of them Photoshop's Help system under Indexed Color.

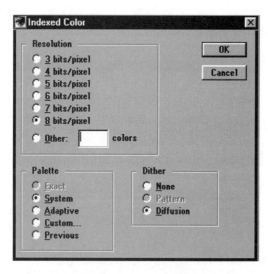

FIGURE 13.12:
The Indexed Color dialog box—use it to resample an image's color depth.

3. Under Resolution, make sure 8 bits/pixel is selected.

4. Under Palette, make sure System is selected.

5. Click on OK to make the change.

If you watched closely, you might have noticed a slight change in hues. Photoshop remapped all the colors in the image to the system palette. It is now ready to save and use in your Director movie.

Saving an Image in Photoshop

Most programs, including Director, do not support Photoshop's native file format. To use it in your movie, you must save it in another format, such as .tif or .bmp. When working with files designed for display on a computer screen, I prefer .bmp, because it was designed by Microsoft primarily for that purpose—displaying on monitors in Windows. Also, it provides a little more control over color depth, letting you choose between 8, 16, and 24 bits when saving the file. When you choose the BMP format in the Save As dialog box, after naming the file and clicking OK, Photoshop displays a dialog box asking you which color depth you want to use. For this image you would use 8 bits.

If you're using the Photoshop demo, you can't save the file we've been working on in this chapter. You'll find saved copies named WWW.psd and WWW.bmp in the Workshop\Chap13\After folder on your hard disk. You'll use the latter in your title in the next section.

Placing Images in Director

You've already placed graphics and several other elements in your title, MYMOVIE.dir. Placing the image you just created is no different, you simply import it into the Cast, go to the place in the Score where you want it to appear, move the cast member to the stage, and then fill in the frames in the Score.

In addition to the graphic you created in Photoshop earlier, you'll also place another, WWW2.bmp, a slightly modified version of WWW.bmp, which will serve as a backdrop to several images I've saved in the Workshop\Chap13\After folder. Since you've already done this procedure a few times, we'll breeze through this exercise:

1. Open Director, and then open the copy of MYMOVIE.dir in the Workshop\Chap13 folder on your hard disk.
2. Choose Import from the File menu.
3. Go to the Workshop\Chap13\After folder on your hard disk.
4. Double-click on WWW2.bmp to add it to the Import list.
5. WWW.bmp is in the After folder too. Double-click on WWW.bmp to add it to the Import list.
6. Click on Import.

7. In the Image Option dialog box select Stage (8 bits) and Same Settings for Remaining Images, as shown in Figure 13.13.

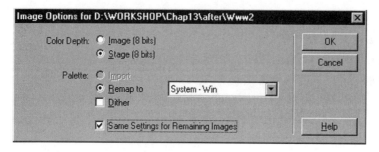

FIGURE 13.13:
Select Stage (8 bits) and Same Settings for Remaining Images.

8. Click OK.

The images are imported as cast members 27 and 28 in the Cast palette. You can now place them in the Score:

9. In the Score, scroll until frame 850 in channel 20 is displayed.
10. Click on frame 850 in channel 20 to select it.
11. Drag cast member 27 from the Cast to the Stage and place it as shown in Figure 13.14.

FIGURE 13.14:
Place cast member 27 as shown here.

12. Return to the Score and make sure frame 850 in channel 20 is still selected.
13. Scroll right to the end of the Score, and Shift-click to select the last visible frame and those in between.
14. Choose In Between from the Modify menu.
15. Repeat steps 13–15 to fill the channel to frame 1174, as shown in Figure 13.15.

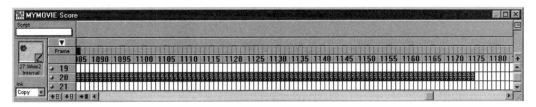

FIGURE 13.15:
Fill the frames to frame 1174.

Now let's place the second image:
16. Go to frame 1169 in channel 21.
17. Click on frame 1169 in channel 21 to select it.
18. Drag cast member 28 from the Cast to the screen and place directly over cast member 27.

TIP Remember that you can use the arrow keys to nudge the image into precise placement.

19. Use the In Between method you've learned so well to fill channel 21 from frame 1169 to 1248.

That's it. Now you'll use Director's Paint window to modify the two images.

Editing Cast Members in Director's Paint Window

Director's Paint window, a small, relatively simple bitmap editor, looks remarkably like Photoshop, and operates much the same. To open the Paint window, you simply double-click on the image on the stage you want to edit:

1. In the Cast window, double-click on cast member 27.

The image appears in the Paint window, as shown in Figure 13.16. This little paint applet allows you to make changes to the cast members—too many to go over here. However, you'll find a rather extensive description of all these buttons and tools in Director's Help system. (Choose Help/Contents, then click on search. Type **paint** in the top field, and then double-click on Paint Window Basics in the bottom list.)

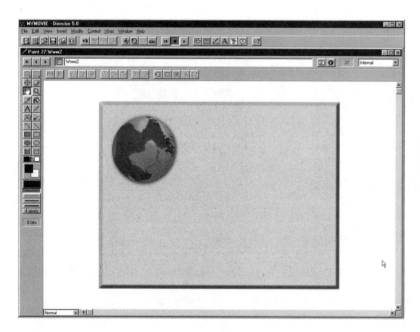

FIGURE 13.16:
Director's Paint window—use it to edit and create graphic cast members.

In this exercise, you'll add a Web site URL (address) to the bottom of the image with the Text tool. Start by defining the text attributes and color of the text to be typed:

2. Double-click on the Text tool icon (The *A* in the first column).

This displays the Font dialog box shown in Figure 13.17. From you here you set font attributes and color.

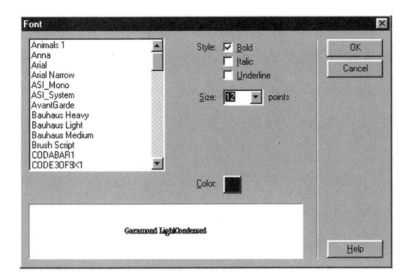

FIGURE 13.17:
Use the Font dialog box
to set text attributes and
color in the Paint window.

3. Find and select Arial in the list of typefaces on the left.
4. For Style, select Bold.
5. In the Size drop-down list, find and select 18.
6. Click on the Color button and then select the seventh color in the first row (red).
7. Click OK to close the dialog box.
8. Click the text mouse cursor in the lower-left corner of the image in the paint window (don't worry about being precise—you'll move the text block shortly).
9. Type **http://www.divine.com** as shown in Figure 13.18.
10. Drag the text to the position shown in Figure 13.19.

NOTE It is important during the drag procedure that you click inside the text box. If you miss, or for some reason click outside the text box, the text will become immovable. If so, you will need to delete cast member 27, reimport it and repeat this process.

11. Click on the X in upper-left corner of the Paint window to close it.

This change in color and font will show up in every frame where this cast member is displayed. Now you need to make the same changes to cast member 28.

12. Double-click on cast member 28 and repeat steps 8 through 11.

FIGURE 13.18:
Type this text in approximately this position.

FIGURE 13.19:
Move the text to the corner of the image, as shown here.

You're through with the image editing portion of this project. Let's move on to creating and placing text.

Working with Text

As mentioned earlier, there are two ways to get text into your Director title: using a word processor, or creating it in Director's Text window. (A third method would be to select the text in your word processor, use the Copy command to place it on the Windows Clipboard, and the use the Paste command in Director to place the text in to the Cast.) Again, the method you use depends on the amount of text you need, or whether the text already exists somewhere in a word processor file.

Creating Text in Your Word Processor

When creating text for Director movies, you work the same as you would with any other word processor document. Simply type the text (complete with headings, paragraph breaks, bolds, italics, and so on) where you want it to appear when placed on the Director Stage.

The only real difference is in how you save the file. Director does not support word processor files directly. In other words, you cannot save your text as a native Microsoft Word or Corel WordPerfect file and then import it into Director. Instead, you export the text from your word processor to a *Rich Text Format* (RTF) file.

RTF files are text files containing some limited formatting instructions, such as text size, style, line breaks, and a few others. But it does *not* support tables, embedded graphics, boxes and lines, and many of the other features supported by your word processor. RTF is cross-platform, meaning that you can easily import it from Macs to Windows machines and back again.

In Word, for example, you export to RTF from the Save As dialog box. Simply choose Save As from Word's file menu, and find the Rich Text Format (*.rtf) setting in the Save As Type drop-down list, as shown in Figure 13.20. When you click on OK, the file will save as RTF. You can now import it into Director.

Creating Text in Director's Text Window

You used the Text window in Chapter 11 to create the text sprites for your animation. While somewhat limited in features, the Text window shown in Figure 13.21, works essentially like a word processor. You simply type text on the page and use the various buttons and drop-down menus to format it. When you close the Text window, the new text automatically occupies the next open position in the Cast.

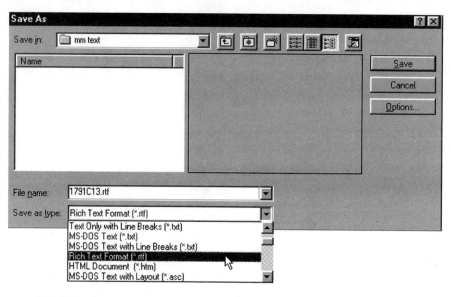

FIGURE 13.20:
When saving text for a Director movie, use the Rich Text Format setting.

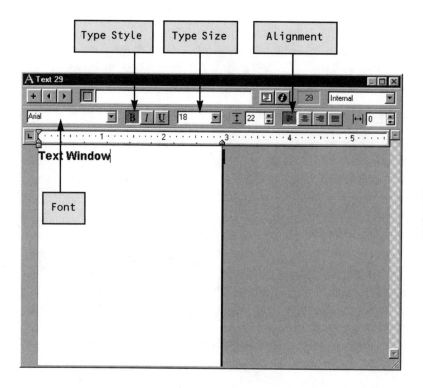

FIGURE 13.21:
Use the Text window to create and edit text inside Director.

As you'll see in a moment, you can also use the Text window to edit and format text you've imported into Director from your word processor.

Placing Text in Director

As you've probably guessed, you place text in Director the same way you would any other cast member—simply use the Import command on the File menu. In this section you will import a file created in Microsoft word, place it on the stage, and then use the Text window to format it.

Let's get started:

1. Begin by opening the saved version of MYMOVIE.dir in the Workshop\Chap13\After folder on your hard disk.
2. Rewind and play the movie.

Behind the Scenes Authoring

As you can see, I've added a few more images to the movie—some screen shots of Web sites. In the next chapter you'll create a menu with several options, one of which will be to branch to this section of the title. This portion of the movie is designed to showcase Divine Concepts' Web site creations.

The screen shots were captured on a Mac, but you can capture screens in Windows simply by pressing Print Screen. This places the contents of your monitor on the Windows Clipboard, so you can then paste the screen shot into your image editing software.

After capturing the screen shots, I cropped them in Photoshop, and then placed them on a portion of the same background used in WWW.bmp. Using layers to keep the screen shots separate from the background, I selected the screen shot and used Alien Skien's Drop shadow plug-in to create a shadow behind the Web page. (Note if you use Corel Photo-Paint, it has a drop-shadow plug-in, too.)

After using Indexed Color to change the color mode to 256 System colors, I flattened the images and saved them as .bmp files, which I then imported into Director and placed at 100-frame increments in the Score.

Behind the Scenes Authoring (continued)

If you own a full version of Director, you can complete this section of the movie yourself. The three screen shots are saved in the Workshop\Chap13\After folder on your hard disk.

---

3. Choose Import from the File Menu.
4. Go to the Workshop\Chap13\After folder on your hard disk.
5. Double-click on WWWtext.rtf to add it to the Import list, as shown in Figure 13.22.
6. Click Import.

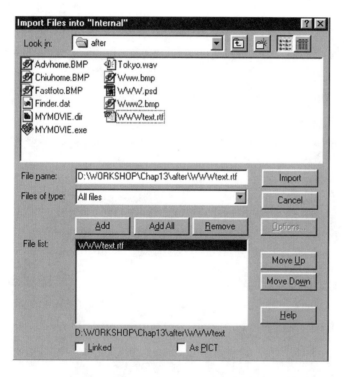

FIGURE 13.22:
Add the file WWWtext.rtf to the Import list, as shown here.

The file is added to the Cast as cast member 32.

7. In the Score, go to frame 1174 in channel 22 and click on it to select it.
8. Drag cast member 32 to the Stage as shown in Figure 13.23.

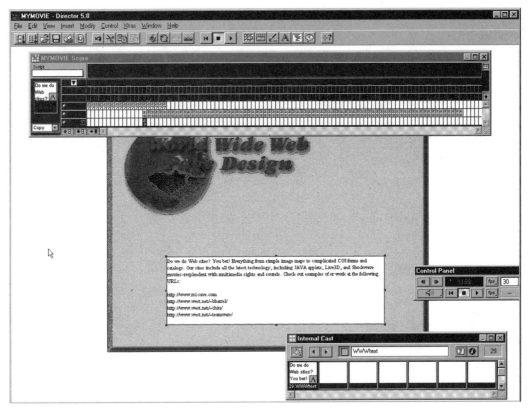

FIGURE 13.23:
Place cast member 32 as shown here.

9. Double-click on cast member 32 in the cast to open the Text window.

The Text window opens displaying the text in WWWtext.rtf.

10. Beginning at the top of the text in the Text window, drag the mouse over the text to select it all, as shown in Figure 13.24.

11. Click on the Center Align button (the second of the four buttons near the upper-right portion of the window) to center the text.

12. In the Font drop-down list select Arial.

13. In the Size drop-down (to the right of the *B, I,* and *U* buttons) list select 18.

14. Click on the Bold (**B**) and Italic (*I*) buttons to turn them on.

At this point your Text window should look like Figure 13.25.

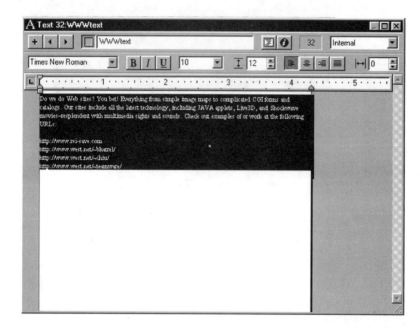

FIGURE 13.24:
Select all the text in
the window.

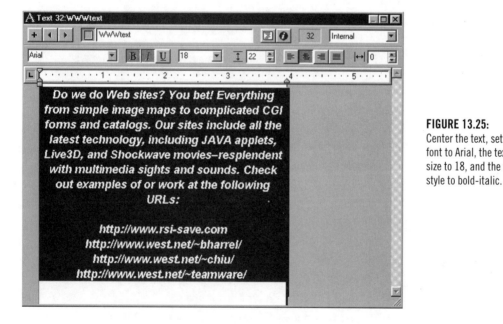

FIGURE 13.25:
Center the text, set the
font to Arial, the text
size to 18, and the text
style to bold-italic.

15. Click on the X in the upper-right corner of the Text window to close it.

The text now has the attributes you set in the Text window. All that's left to do is resize the text box and make the background transparent.

16. Using the center handles on the text box, resize the text box as shown in Figure 13.26.

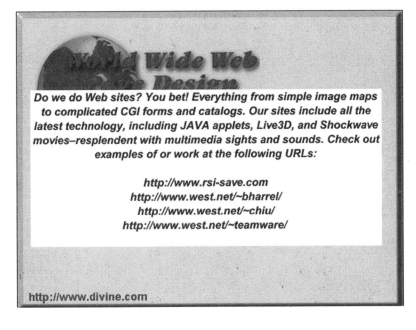

FIGURE 13.26:
Resize the text box as shown here.

 **TIP** If you miss the handle and accidentally move the background, before doing anything else, choose Undo Score from the Edit menu to return your stage to the previous state.

17. From the Ink option in the Score, choose Bkgnd Transparent.
18. Drag the text box into the position shown in Figure 13.27 (use the left and right edges of the stage to center the box).
  Now all you need to do is in-between the frames to the end of the movie.
19. Make sure that frame 1248 in channel 25 is still selected.
20. Shift-click on frame 1248 in channel 25 to select all the frames in between, as shown in Figure 13.27.
21. Choose In Between from the Modify menu to fill the frames.
22. Rewind and play the movie.
  You probably noticed that there is a blank spot after the digital video clip plays, we'll fill that in the next chapter.

FIGURE 13.27:
Place the text box
as shown here.

Saving Your Work

As in the previous chapters, to save your work you simply choose Save from the File menu to update the current file, or choose Save As to change the file name or location. If you're working with a demo of Director, you'll find the file containing the changes we just made (and a few others) in the Workshop\Chap14 folder on the *Multimedia Authoring Workshop* CD.

In the next chapter we will make the title interactive using Director's Lingo scripting language.

CHAPTER 14

Making Your Title Interactive

Featuring

- What makes a title interactive?
- An overview of Director's Lingo scripting language
- Creating a menu
- Providing additional user control of the title's flow

U ntil now you've added cast members to your movie so that they display and play in a linear fashion—one element after another. In this chapter you'll add a menu to your title, allowing your audience to navigate through the movie and its sections. In essence, this type of interactivity is what distinguishes multimedia titles from plain old animations and presentations.

This chapter is an introduction to Director's scripting language, *Lingo*, which allows you and your audience to control the behavior of your titles. Lingo *scripts* are miniature programs that Director executes to perform various actions. Scripts can be written for simple tasks—like pausing a movie or jumping to a frame in the Score; or more elaborate ones—like performing mathematical functions, querying databases, and returning answers to user questions.

NOTE Lingo is an extensive language that requires some time and dedication to master. The intent of this chapter is to introduce you to Lingo and provide a basic overview of how it works. Director's Help system provides extensive information about Lingo, but you still might be better served by purchasing a book specifically about Director.

What Is Interactivity?

On the surface, *interactivity* is a simple concept. It simply means that the title responds to user or audience input. For instance, if the user clicks on a menu item, the movie jumps to that portion of title. Depending on the type of title, interactivity can be just about anything. Multimedia encyclopedias, such as Microsoft *Encarta*, provide interactivity by responding to your requests for information. Courseware provides interactivity by giving you information and then testing you on how well you retained the data. Multimedia titles like MYMOVIE.dir, the one you're creating in the Workshop, provide interactivity by allowing users to select and view data that has been divided into various topics.

Games are prime examples of interactivity because they are constantly responding to input from the user. A quiz game asks questions and then waits for your answer. If you respond correctly, the title responds in one way; if you answer incorrectly, it responds in another. Some quiz games carry interactivity even further by tallying your right and wrong answers and providing you with a score. Perhaps it even compares your score with others who have played the game and shows you how well you stack up against them.

Director, and products like it, allow you to create interactivity in your titles. The extent of the interactivity you provide depends on the nature of the movie and the dedication you apply to learning the vehicle used to create it—in this case, Director's Lingo.

Getting to Know Lingo

Basically Lingo is a scripting language. Scripts are combinations of words that convey information and instructions to Director. Used together, the words in scripts form *statements*. Like grammar, Lingo scripts—words and statements—conform to certain rules. Unlike spoken or written language, though, Lingo requires precision. Often when you break the rules of grammar and spelling, your meaning is still understood. However, when you break the rules in a Lingo script, Director cannot execute the script.

Fortunately, as you'll soon see, Director provides many ways to help you ensure that your scripts are written correctly. Before actually writing any scripts, though, there are several concepts about Lingo you should be introduced to, many of which you'll recognize if you are familiar with programming.

The Scripting Process

In Director, Scripts are created in the Script window, as shown in Figure 14.1. Depending on the type of script you're writing, you get to this window any number of ways. Basically, this is a text window for entering words and statements, and you can write scripts either by typing or by using one of the drop-down lists, which I'll show you later in this chapter.

We'll look at each of the components of the Script window as we use them. The Script window in the figure is a *Script of Cast Member*. Lingo supports three other types of scripts: Score Scripts, Movie Scripts, and Parent Scripts. This chapter covers Scripts of Cast Members and Score Scripts, which are the most common types. For a full description of the other two, look in Director's Help system under the appropriate topic.

Types of Scripts

There is a simple distinction between Scripts of Cast Members and Score Scripts. The former is assigned to an individual cast member, such as a button, and controls its behavior.

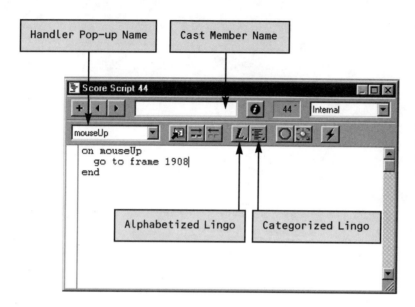

Handler Pop-up Name

Cast Member Name

Alphabetized Lingo

Categorized Lingo

FIGURE 14.1:
Director's Script window—use it to create scripts.

For example, when you assign a script to a button, Director executes the script when you click on the button. The latter, Score Scripts, generally affect the behavior of the entire movie when the playback head enters the frame containing a script. A common Score Script, *pause*, pauses the movie and waits for user input, such as mouse click or keystroke, before it executes.

Used in conjunction, these two types of scripts are used most often for creating interactivity. A typical scenario is to use a Score Script to pause the movie, and a Script of Cast Member to advance the movie to another frame or to load another movie.

NOTE

The situation just described is Lingo in its most common and simplest form. You can also use Score Scripts and Scripts of Cast Members to execute animation sequences, load sound and movie files, make text and other sprites appear, disappear and change colors, and perform many other functions.

Scripting Handlers and Messages

While Lingo scripts can contain many components, for our purposes the two most significant are *handlers* and *messages*. A handler is a set of Lingo statements assigned to an object, in this case a cast member or frame in the Score, that executes when a corresponding message occurs.

Figure 14.2 shows a typical Score sprite containing a handler and message. When the playback head enters the frame containing the script, it executes the message and then ends the script.

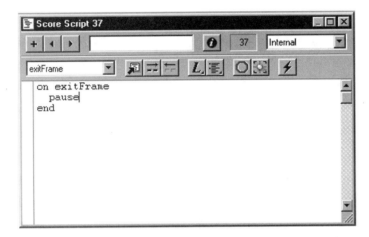

FIGURE 14.2:
A typical Score script

Handlers begin with *on,* followed by the handler statement. In the figure, Director reads the script, which tells the program to perform the following actions:

"When you exit this frame (on exitFrame) pause (pause) the movie, then stop running the script (end)."

Note that the actual Lingo statements are in parenthesis; the text in quotes are my explanations of what the statements mean.

The movie will then wait for another action, such as a mouse click or keystroke to decide what to do next. Most often, the next action will be determined by another script, such as a Script of Cast Member, telling the playhead to begin moving again or to jump to another frame in the score.

Managing Scripts

A movie can contain an unlimited number of scripts. In addition, many movies will use the same script in several different places. For instance, it's common to pause a script in several places, providing the user with navigational options, such as returning to the main menu, or exiting the movie.

Score Scripts are cast members and reside in the Cast window, similar to text, graphics, sounds, and so on. You can reuse them simply by dragging them to the desired frame in the Script channel in the Score. Scripts of Cast Members are assigned to individual cast members. You can reuse the cast member containing the script as you would any other cast member, simply by dragging the cast member to the Stage while having the desired frame in the appropriate channel selected. Director will execute the same script no matter where in the movie you use the cast member.

You can also copy and paste Scripts of Cast Members from one cast member to another by selecting all the text in the Script window you want to duplicate, choosing Copy from the Edit menu, opening a Script window for the cast member you want to copy the script to, selecting the text in that window, and then choosing Paste from the Edit menu.

Score scripts can also be duplicated in any frame in the Script channel from the Script drop-down list in the Score window. Simply select the frame in the Script channel where you want to reuse the script, and then choose the desired script from the list, as shown in Figure 14.3.

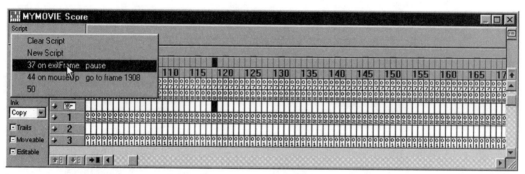

FIGURE 14.3:
Use the Script list to reuse, manage, clear, and create scripts in the Score.

Creating Your Main Menu

A typical component of a multimedia title is the main menu, the place in the movie where users control the direction the title takes. In this section, you will use a Score Script to stop the action at a menu screen, and then use Scripts of Cast Members to assign choices to the menu. Let's begin:

1. In Director, go to the Workshop\Chap14 folder and open MYMOVIE.dir.
2. Rewind and play the movie.

In this section, the menu has four menu items, as shown in Figure 14.4. However, to save space (and forests) we are working only with first item, so only that one actually advances the title to another section of the movie. Were you creating an title for distribution, all four choices would take the user to different sections.

 NOTE If we were to include all four sections, the movie score would become quite lengthy, making the title too large to load quickly and the score too long to manage comfortably. In these situations most multimedia authors would create separate movies for each title, and then write scripts that would load another movie when the menu item is clicked, rather than include the sections all in one Director movie. The Lingo for launching a movie from within a movie is shown in Figure 14.5. You would replace the "whichMovie" placeholder in the message with the name of the movie you want to play when the user clicks on a sprite.

3. In the Score, go to frame 847 in channel 27.
4. Select frame 847 in channel 27.
5. Drag cast member 35 from the Cast and place it as shown in Figure 14.6.

 **NOTE** Depending on the speed of your system, as you play the movie, Heidi.mov may be cut short. Don't worry, when we create a stand-alone movie in the next chapter, it will play correctly.

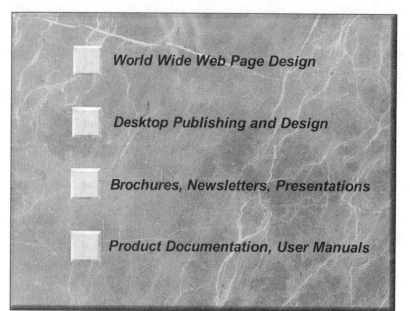

FIGURE 14.4:
A typical main menu. In our movie only the first item will be available.

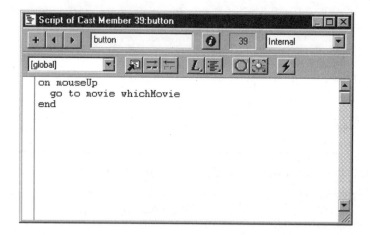

FIGURE 14.5:
Lingo used to load and play another movie from within the current movie.

Behind the Scenes Authoring

As you watched the movie play, you undoubtedly noticed that I've added a few cast members—namely a marble background, some buttons, and a few transitions. You've already imported and placed these kinds of elements several times, so I didn't have you do it again. The graphics were created from stock photography textures in Photoshop.

In addition, I added several transitions. Notice, also, that cast members 37–45, the marble background, buttons, and menu text, are placed only in one column of frames (number 848). Since we will be pausing the movie here, only one frame is required. The playback head will stay in frame 848 until another script tells it where to go next. This will become clearer in the upcoming exercise.

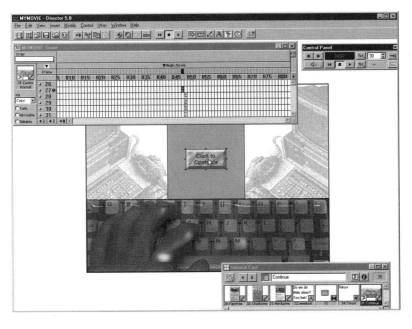

FIGURE 14.6:
Place the sprite as shown here.

TIP Use the Grid (View/Grid/Show) to help center the graphic between the two computers. The button should be placed in the center of the video, but don't worry about being too exact.

6. Choose Cast Member from the Modify menu, and then choose Properties from the submenu.

7. In the Bitmap Cast Member Properties dialog box, check Highlight When Clicked, as shown in Figure 14.7. This tells Director to make the button change colors as though it has been pushed.

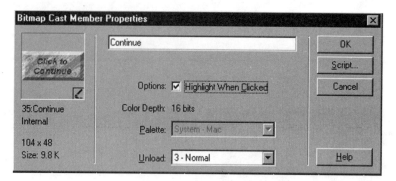

FIGURE 14.7:
Use the Highlight When Clicked option to give the button the effect of being pushed when the user clicks on it.

8. Click on the Script button to go to the script window.

You could have also chosen the Script command. I'll show you how that works a little further on.

9. Click on the Categorized Lingo button, as shown in Figure 14.8.

This drop-down list allows you to select Lingo handlers, messages, and other options by situation. Were you're working with sounds, for example, you would scroll down to the Sounds and Transitions option. In this case, we're working with user interaction with the mouse.

10. Scroll down to User Interaction (Mouse).

Director enters the appropriate handler and flashes the cursor where the message should appear. This time we'll choose from the Alphabetized Lingo list. The primary difference between the two lists is how they are arranged.

11. Click on the Alphabetized Lingo button, as shown in Figure 14.9.

12. Scroll to G H.

13. Select "go to frame" from the submenu.

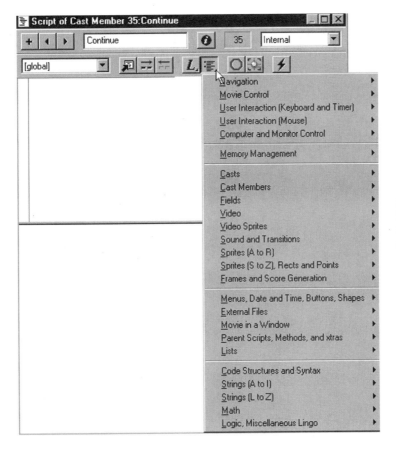

FIGURE 14.8:
Use the Categorized Lingo list to choose Lingo statements by context.

Director enters the proper syntax, providing you with the whichFrame placeholder. All you do is type in the frame number you want the movie to advance to when the Click to Continue button is selected.

14. Type **848**.

TIP

There are several other Lingo options you can use to jump the movie ahead. "Go to labelname," for example, will advance the movie to the frame with a label marker (as discussed in Chapter 9). You can also use the "continue" command to advance the movie to the next frame.

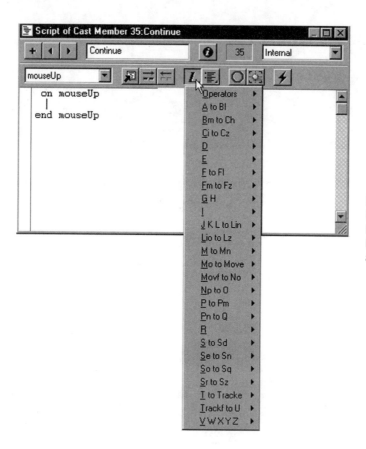

FIGURE 14.9:
Use the Alphabetized Lingo list to choose lingo statements alphabetically.

15. Close the Script Window.

Notice that cast member 35 now displays a small script icon in the lower-left corner, as shown in Figure 14.10. This tells you that this cast member has a script associated with it.

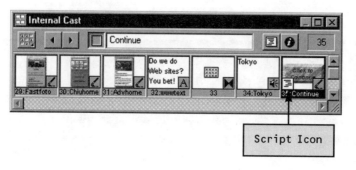

FIGURE 14.10:
This small icon tells you that the cast member has a script attached.

Script Icon

Pausing Your Movie

If you were to rewind and play this movie right now, the playhead would zip past the screen with the Click to Continue button on it. That will do us no good. Instead, we want the movie to stop in frame 847 to give the user a chance to click on the button. In this section you'll create a Score Script to pause the movie in frame 847.

1. Scroll to the to top of the score until the Script channel is available.

TIP To move to the top of the score quickly, click on the button directly above the Up scroll arrow on the right side of the score—the one with the arrow pointing up at a set of double lines.

2. Select frame 847 in the Script channel.
3. From the Script drop-down list in the Score window, click on New Script, as shown in Figure 14.11.

FIGURE 14.11:
Click on the Script drop-down list and select New Script.

When you do this, three things should happen: Director adds a script cast member to the cast window; then it places a cell in frame 847 in the Script channel; and finally, the Score Script window opens. Notice that Director has anticipated that you want to use the "on exitFrame" handler. All you need to do is add the message:

4. Click on the Alphabetized Lingo button.
5. Scroll to P to Pm, and select pause.
6. Close the Script window.
7. Rewind and play the movie.

TIP

If you're getting tired of watching the entire movie over and over again, you can play from directly before the button appears by placing the playback head in frame 846. Simply click in the desired column, instead of clicking the Rewind button.

8. When the movie pauses, click on the Click to Continue button.

The movie jumps to frame 848 and continues playing. However, we want it to pause again at the main menu in frame 848. To make this change, we'll simply use the same script in frame 848.

9. Select frame 848 in the Script channel.
10. From the Script drop-down list in the Score window, select "46 on exitFrame" pause, as shown in Figure 14.12.

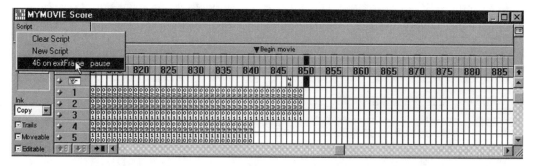

FIGURE 14.12:
To reuse the script, select the desired frame, and then select the script from the Script drop-down list.

11. Rewind and play the movie.
12. When the movie stops, click on the Click to Continue button.
13. When the movie pauses again, click the Stop button in the Control window to stop the playhead.

Getting the hang of this? Now we'll make one of the buttons and the corresponding line of text jump to the World Wide Web section of the Divine Concepts title.

Making the Menu Interactive

After the introduction plays, we want the user to choose which section of the title to play next. Hence, we provide him or her with four choices: World Wide Web Page Design; Desktop Publishing and Design; Brochures, Newsletters, Presentations; and Product Documentation, User Manuals. Remember that we are making only the first choice interactive in this Workshop. To do so, you'll use the same procedure you used earlier to create the Sprite of Cast Member for the Continue button:

1. On the Stage, click on the first button to select it.
2. From the Modify menu, choose Cast Member, and then choose Script from the submenu.

This displays the Script of Cast Member dialog box for the button shown in Figure 14.13. Notice that when we use the Script option, rather than beginning with Properties, Director anticipates that we want an on mouseUp handler.

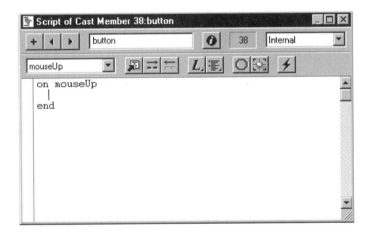

FIGURE 14.13:
The Script of Cast Member window waiting for the handler message.

3. Click on the Alphabetized Lingo button.
4. Scroll to <u>G</u> H.
5. Choose go to frame from the submenu.
6. Type **850**.
7. Close the Script window.
8. Choose Cast Member/Properties from the Modify menu.
9. Select Highlight When Clicked, and the click OK to close the Cast Member Properties dialog box.

10. Click on the text next to the top button to select it.
11. Repeat steps 2 through 8 to assign the same script to that cast member.
12. Rewind and play the movie.
13. When the movie pauses on frame 847, click on the Click to Continue button.
14. Click on the top button on the menu.

You'll see that the World Wide Web sequence plays to the end and the movie stops. However, when you create a *projector* (a *stand-alone* version of the title) to make the movie self-running (outside of Director), the movie will stop *and* quit at this point. Clearly this is not the effect we want. You want the movie to return to the main menu, allowing the user to view other sections of the movie if he or she wants. You've also got to give the audience a way out of the title—it's good, but they may eventually want to use their computers for other tasks! Let's look at how to do this in the next section.

Navigating Back to the Main Menu

Once the user has checked out one section, you should provide him or her with a means to return to the main menu—*and* you should provide a way to exit the title. There are no hard and fast rules for when and where to provide navigation in a title—it's completely up to you. The point is to make the title as user-friendly as possible. So, you'll want to give the user enough options to make the journey through your title comfortable and enjoyable.

In this section, rather than using imported graphics to create your buttons, you'll use Director's built-in control features. In addition to allowing you to create buttons, the program also allows you to make radio button and checkboxes. All you'll need for this title is a couple of buttons—one to return the title to the main menu at the end of the World Wide Web sequence, and another on the main menu itself to exit the title. Here's how we do that:

1. In the Score, scroll to frame 1248 in the Script channel.
2. Select frame 1248 in the Script channel.
3. From the Script drop-down list in the Score, select 46 on exitFrame pause, as shown in Figure 14.14.

This is the end of the movie. We're pausing the movie here to allow the user the option of returning to the main menu—otherwise, the completed movie would simply end and quit.

4. Scroll in the Score until frame 1174 in channel 26 is displayed.
5. Select frame 1174 in channel 26.
6. Choose Control from the Insert menu, and then choose Push Button from the submenu.

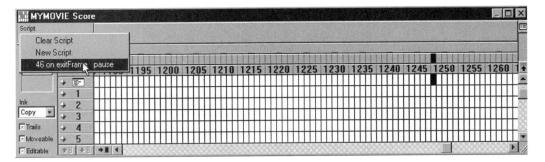

FIGURE 14.14:
Select the pause script to insert a copy of the script in this frame.

Director places a button in the center of the stage, as shown in Figure 14.15. You can type whatever text you need in this button, format the text as desired, resize the button, and move it to any position on the stage.

FIGURE 14.15:
Choosing Push Button from the Control submenu places a button on the stage. You can format the button text, resize the button, and move it as needed.

7. Choose Font from the Modify menu.

This displays the Font dialog box shown in Figure 14.16. From here you set the attributes for your button text.

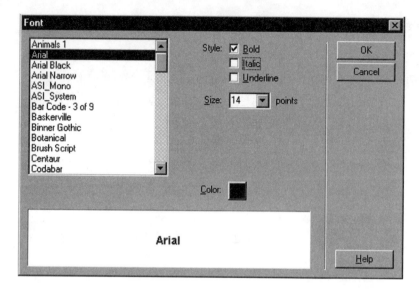

FIGURE 14.16:
Use the Font dialog box to set the attributes for your button text.

8. Set the typeface to Arial from the list of typefaces in the upper-right portion of the dialog box.

9. Set the Style to Bold.

10. Set the Size to 14.

11. Click OK to close the dialog box.

12. Type **Main Menu**.

13. Resize and move the button the same way you would any other cast member. It should be in the position shown in Figure 14.17.

The button is somewhat homely in its current state. Let's use one of the options on the Scroll Ink drop-down list to change background of the button to transparent:

14. Choose Bkgnd Transparent from the Ink drop-down list in the Scroll window.

Now lets assign a script to the new button:

15. Making sure the button is still selected, Choose Cast Member/Script from the Modify menu.

16. From the Alphabetized Lingo drop-down list, choose G H, and then choose Go to Frame from the submenu.

17. Type **848.**

18. Close the Script window.

19. Use the In Between on the Modify menu to fill the frames in channel 26 between 1174 and 1248.

Do we do Web sites? You bet! Everything from simple image maps to complicated CGI forms and catalogs. Our sites include all the latest technology, including JAVA applets, Live3D, and Shockwave movies–resplendent with multimedia sights and sounds. Check out examples of or work at the following URLs:

http://www.rsi-save.com
http://www.west.net/~bharrel/
http://www.west.net/~chiu/
http://www.west.net/~teamware/

http://www.divine.com

FIGURE 14.17:
Resize and move the button as shown here.

Great! We've got one more thing to do, and then you're movie will be finished. Before rewinding and playing the movie, let's go back to the main menu and create an Exit button:

1. Scroll in the Score until frame 848 in channel 37 is visible.
2. Select frame 848 in channel 37.
3. Choose Push Button from the Insert/Control submenu.
4. Select Font from the Modify menu.
5. Change the typeface to Arial.
6. Set the Style to Bold
7. Set the Size to 14.
8. Click OK, to close the Font dialog box.
9. Type Exit.

Your Stage should look like Figure 14.18. All that's left to do is resize and place the button, and then write a script that quits the movie.

10. Resize and move the button as shown in Figure 14.19.

Again, we've got a homely button. This time, lets make the background transparent and the text white, so that it will show up well on the marble background.

11. Choose Ghost from the Ink drop-down list on Score window.

To create a script that quits the movie, follow these steps:

12. Choose Modify/Cast Member/Script from the Insert menu.

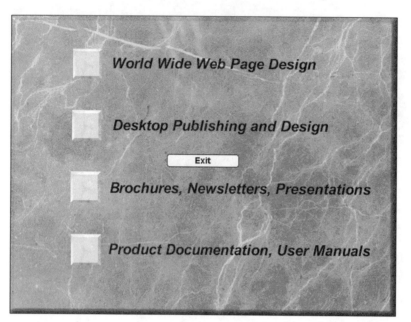

FIGURE 14.18:
So far, your button should look like this.

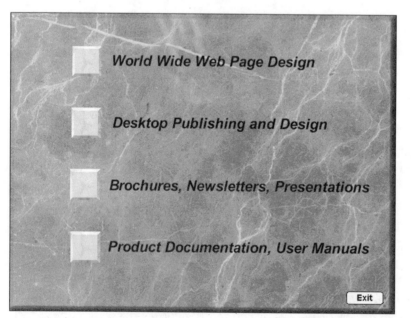

FIGURE 14.19:
Resize and move the button to the bottom-right corner of the Stage.

13. From the Alphabetized Lingo drop-down list, choose <u>Pn</u> to Q, and then choose quit from the submenu.

Your script should look like Figure 4.20.

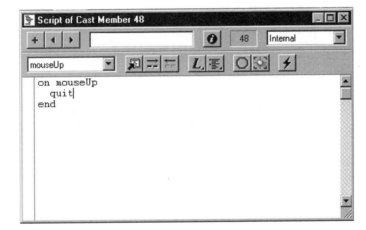

FIGURE 4.20:
Use this script to create an Exit or Quit button.

14. Close the Script window.

That's it—we're done. You are now ready to rewind and playback your work:

1. Rewind and play the movie.
2. When the movie stops on the Click to Continue screen, click the button.
3. When the movie stops on the main menu, click on the World Wide Web Page Design button.
4. When the movie stops on the final text scene, click on the Main Menu button.
5. When the movie stops on the main menu DO NOT click on the Exit button. Depending on which version of Director you're using—demo or full—the Exit button will behave differently while inside the application. In the full version, for example, the program queries you to save the movie before exiting the program.

The purpose of this button is to allow users to exit your title when running outside of Director.

NOTE Is all this stuff about running inside and outside Director confusing? Have no fear, we look at turning your title into a stand-alone multimedia title in the next chapter.

Saving Your Work

As in the following chapters, saving your title after completing your scripting is simply a matter of choosing Save or Save As from the File menu. Now that you've finished laying out your title, the next step is to create a projector, so that the movie can be played on computers that don't have Director installed. This is an important part of the authoring process, as you'll see in the first section of the next chapter.

CHAPTER 15

Publishing Your Title

Featuring

- Creating a stand-alone projector
- Preparing a master CD-ROM
- Creating multimedia titles with Shockwave for Director

Over the past five chapters you've used Macromedia Director and several other applications to create an electronic brochure. Now that it's finished, you're ready to enter an all new phase of the multimedia authoring process—publishing your work so that others can use it.

Usually, this is a two step process: First, you use Director's Create Projector feature to turn the movie into a stand-alone application that will run without Director. Then you create a master CD-ROM. The bulk of this chapter covers these two steps.

In addition to publishing on CD-ROM, you can also convert your Director movies to play on the World Wide Web. While this kind of technology is still in its early development stages, we'll spend a few pages at the end of this chapter discussing how you can show multimedia titles on your Web pages with Shockwave for Director.

Making Your Titles Stand-Alone Applications

Whether you create games, edutainment titles, electronic brochures or catalogs, the whole point is to show your creations to other people. Director allows you to distribute your titles freely through a vehicle called a *projector*. Basically, a projector is a version of your movie that will play without Director being installed on the system running it. The process for creating a projector is quite easy: Simply choose Create Projector from the File menu, choose the movies you want to include in your projector, then name the projector. Director does the rest.

However, depending on the complexity of your title—whether it contains linked video clips, graphics, sounds, or other Director movies—you often need to do some preliminary preparation before creating the projector to make sure the movie runs correctly.

Preparing to Create a Projector

The primary concern when creating a projector is making sure that it can find and play all of its supporting files. A Director movie looks for its supporting, or linked, files much like every other program. It remembers the location on your hard disk where the digital video, sound, supporting Director movie, or image resided when you imported it into the movie. If it's not there, and not in the folder containing the projector file, the movie queries the user of the title for the location of the file in the Where Is...? dialog box, as shown in Figure 15.1.

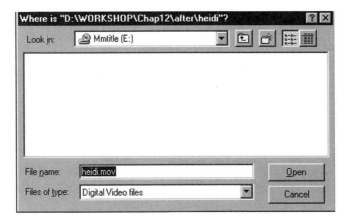

FIGURE 15.1:
This is what happens if a Director movie can't find a supporting file.

As you can imagine, if your projector can't find its supporting files when your audience runs the title, and the users get this disastrous message, it will ruin the effect of your title. So when preparing to turn your movies into projectors, your primary concern is to ensure that all of your supporting files are accounted for. For short titles without a lot of supporting files, the easiest way to do that is to create the title with all the supporting files in the same folder as the Director movie.

For example, in MYMOVIE.dir, the only linked file is Heidi.mov, so that's the only file Director needs to find. It's simple to copy the video file to the folder in which you'll be creating your projector, as I've done in Figure 15.2. You'll see that I've copied Heidi.mov and the projector into the same folder. As long as I keep these two files in same folder, the title will run properly.

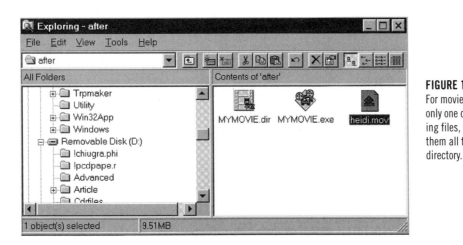

FIGURE 15.2:
For movies that contain only one or a few supporting files, you can copy them all to the same directory.

However, if your movie contains several supporting files, such as multiple videos, Director movies, or linked graphics and sound files, you should plan ahead—preferably at the beginning of the authoring process. If you wait until the end, the process of copying all of those files could take a very long time. This is especially true of titles you plan to distribute on CD-ROMs or other media.

Here's another example: Perhaps you've noticed during the Workshop that no matter which folder—Chap12, Chap13, or Chap14—on your hard disk you load MYMOVIE.dir from, Heidi.mov still plays. This is because the MYMOVIE.dir file contains a pointer to the original Workshop\Chap12\After folder, no matter where we save the Director movie file. If you break the link by moving the video clip or deleting it, the movie won't be able to find the video file (unless you move it into the folder containing MYMOVIE.dir).

The pointer remembers the exact location of the supporting file: Drive:\Folder\Subfolder; however, this is not the manner in which the movie looks for the file. It first looks in the folder containing MYMOVIE.dir. If it's not there, then it looks within its own folder structure, and finally, when all else fails, it looks to the drive and folders where the movie was originally imported from.

What do I mean by folder structure? Again, the Workshop folders are a good example. All of the chapter folders (Chap11, Chap12, etc.) are subfolders of the Workshop folder. The *Before* and *After* folders are subfolders of the chapter folders. MYMOVIE.dir and supporting files all reside within main folder, Workshop. So, when MYMOVIE.dir looks for Heidi.mov, it looks in the Workshop\Chap12\After folder, because it is part of the same folder structure. Were you to import the movie from the CD-ROM, MYMOVIE.dir would still look first within its own *file structure*—the Workshop folders and subfolders—and then look in the Workshop folders and subfolders on the CD.

Basically what I'm trying to stress is that when creating your titles, you should keep all of your supporting files—and the movie itself—within the same folder and file structure.

Planning a File Structure

Most multimedia authors create a folder structure at the beginning of the process. As you begin a title, simply create a set of folders to hold like supporting files. The best, most foolproof method is to keep supporting files inside subfolders of the folder that will contain the projector, as shown in Figure 15.3. In this way, you can create your projector in the same folder as the .dir file and easily maintain all the links. You can then move the entire structure without breaking the links. Keep in mind, though, that this structuring should be created and maintained *while creating the movie*. You can't copy the supporting files to the subfolders from other locations scattered about your hard disk *and* maintain the links after the movie is laid out.

TIP

You can also copy all the supporting files to the same folder as the movie or projector file. The title will then find and load them from there.

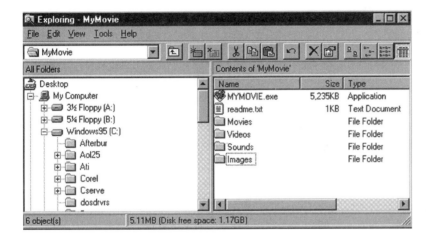

FIGURE 15.3:
This is a common folder structure for arranging movies and supporting files.

Using the Create Projector Command

As mentioned, creating a projector in Director is as simple as choosing the Create Projector command from the File menu and then saving the file. There's really not very many decisions to make. In this section, we'll look at the Create Projector dialog box and some of its options.

NOTE

If you're using the demo version of Director, you can't, of course, create a projector from MYMOVIE.dir. So, rather than walk you through the step-by-step procedure, this section will provide an overview of the process.

Once you've finished laying out your movie and have all the timing and transitions where you want them, you simply choose Create Projector from the File menu, which brings up the Create Projector dialog box shown in Figure 15.4. From here you choose the movie(s) you want to include in your projector.

FIGURE 15.4:
Use the Create Projector dialog box to create a stand-alone version of your Director movies.

NOTE Two things: If you haven't saved the current open movie before choosing Create Projector, Director will prompt you to do so before opening the Create Projector dialog box. Also, it is not necessary to have the movie from which you want to create a projector open in Director. You can create projectors from any Director (.dir) file on your system.

The Create Projector dialog box allows you to create a projector from one or several movies. You simply double-click on the movies you want to include in the projector, and then use the Move Up and Move Down buttons to arrange them in the order you want them to play. However, if you've linked to movies with the Import command or referenced them in Lingo scripts (such as, "on mouseUp play whichMovie"), you do not add them to the projector. You simply make sure you maintain the file structure so that the projector can find the supporting movies.

TIP

When creating titles that contain several movies, the standard, pre-ferred method is to create a small projector that uses Lingo scripts to load and play other movies. In other words, your titles are creat-ed in small pieces or segments. This keeps files small, which makes them load faster, easier to manage, and saves you from having to navigate through long Scores.

When creating projectors, you should also consider how to set options, such as whether the movie should play in a window or full-screen, or whether to include a Windows title bar. Options are controlled from the Projector Options dialog box, shown in Figure 15.5. You get here by clicking on the Options button in the Create Projector dialog box.

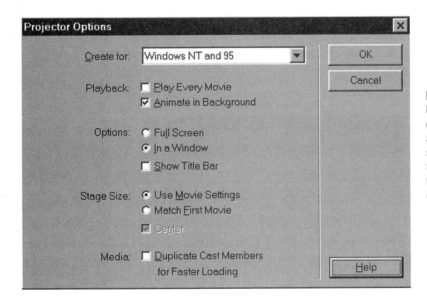

FIGURE 15.5:
Use the Projector Options dialog box to set various attributes for your title, such as which operating system the title will run under, whether to include a title bar, and so on.

Depending on the type of movie you've created, all of these options may be important; for MYMOVIE.dir we are concerned with only a few: operating system (Windows 3.1 or Window 95 and NT) and title bar.

Choosing the Right Operating System

In Director, you have two options for creating a projector: Windows 95 and NT or Windows 3.1. (To create projectors to run on a Mac, you'll need a Mac version of Director.)

If you're sure your title will always run under Windows 95, choose Windows 95 and NT. This option creates a 32 bit version of the projector, which will run faster and more efficiently in 32 bit environments, such as Windows 95. Keep in mind that projectors created with this setting will not run on machines running Windows 3.1.

If you think your title might be run in both environments—Windows 95 and Windows 3.1—choose the Windows 3.1 option. This will assure compatibility on all Windows machines.

To Title Bar or Not to Title Bar

After all is said and done, after you turn it into a projector, a Director title becomes a Windows application. Most Windows applications have a title bar across the top that gives the name of the application. Figures 15.6a and 15.6b show MYMOVIE.dir with and without a title bar.

In a title like MYMOVIE, the primary advantage of the title bar is that the user can close the movie easily by clicking on the close button. Also, when playing the title on a screen set to a higher resolution than the movie window, it makes moving the movie around on the screen possible. If you don't include a title bar, the user must wait for an interactivity option (such as the Exit button on the main menu in MYMOVIE), and the movie cannot be dragged around on the monitor.

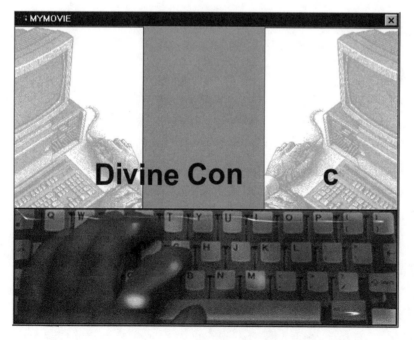

FIGURE 15.6a:
MYMOVIE.dir with a title bar.

FIGURE 15.6b:
MYMOVIE.dir without
a title bar.

If you want the optimal control over when the title can be closed and where it plays on the monitor, don't use a title bar. If you want to give your audience these controls, include the title bar. For MYMOVIE, my choice is no title bar, for two reasons: One, I don't want to give up the control of when and where the title plays, and two, I think the movie is more attractive without the title bar.

To include a title bar, you must also select the In A Window option.

Naming and Saving the Projector

Once you've imported your movie files and set the options, you are ready to create the projector. First click OK to save the options and close Projector Options, then click on Create. This displays the Save Projector As dialog box shown in Figure 15.7. From here you choose the folder for the projector, name it, and save it.

That's it. As long as your file and folder structures are in tact, as explained earlier, all you have to do is double-click on the projector .exe file to run the title. It's ready for distribution.

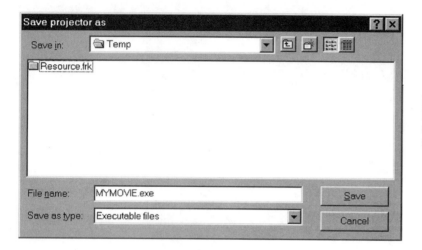

FIGURE 15.7:
Use the Save Projector As dialog box to name and save your projector.

Going to CD-ROM

As discussed in Chapter 5, you have a couple of options for getting your title from your desktop computer to a CD. You can either take the files on some type of removable media, such as a Bernoulli or Jaz disk to a service bureau, or you can you can buy a personal CD-ROM recorder (CD-R) and *burn* your own discs. Let's discuss the procedures and merits of both methods.

Off to the Service Bureau

Taking your titles to the service bureau—if you plan on producing more than a few titles—is by far the most expensive option. Service bureaus charge by the amount of time they must spend on a procedure and for the time your job ties up their equipment. Creating a CD-ROM master, even on the fastest of CD-R devices, takes time—period. To create a master that requires all or most of the CD can cost upwards of $100, rendering this option viable only for creating masters that you will use either to transfer a title from computer to computer, or for taking to a CD-ROM publishing firm for mass reproduction.

 **NOTE** If you plan to create more than seven or eight titles, you'll save in the long run by purchasing your own CD-R. The prices have fallen well below $1,000 for these devices, and having your own provides a wealth of freedom for experimenting and updating your work.

By far, the easiest way to transport the often huge sets of files that make up a CD, is with a removable media of equal size or greater than the capacity of a CD—650 megabytes or more. As discussed in Chapter 5, these include Iomega Jaz, transportable hard disks, and Syquest SyJets. Some service bureaus also support the DAT tapes used in popular tape backup drives. The benefit of using large media is that you can transport the entire folder and file structure intact, so you won't have to depend on the service bureau to reconstruct the file structure from several small-capacity disks.

If you already own a smaller capacity removable, such as a Zip, Bernoulli, or Syquest drive, all is certainly not lost. You can easily copy the folders and files to several disks and provide the service bureau with a directory structure map. You can either draw the structure by hand or in a word processor, as shown in Figure 15.8.

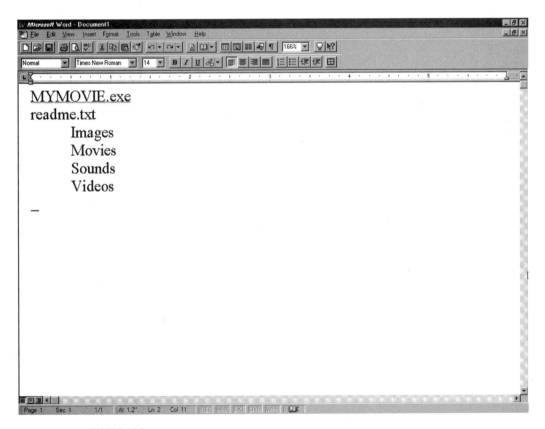

FIGURE 15.8:
An example of a file structure map—indented names represent folders. You can indicate subfolders by using additional indents.

Or you can simply take a screen shot of the structure in Windows Explorer, as shown in Figure 15.9. To take a screen shot of a Windows screen, press Print Screen. Then use the Paste command on your image editing software's Edit menu to copy the image, crop the image if you want, and then print it out.

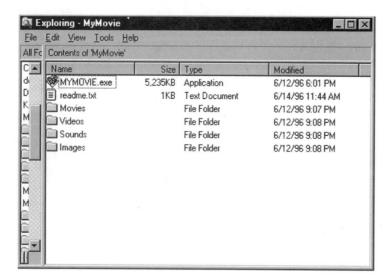

FIGURE 15.9:
An example of a screen shot of the title's file structure.

A third option is to create a simple readme.txt file containing the file structure that the service bureau can open and read.

Even though Windows 95 supports long file names, most CD-ROM recording software does not. Also, titles designed to work with Windows 95 and Windows 3.1 will not work properly in Windows 3.1 with long file and folder names. When creating a title destined for a CD-ROM, you should stick to the standard DOS file naming conventions of eight character names with three character extensions: filename.ext, e.g., MYMOVIE.exe.

Burning CDs at Home

Just a couple of years ago, it was difficult to imagine burning your own CDs at home. Lately, the price of this technology has come way down. Vendors are selling so many CD-Rs that—like any highly competitive product—the costs will probably continue to drop. It's foreseeable that CD-Rs may soon be selling for as little as $500.

The advantages of owning your own CD-R: If you plan to make a habit of creating your own CD-ROM titles, you'll save money, be able to experiment relatively inexpensively with timing and video playback, and update the master quickly and easily. Secondly, for titles like MYMOVIE, which is designed for small distribution, you can easily burn a disc as needed upon request. You can also burn the disc per your audience's request—Windows 95 or Windows 3.1, Mac, and so on. Another advantage of owning your own CD-R is that they are splendid backup and archiving tools. The media (discs) are relatively cheap and durable.

NOTE   Distributing CDs in the manner just described has its drawbacks as well. It's time-consuming and at about $8 a pop, expensive. It takes from 30 to 45 minutes to burn a disc full (650 MB) of data. Conversely, you can get CDs mass reproduced for as little as a dollar or two apiece, depending on quantity. However, like hard copy brochures, when CDs are mass produced, you're stuck with them—you can't change or update the copies. So, as you can see, deciding how and when to create CDs is a juggling act. What you should do depends on one important factor: How many discs do you need?

The CD-ROM Burning Process

As discussed in Chapter 5, the simplicity and painlessness of the CD-ROM recording process depends primarily on the recording software. For Windows, one of the easiest programs is Corel's CD Creator, shown in Figure 15.10. It provides CD-recording wizards that walk you through the process, making it nearly foolproof.

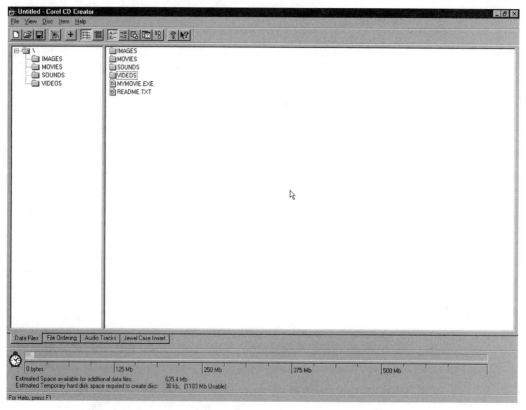

FIGURE 15.10:
Corel CD Creator in preparation to burn a CD-ROM.

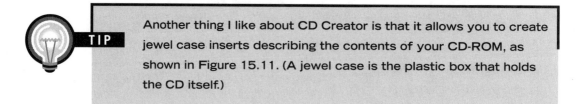

TIP Another thing I like about CD Creator is that it allows you to create jewel case inserts describing the contents of your CD-ROM, as shown in Figure 15.11. (A jewel case is the plastic box that holds the CD itself.)

Depending on the software, the process for creating a CD is simple. Usually, all you do is select the files and folders you want on the disc, and then, you can use the recording software to arrange them into the desired structure, similar to moving files and folders around in Windows Explorer (or File Manager). Most programs allow you save a *disc image* file that keeps track of your files and folders and how you want them arranged. This lets you make copies of your CDs whenever you want, and it allows you to update files within the structure to keep your titles current.

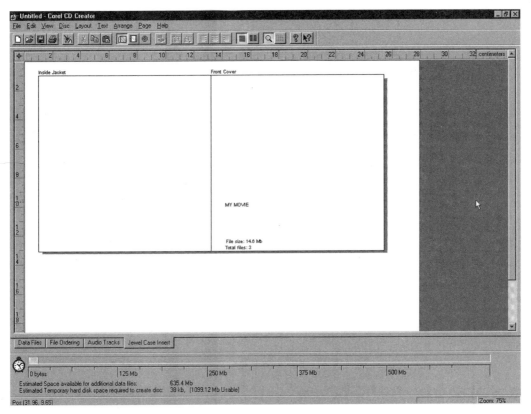

FIGURE 15.11:
Corel CD Creator helps you create inserts for your titles.

It's easy, but there are two things you should keep in mind:

- To burn a CD-ROM, one of your drives, either your hard disk or removable, must contain enough space to hold the entire title. The CD-R requires a steady stream of data from beginning to end. You can't stop and copy to the disc from multiple removable disks as you can most other types of media.
- Burning a CD-ROM requires the complete dedication of your computer. Any multitasking, printing, network activity, or working on documents in the foreground can interrupt the data flow to the CD-R, rendering the disc unuseable.

NOTE I can hear you thinking: Today's CD-Rs and CD-ROM drives are multisession, right? Multisession is, of course, the ability burn several times—or sessions—to the same CD. In other words, you can burn 100 megabytes in one session, some more data during another session, and so on, until the disc is full. While it's true that most of the drives and recorders do support multisession, this feature is best used for archiving data, rather than creating multimedia titles. Multisession CD-ROM discs mount several drives—one for each session—on a computer. In other words, if the disc contains three sessions, three drives (D:, E:, and F:) will show up in the user's Windows Explorer. This can be very confusing for users of your title, and multisession drives often require a special software driver to display all the sessions.

Keeping these few drawbacks in mind, if you have enough hard disk or removable space, and can afford the CD-R, it's the most efficient, cost-effective way to go.

Using Your Director Titles on the Web with Shockwave

One of the most exciting opportunities available to multimedia designers is the World Wide Web. This technology is emerging as I write this. So far, the standards are still under development and it remains to be seen just how things will shake out. In the mean time, Macromedia has provided a way for Web surfers to view your titles via a technology known as *Shockwave*. Basically, what Shockwave does is convert a Director .dir file to a format supported by the leading WWW browsers: Netscape Navigator, Microsoft's Explorer, Apple's CyberDog, etc.

Be forewarned, though, this is not a seamless approach. Several key factors must be considered and resolved before your movies can play on the Web:

- Netscape Navigator's *plug-in* technology
- Converting Director movies with Macromedia *Afterburner*
- Downloading (*bandwidth*) considerations

Overview of Netscape Navigator's Plug-In Technology

Netscape Navigator (and Netscape compatible programs, such as Microsoft Internet Explorer) is the application that the majority of Web surfers use to view sites on the World Wide Web, and it uses a technology called *plug-ins* to increase functionality. (Perhaps you'll remember plug-ins from Chapter 13. Adobe Photoshop uses a similar technology.) Basically, plug-ins allow Netscape Navigator to display and play images and media clips that would otherwise be unavailable.

For example, to play QuickTime movies from inside Netscape Navigator, you would use a QuickTime plug-in. To play various sound formats, you would use help apps, which are similar to plug-ins, except that they play clips in a separate window, rather than directly on the Web page itself. To play Director movies, the required plug-in is Shockwave for Director. A Web page containing a Shockwave movie is (in Macromedia terms) called *shocked*. Figure 15.12 shows a shocked Web page.

Though you can't tell by the figure, several things are happening on this page: The graphic on the left of the *People Magazine* logo spins, flipping back and forth between *People* and *Online* so that the image is continually reading *People Online* over and over. Every few seconds the photograph on left the switches, highlighting one of the stories in the current issue. All of this is done in sync with the sound of a fast-paced cowbell.

TIP

So my description of the "People Magazine" home page is lacking? Want to see the site in action? Go to the site and see it for yourself at: http://www.pathfinder.com/people/shock.html. However, if you're not familiar with Shockwave, the plug-in is probably not installed on your system, so finish reading this section before you try to visit the site.

In order to view shocked sites, the viewer must have the Shockwave plug-in installed on their system and be using a browser that supports it (Netscape Navigator 2.0 or 3.0, or a compatible browser). As a designer, you have little to no control over which browser and plug-ins your site visitors use. Consequently, not everybody who comes to your site will get to see your movies.

When a Netscape user without the plug-in installed comes to a shocked page, Netscape informs him or her that they are about to access a page containing data for which a plug-in is not installed on their system, and then provides them with the option of obtaining the plug-in. If the user clicks Get Plug-In, they are then returned to a page on the Netscape site that explains plug-in technology and provides them with an opportunity to go to the Macromedia home page to download Shockwave (shown in Figure 15.13).

FIGURE 15.12:
An example of a shocked Web Page.

TIP

Does the above procedure sound complicated? The whole point of the description is to show you what a pain it can be for visitors to a Web site to see a movie—they have to be pretty dedicated. The best you can hope for is that some of the visitors to your site have already installed Shockwave. You can install it on your system by going directly to the Macromedia site: http://www.macromedia.com. Simply download the file and double-click on the file icon to install it.

Granted, the Shockwave plug-in is not without its drawbacks, but as I write this it's one of the only ways to put full-featured movies—animation, sound, and interactivity—onto a Web page.

FIGURE 15.13:
The Macromedia home page. Start here to download the Shockwave plug-in.

Making Director Movies Web-Ready

In order for your Director movie to run on the Web, you'll need to do two things:

- Make sure that your Web server (or *Internet provider*) is configured properly.
- Use Macromedia Afterburner to covert your movies.

Getting the Server Ready to Run Shocked Sites

Most Internet providers should be configured to run Shockwave movies. However, if your company has its own server, or if your Internet provider does not yet support shocked sites, you (or the provider) can get detailed information on how to do so from the Shockwave for Director: Getting Started page at the Macromedia Web site:

http://www.macromedia.com/Tools/Shockwave/Director5/getstart.html.

Most Internet providers should be happy to make these changes for you—it doesn't cost them anything but a little time.

TIP

If this brief introduction to Shockwave doesn't provide all the help you need, check out the Macromedia Shockwave for Director Developer's Guide at: http://www.macromedia.com/Tools/Shockwave/Director5/contents.html.

Getting and Using Afterburner

To convert your Director movies to Shockwave movies, you'll need a Director Xtra called Afterburner, which is available on the Macromedia Web site at: http://www.macromedia.com/Tools/Shockwave/Director/aftrbrnr.html. *Xtras* are similar to plug-ins in that they provide additional functionality to Director. The primary difference is that Macromedia calls them *Xtras*, rather than *plug-ins*. The Web page is shown in Figure 15.14.

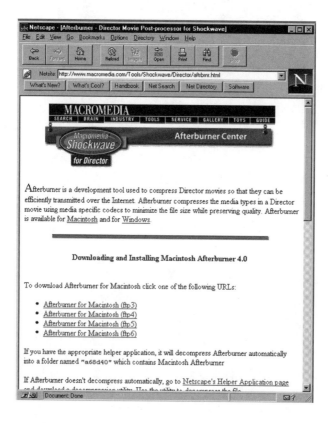

FIGURE 15.14:
Go to this page on the Macromedia Web site to download Afterburner for Director.

Once you've downloaded Afterburner, simply move the file to an empty folder, double-click on the file icon (a16d40.exe) to uncompress it. Then double-click on Setup.exe to install the Xtra into Director.

Now you're ready to convert your movies. Afterburner converts a Director .dir file to a Shockwave .dcr file (.dcr files are projectors designed to run on the Web). It also compresses the movie so that it will download faster over phone lines (see the next section, *Downloading (Bandwidth) Considerations* for an explanation of bandwidth).

From here on the process is simple. Open the movie you want to convert, then choose Afterburner from the Xtras menu, as shown in Figure 15.15. Director displays the Save As dialog box. From here all you do is name and save the .dcr file.

FIGURE 15.15:
To convert a movie with Afterburner, simply open the movie and then choose Afterburner from the Xtras menu.

Shockwave does not support all of Director's features, especially some Lingo options. For a list of unsupported features, refer to the "Creating Director 5 Movies for the Web" at the Macromedia site.

Shocking Your Web pages

Before going into how to use Hypertext Markup Language (HTML) codes to place your Shockwave movies on your Web pages, let me begin by saying that if you do not already create Web pages, this discussion is way over you're head. While HTML coding is not difficult, you must know how to use it to create Web pages—as well as include movies on your web pages. (If you don't know HTML, you should find a good book on it, such as Sybex's *Do-it-Yourself Web Publishing with HoTMetaL.*)

A recap: To view a shocked Director movie, users need the Shockwave for Director plug-in and a Netscape-compatible browser: Netscape 2.0, Netscape 3.0, or any other browser that supports Netscape plug-ins. Also, the Web server must be configured before the movie will play. To add a shocked Director movie to an HTML page, use the HTML tag EMBED. The EMBED syntax for a shocked Director movie looks like this:

<EMBED SRC="path/filename.ext" WIDTH=pixels HEIGHT=pixels PALETTE=background BGCOLOR=color>

Let's break this statement down into individual components:

- **EMBED SRC="path/filename.ext"** designates the actual shocked movie file and its location on the server. The movie filename must have a .dcr extension (mymovie.dcr); this is what tells Netscape to evoke the Shockwave plug-in.
- **WIDTH=pixels HEIGHT=pixels** designates the size in pixels of the window on the Web page in which the movie plays. Usually, this is the same size of the movie itself. As you'll see in the discussion of downloading and bandwidth considerations in the next section, this size is seldom as large as movies designed to play on monitors.
- **PALETTE=background** prevents the palette of the Director movie from loading and uses the system palette instead.
- **BGCOLOR=color** determines the color of the window in which the movie plays. Usually, this is the color of the window that displays before the movie plays.

Here's an example of a movie embedded to play on a Divine Concepts home page:

<EMBED SRC=" /movies/mymovie.dcr" WIDTH=335 HEIGHT=255 PALETTE=background BGCOLOR=red>

TIP

If the user's browser doesn't support the Shockwave plug-in, the NOEMBED tag allows you to substitute a JPEG or GIF image in place of the movie. The NOEMBED tag looks like this:

<NOEMBED> <IMG SRC="path/filename.ext"> </NOEMBED>

Basically this tag substitutes the image for the movie—which is much better than the broken image icon that would display otherwise. (Again, if you're totally lost in this discussion of HTML tags, you should read up on creating Web pages with HTML.)

Downloading (Bandwidth) Considerations

A major impediment to creating movies for the Web is the speed at which modems download data from the Internet, known as *bandwidth*. Nowadays, movies delivered over the World Wide Web are limited in file size primarily because the majority of users logon at relatively slow speeds—14,400 and 28,800 bits per second (bps). The bps is the connection's bandwidth. At these bandwidths, the user can receive about only 1K of information per second. In other words, it takes one minute to transfer a 60K file.

These numbers are under optimal conditions. If there is heavy traffic on the Internet host or if the network is congested, the transfer rate drops considerably. So, to deliver movies over the Web effectively, it is important that you keep the filesize of your movies small.

Granted, as discussed, Afterburner compresses a movie's file size, but only by about half. Take MYMOVIE.dir,—without the supporting file, Heidi.mov, the filesize is about 4 MB. With the supporting video, it's even larger, closer to 5MB. This movie could take a half hour or longer to download to your site visitors' computers—believe me, few (if any) Web surfers will wait that long to see your movie. If you can get them to wait a minute or two, you're lucky.

NOTE By now you're probably wondering: So how would I get MYMOVIE.dir to play on the Web? Well, you wouldn't. When designing movies for the Web, you will usually start from scratch, keeping file size constraints uppermost in your mind during the design process.

Everything you've learned about keeping the components of your movies—and the movies themselves—small in file size are doubly pertinent when creating titles for the Web. Here's a list of ways to keep your movies small:

- Begin by designing the movie at the smallest possible Stage size. Remember from Chapter 9 that you control the size of movie's view area with the Stage Size option in the Movie Properties dialog box (choose Movies on the Modify menu, and then choose Properties from the submenu). For Web pages, you'll usually use a custom size, as shown in Figure 15.16. The size you should use depends primarily on the content of the movie—a tradeoff between how much viewing area is needed to display details and filesize.

- Use very short sound files, if any. Loop them, as shown in Figure 15.17, by selecting Cast Member/Properties on the Modify menu. You should also resample sounds to play at the lowest possible settings: 11kHz, 8-bit mono.

- Use an 8 bit stage to keep color depth down (design the movie with your computer's display settings set to 256 colors, as discussed in Chapter 9). Also, use your image editing software to index your images to the lowest number of colors possible. Again, this is a tradeoff between filesize and quality.

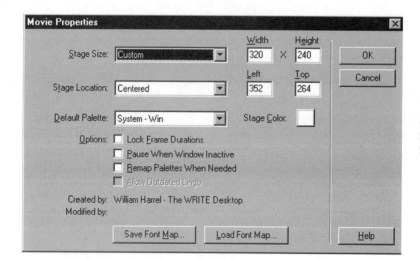

FIGURE 15.16:
Create a Custom Stage Size for your Shockwave movies.

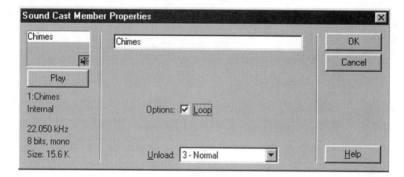

FIGURE 15.17:
Use short sounds and loop them in Sound Cast Member properties to keep the file size down.

- Keep your movies as short as possible. Most movies for the Web are only about 20 to 30 seconds long, and they repeat, looping while the page they are embedded in displays. There are a number of ways to loop movies—either with the Lingo "loop" message, or you can loop one or more objects with the Film Loop command on the Insert menu. (There's a great description of Film Loop in Director's Help system. Simply search for "loops (film), creating".)

How big should your titles be? The only answer I can give you is, as short as possible. Anything longer than about 300K (after compression with Afterburner) will probably cause your visitors to get discouraged and go somewhere else. Some won't even wait that long.

TIP You'll find a lot of great information on downloading considerations and ways to keep filesizes down on the Macromedia site.

Right now, the primary problem with Shockwave movies is that the user must wait for an entire movie to download before it begins playing. However, Macromedia is working on a technology called *streaming* that will allow movies to begin playing shortly after the first few seconds of beginning the download, with the rest of the movie downloading in the background. This will make a huge difference in how big your Shockwave movies can be. Keep in touch with the Macromedia Web site for updates on this technology.

Within the next few years, new technologies such as cable modems (hooked onto you TV cable lines) will dramatically boost the speed of the Internet. The size limits imposed by the current snail-paced technology will no longer be an issue. Multimedia authors will be able to deliver CD-ROM size—and larger—titles in real time across the World Wide Web. For now, though, keep the filesizes small.

When you sit down to begin your projects keep in mind all of the possibilities that multimedia authoring offers, but don't lose sight of your overall goal. Use restraint when designing your title; don't clutter it up with needless bells and whistles, all multimedia elements should serve a desired purpose. Most of all, don't forget to have fun, and brush up on those multimedia authoring talents! Good luck.

GLOSSARY

3-D sound: A sound card feature similar to the Surround Sound feature found in many of today's home entertainment systems and movie theaters. 3-D sound comes in two standards: SRS and Q-Sound.

actor: A graphic or figure that makes up part of an animation sequence. Usually, actor refers to one of several graphics (actors) that make up an action sequence, such as a dog barking, a bird in flight, and so on.

Afterburner: A Director Xtra that allows you to convert your Director movies into a file format (.dcr) useable on the Web.

Apple QuickTime for Windows: A file format that allows Windows to display video files. QuickTime is cross-platform, meaning that you can also use it on Macs.

applet: A small computer application that allows you or a remote viewer to run an electronic presentation without owning the program that created it. Microsoft PowerPoint, for example, ships with PowerPoint Viewer, a royalty-free runtime viewer that shows PowerPoint presentations.

bandwidth: Refers to the rate at which phone lines and modems transfer data, measured in kilobytes per second (kbs).

Bernoulli drive: A removable disk technology manufactured by Iomega. Bernoulli drives support sturdy, plastic-encased disks that come is sizes ranging from 35 to 250MB.

bitmap graphics: Pixel-based graphic images created by scanners and in paint-type programs such as Adobe Photoshop.

build slides: These are slides that introduce topics point by point so that your audience can't get to the finale ahead of you.

burn: A term used to described the process of copying files to a CD-ROM, called so because the CD-R device uses a laser beam to record the information.

business presentation: Business presentations are typically created with business presentation software, such as Lotus Freelance Graphics, Microsoft PowerPoint, and Harvard Graphics, and include an electronic screen show.

business presentation program: A dedicated software application designed to create slide and screen show presentations. Two of the more popular are Microsoft PowerPoint and Lotus Freelance Graphics 96.

bus type: In and out buses on computers bring data into and out of the processor. Typically an I/O bus is a slot on the computer motherboard (PC) or logic board (Mac) where you insert cards, such as video, video capture, and others. I/O buses come in several standards, but the prevailing type right now is PCI.

caddy: A small case, or carriage, that some types of drives require you to put a CD-ROM in before you slide it into the drive.

capture variables: Elements that impact the quality of a captured video sample, such as frame rate, frame size, and color depth.

cast member: Sometimes called a sprite, this is a graphic, clip media, or other element used in a Director movie. Cast members are held in the Cast window.

Cast window: A window in Director that holds the cast members of a movie, including sound, graphics, transitions, and scripts.

CD-R: Recordable CD-ROM technology. A CD-R drive uses a laser beam to "burn" CD-ROMs.

cel-based animation: Animation production technique based on the process of using celluloid layers to overlay active elements in an animation frame on a static background. Referred to as onion skinning.

cell: The unit of information about a sprite or cast member contained within a frame in the Director Score window. Cells hold size, color, placement, and other information about the cast member during its current position on the stage or movie.

channel: A row of frames in the Director Score window for defining movie elements and how long they display on the Stage, or how long they play (such as sound files).

choose: I use this term when you have a list of choices, such as a menu or in a dialog box. It is used interchangeably with *select*. For example: If I say, "Choose Save As from the File menu" you would click on the File menu and then click on Save As from the list of options on the menu.

clip art: Ready-to-use graphics images that typically come in collections or with graphics programs.

clip media: Ready-to-use audio, video, and/or animation clips, usually royalty-free, including graphic images.

CODEC: Compression/decompression. A set of drivers that reduces the video file size to make them manageable by a computer.

color depth: Refers to the number of bits per pixel a computer's display system is capable of. The higher the color depth, the more colors a computer can display.

compression: The process of making the video file size small enough during capture to be managed by computers.

Color window: A set of colors (typically 256) being used by the computer display. Typically, a Director movie uses only one window (like the Windows system window) and all images it uses must be mapped to the same window.

Construction window: The window in Premiere where you layout the elements of your project. Use this window to place the various clips, still images, and transitions that comprise the video project.

Control Panel (Director): A VCR-like window in Director that allows you to play back, rewind, and stop the play of a movie, among other options.

Control Panels (Windows): A set of utilities in Windows that allows you to configure the Windows environment options. Display options, for example, are controlled with the Display Control Panel.

Controller window: A VCR-like window that lets you play, rewind, stop, and mark digital video clips.

courseware: A form of multimedia title designed to instruct. Popular for training in large corporations, multimedia courseware takes the place of an instructor. It provides lessons, reinforces examples, and gives tests.

CPU: Central Processing Unit: The brains of your computer.

demo: Sometimes called tryouts or save-disabled, these are demonstration copies of various popular programs functional in most ways, except that you can't save your work. *Demo* is the term used in this book.

destination application: A term associated with Windows OLE referring to an application that is capable of linking to or embedding a file from an OLE-aware server application.

digital-to-analog converter: A device that converts computer video output to a format that can be used by a TV or VCR.

digitize: The process of converting analog signals from video (VCR, TV, camcorder) to a format represented by 1s and 0s, thus useable by computers.

dot pitch: Refers to the fineness of the dots that comprise a monitor, i.e., .31, .28, .26.

double-click: Place your mouse on the object I tell you to "double-click on," and click the left mouse button very fast. Double-clicking is usually used to open a program, a file folder, or a dialog box.

drag: Click and hold the left mouse button on the object I tell you to "drag," and hold the mouse button while moving the mouse to the position I tell you to drag to. Dragging is used to move objects across your monitor, such as a graphic from one place to another.

edutainment: A form of multimedia title designed to instruct and entertain at the same time. Common edutainment titles include interactive encyclopedias, such as *Microsoft Encarta* and children's books and puzzles, such as *My First Dictionary*.

element: A term I use throughout this book to refer to the graphics, sounds, and other objects that make up your multimedia titles.

EZ drive: A removable disk technology manufactured by Syquest, the EZ drives support relatively inexpensive 100MB and 135MB Winchester-type disks. This new disk type is likely to become the new standard for Macintosh systems.

file structure: The arrangement of files and folders used to hold your movies and supporting files. Keeping all of the components of a title within the file structure allows you to easily move the title or create CD-ROMs.

flowline: A flowchart-like environment for creating multimedia applications. Icons are dragged and dropped to the flowline and then assigned multimedia content. Authorware, IconAuthor, and MetaTools Interactive use flowline interfaces.

FM synthesizer: A form of MIDI sound reproduction that simulates musical instruments. This is an older, inferior form of sound card technology. The industry standard is now wavetable.

frame rate: The frame rate measures the number of frames per second (fps). The illusion of movement is achieved in video by the rapid succession of frames being viewed.

frame-based animation: Animation production technique approximating digital video.

Green PC: An energy saving standard for monitors and computers.

handler: A set of Lingo statements attached to an object, such as a score script, or to a cast member. All handlers begin with *on*. For example, *on mouseUp,* meaning "when the mouse button is released."

I/O: Input/output. These are the ports on your computer that allow you to print, play sound, capture video, and so on.

Indexed Color: An Adobe Photoshop feature that allows you to map the colors in an image to either the system palette or adapt the palette to the image.

interactivity: In a multimedia title, this refers to the ability of the title to respond to user input. The most common interactivity is allowing the user to navigate through the title.

Internet provider: A vendor that supplies Internet access for a fee. Many Internet providers also have space on their server for housing Web sites.

Java: A programming language developed by Sun Microsystems for programming events on the Internet. Java is often used to program multimedia content on the World Wide Web.

Jaz drive: A relatively new removable disk technology by Iomega that supports inexpensive 1GB disks.

jewel case: The plastic case that holds a CD.

key frame: A reference frame in a video clip used by the CODEC (compression/decompression) scheme to determine the presence of redundant information.

keyboard shortcut: Windows applications allow you to use certain commands or functions by pressing combinations of keys, such as Ctrl+A for Select All.

kiosk: Sometimes called *point-of-sale kiosks*, a kiosk is a multimedia device, such as touch-screen monitor, that advertises products or provides information. In a large shopping mall, for example, a kiosk might direct patrons to specific locations in the mall.

layering: A feature of Adobe Photoshop and other image editing software that allows you to keep the objects you place on the canvas separate, similar to acetone sheets used in color keys in print shops.

LCD screen: Liquid Crystal Display is a screen for viewing electronic presentations from a computer through an overhead projector.

link: Programs like Director allow you to create links to large files, such as 24-bit images and video clips, rather than import the file itself into the movie file. This makes for smaller document filesizes.

loop: A computer term meaning to run over and over, it is the process of repeating a movie or sound clip continuously.

map: A term used to describe how colors in a palette are assigned and defined.

master CD-ROM: When multimedia authors finish a title, they burn a master disc, which is then duplicated for distribution.

message: Lingo instructions used to direct handlers, for example, *go to frame 2005*. Handlers look for and execute corresponding messages.

Microsoft Video for Windows: A file format that allows Windows to display video files.

MIDI: A technology used to reproduce musical instruments on a computer sound card. There are two types: FM synthesizer and wavetable.

mix: The process of combining two or more sounds so that they play simultaneously.

modes: The various resolutions and color depths supported by a display system.

Movie (Director): The term used to designate a Director document or file. This can be a short animation or an entire multimedia title.

Movie (Premiere): In Premiere, the completed project is rendered into a "movie" (QuickTime or Microsoft Video) with the Make Movie command. This is different from Director in that the document in which you compile the multimedia elements itself is called a movie.

multi-direction animation: An animation sequence where the sprite moves in more than one direction, such as left, then up, then right, and so on.

multimedia: Technically, the combining of two or more types of media. For computer purposes, however, it refers to the combining of sound, animation, and video.

multimedia authoring: The process of creating multimedia titles.

multimedia authoring software: Software for creating interactive projects with sound, video, text, and animation, such as Macromedia Authorware, Director, and Asymetrix ToolBook.

Multimedia PC Marketing Council (MPC): A consortium of multimedia hardware and software vendors that sets the standards for multimedia computers.

multimedia presentation program: Similar to business presentation software, presentation programs allow you to create screen shows that contain a lot of multimedia content. Typically, these programs provide more control over multimedia events and animation.

multimedia title: A document created by combining sound, graphics, animation, and video. Multimedia titles can be interactive games, edutainment, presentations, interactive books, and so on.

multimedia upgrade kit: A combination package of multimedia peripherals, such as a CD-ROM drive, sound card, speakers, and microphone designed to work together to make computers multimedia ready.

object linking and embedding (OLE): A technology built into Windows that allows OLE-aware applications to exchange information, by either linking a file to a server (originating) program, or creating a pointer from an embedded file to the server application. The current standard for Windows is OLE2.

on-the-fly-resolution switching: The ability to change display resolution without restarting the computer.

palette: A device used by Windows, image editing software, multimedia authoring software, and other programs to define and assign (map) colors.

panning: Also known as *virtual desktop*, the ability to move your desktop to provide more viewing real estate.

pixel: The smallest displayable unit of color on a computer screen. Pixels are round on the Macintosh and square on the PC.

pkzip: A form of file compression technology popular on the PC.

plug-in: A utility that adds functionality to an application. For example, a Web browser plug-in allows the browser to play files, such as multimedia events, that it would not otherwise be capable of.

pointer: A reference within a document file (such as a Director movie) that remembers the location of a supporting linked file.

presentation software: Programs designed to create business presentations, such as Microsoft PowerPoint or Harvard Graphics. These programs typically allow users to create presentations based on a slide metaphor.

Preview window: The window in Premiere where you playback your project to view progress and the effects of your edits as you work with the Preview command.

project: In Premiere, it is the ongoing document where you edit clips and combine elements.

projector: The process of creating a projector in Director turns the movies you layout into stand-alone titles that other people can then run on their own computers without needing a copy of Director.

RAM: Random Access Memory. The memory chips in your computer that hold data for processing by the CPU.

refresh rate: The rate at which a computer refreshes the monitor display. Slow refresh rates can be hard on the eyes.

removable media: A generic term for all the various types of storage media capable of being removed from the computer for transporting and storing data.

resolution: When referring to monitors, resolution defines the number of pixels per inch, such as 640x480, or 800x600.

Rich Text Format (RTF): A cross-platform text file format that supports some limited formatting information, such as tabs, bolds, italics, and text size. RTF is the format of choice with Director.

sampling frequency: The cycles per second at which digital audio files are recorded: 44.1kHz, 22.05kHz, and 11.025kHz.

save-disabled: Sometimes called demos or tryouts, these are demonstration versions of popular programs that are functional in most ways, except that you can't save your work.

Score Scripts: Lingo scripts assigned to frames in the Score's Script channel that control the behavior of the movie. A common Score Script is the pause script, which pauses the playback head to wait for user input.

screen show: An electronic presentation created in a business presentation program and shown on a computer screen, TV monitor, or LCD panel.

script: Small programs multimedia programmers write with a multimedia authoring program's scripting language, such as Director's Lingo or ToolBooks OpenScript.

Scripts of Cast Members: Lingo scripts assigned to cast members that control the behavior of the cast member. For example, you can assign scripts to buttons and other sprites that control the flow of the title.

select: Similar to *choose*, I use this option to tell you to click on a command or another option to turn it on or open a dialog box. Another way in which *select* is used is to tell you to make an object active such as, "Click on the text block to select it." When an object is selected it's active. Depending on the program and the object, selected objects are highlighted in some manner.

Shift-click: Hold the Shift key while clicking on the object indicated. This is used most often for selecting multiple objects.

shocked: A term used by Macromedia to describe movies and Web sites designed to play Director Shockwave movies.

Shockwave for Director: The Netscape Navigator plug-in that allows Web browsers to play Director movies on shocked sites.

Shockwave: A Web browser plug-in that enables Director movies to play on the World Wide Web. Shockwave for Freehand is also shipping, which gives users the ability to pan and zoom on EPS files over the net.

source application: In a Windows OLE environment, the source application is the application in which a file is created. In object linking, the file (e.g., graphic) remains in its source application, and is pulled up by clicking on a hot object in the destination file.

SoundFonts: A form of sound technology that allows you to store wavetable sounds in the RAM on a sound card. SoundFonts are usually used to enhance the musical capabilities of sound card.

stand-alone: This simply means that the user does not need a copy of Director to run the movie.

statements: Combinations of Lingo words and handlers that become Lingo scripts.

streaming: A process of downloading where a movie (or other clip) begins to play shortly after the download begins, while the remainder of the file downloading in the background.

subwoofer: A device that you connect into a speaker system that enhances its bass capabilities. The sound quality of many of today's low-watt speaker systems is greatly increased by adding a subwoofer.

Syquest: A company and a removable media technology based on Winchester disks. Syquest also makes EZ drives.

timeline: Part of a presentation construction environment that allows you to control events and scenes, such as when elements appear and for how long they are displayed.

title bar: The solid-colored strip above a window that gives the name of the window and often the name of the current document. You can use it to move windows around on the screen.

Title window: Sometimes called the Title Maker, the Title window is a small graphics utility in Premiere that lets you create simple graphics and titles for you projects.

tops and tails: The process of cutting one or both ends of a media clip to shorten it or trim away unwanted data.

track: Similar to Director's channels, tracks are areas in the Premiere Construction window where you place elements, such as audio, video, still images, and transitions.

transfer rate: The speed at which devices transfer data. CD-ROM drives are rated in transfer rates. 1x drives have a transfer rate of 150bps, for example.

transition effect: Sometimes called *transitions*, this refers to the way an object or page appears on the screen. Transitions can include wiping away the current object with a new one, fade in, fade out, fade to black, and a host of others.

tryouts: Sometimes called demos or save-disabled, these are demonstration versions of popular programs that are functional in most ways, except that you can't save your work.

tween: Tweening is the process of defining the cells in an animation sequence from one point in the animation to another. For example, when a sprite moves across the stage, Director's tween feature figures the distance the object should move from frame to frame.

vector graphics: Mathematically drawn graphic images drawn in draw, 3D modeling, and CAD programs.

VGA and Super VGA: Display system standards. VGA is 640x480 resolution; Super VGA is 800x600.

video capture board: A bus card used to capture and display video from a camcorder, VCR, or TV.

VideoRAM (VRAM): A faster form of memory chip used on video adapters.

viewer-interactive presentation: A presentation where the viewer controls the information flow by clicking on buttons or with keystrokes. These are akin to interactive multimedia titles, though usually not as multimedia-rich and sophisticated.

VRML (Virtual Reality Modeling Language): A computer language used on the World Wide Web to create 3D graphics and animation.

wavetable: A form of MIDI that enables computers to reproduce the sounds of musical instruments via a sound card. Wavetable technology actually stores samples of various instruments in chips on the sound card, allowing for a more true-to-life reproduction than the alternative MIDI technology, FM synthesizer.

Web browser: A software application, such as Netscape Navigator or Microsoft Internet Explorer, used to navigate the World Wide Web and display Web pages.

Winchester: A form of disk technology based on plastic-encased mechanisms made popular by Syquest.

window: A floating dialog box in an application that allows you to modify or control certain aspects of a document. In Director, for example, the Cast window holds cast members.

World Wide Web: A graphics-rich service on the Internet for conveying information. The World Wide Web is rapidly becoming a multimedia environment and expanding exponentially.

Xtras: Small applets or utilities that add functionality to Director and other Macromedia products, similar to plug-ins in other applications.

zip drive: A relatively new type of removable media based on Iomega's small, 100MB, floppy-sized disks.

INDEX

NOTE: Page numbers in *italics* refer to figures or tables; page numbers in **bold** refer to significant discussions of the topic

About the CD

The CD-ROM included with this book contains everything you need to complete the Workshop portion of this book. In addition, there are several image and animation files you can use in future projects.

The directories on the CD are organized as follows:

Directory	Contains
\Adobe	
\Photoshp	Adobe Photoshop demo installation files
\Premiere	Adobe Premiere demo installation files
\Corel	Images from Corel Stock Photo Library 2
\ImgClb	
\ClipArt	Image Club Graphics images in EPS format
\Photos	Image Club Graphics photos in TIFF format
\Jasmine	AVI videos from The Making of Jasmine*
\Macromed	
\Dir-win	Macromedia Director 5 demo installation files
\SF	Sonic Foundry Sound Forge XP demo installation files
\Workshop	Files for completing all Workshop exercises, along with the completed Workshop Director 5 movie and stand-alone projector

*These videos are saved in Microsoft Video AVI format. They will import directly into Director or Premiere, or you can view them with Windows 95's Media Player. In Windows 3.1, you will need Microsoft Video for Windows to view them.

The demo programs on the CD are all save-disabled, which means that they are fully functional, but you cannot save your work. You can get full versions from the vendors.

SYBEX®